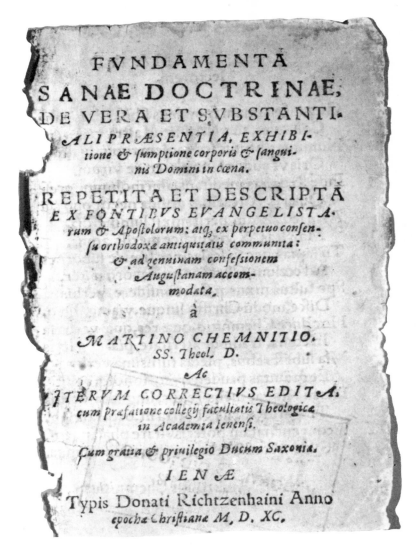

FVNDAMENTA
SANAE DOCTRINAE,

DE VERA ET SVBSTANTI-
ALI PRÆSENTIA, EXHIBI-
tione & sumptione corporis & sanguinis Domini in coena.

REPETITA ET DESCRIPTA
EX FONTIBVS EVANGELISTA-
rum & Apostolorum: atq; ex perpetuo consen-
su orthodoxæ antiquitatis communita:
& ad genuinam confessionem
Augustanam accom-
modata,

à

MARTINO CHEMNITIO.
SS. Theol. D.

Ac

ITERVM CORRECTIVS EDITA,
cum præfatione collegij facultatis Theologicæ
in Academia Ienensi.

Cum gratia & priuilegio Ducum Saxoniæ.

IENÆ

Typis Donati Richtzenhaini Anno
epocha Christiana M, D, XC,

The title page of the second (1590) edition, published by Donatus Richtzenhain at Jena, Germany. This very rare book belongs to the library of Concordia Theological Seminary, Fort Wayne, Indiana. The first edition appeared at Jena in 1570. There were at least eight editions, all in Latin, between 1570 and 1690. As far as we know, there were no editions after that and the work has never before been translated into any language.

The Lord's Supper

De coena Domini

MARTIN CHEMNITZ

TRANSLATED BY **J.A.O. Preus**

INDEX BY **Delpha Holleque Preus**

The foundations of sound teaching concerning the true and substantial presence, distribution, and reception of the body and blood of the Lord in the Supper.

Derived from and described according to the fountains of the evangelists and apostles, and delivered to us on the basis of the continuous consensus of orthodox antiquity and taught in accord with the Augsburg Confession.

by Martin Chemnitz S.S. Theol. D.

and again edited more correctly, with a preface by the members of the theological faculty of the University of Jena.

Published by the grace and favor of the Duke of Saxony.

Jena
Donatus Richtzenhain, Publisher
A.D. 1590

Publishing House
St. Louis

2 3 4 5 6 7 8 9 10 11   WP   90 89 88 87 86 85 84 83 82 81

A translation of *De coena Domini,*
published in Jena, Germany, 1590

Concordia Publishing House, St. Louis, Missouri
MANUFACTURED IN THE UNITED STATES OF AMERICA

Library of Congress Cataloging in Publication Data
Chemnitz, Martin, 1522-1586.
    The Lord's Supper = De Coena Domini.

    1. Lord's Supper—Early Works to 1800. I. Title.
BV824.C4313   264'.3   78-27499
ISBN 0-570-03275-X

To Delpha
whose loving assistance and patience
have helped immeasurably

Contents

Translator's Preface

This translation is based on the Jena edition of 1590, the second edition of the work. It bears the title *Fundamenta sanae doctrinae de vera et substantiali praesentia, exhibitione & sumptione corporis & sanguinis Domini in coena* (translated on our title page). The first edition, also published at Jena, appeared in 1570. In all at least eight editions appeared between 1570 and 1690.

Since this is the second work of Chemnitz which we have translated, we have learned several idiosyncrasies of Chemnitz and his printers and editors. For instance, Chemnitz follows no version of the Bible literally. Hence we have made no effort to square his Biblical citations with any existing English version. Biblical names, as well as chapter and verse designations, are according to the Protestant tradition.

Chemnitz always cites Biblical references by chapter only. We have generally added the verse(s). We have also added references in many places where he had none. These are enclosed in brackets.

Chemnitz or his printer made a number of errors (although not nearly as many as in his *De duabus naturis*) in the titles and numberings of patristic citations. These we have attempted to correct, and without comment. As an aid to the modern reader we have used footnotes to indicate the locations of most of these quotations in modern available editions. In almost all cases we have used Migne's *Patrologia Graeca et Latina* as the modern reference. In a few cases we have used other editions. There are many cases where Chemnitz merely cites an ancient authority without reference to any title. Here we have not searched for the citation and have used a footnote only when we happened to locate it. In some instances, perhaps because he was using other editions not available to us or because he made an error, we have not been able to locate certain citations, even when a title is given. In these cases we have simply indicated our inability to locate the citation. Thus the reader will discover, and we hope pardon, some lack of uniformity. Our general practice is to give the reader all the useful and accurate information we have been able to gather.

At this point we list full bibliographic data regarding the editions in which the patristic quotations appear, using standard abbreviations. In the notes only the abbreviations appear. In a few instances bibliographic data is given in a note.

MPG *Patriologia Graeca,* ed. J. P. Migne, 161 vols. (Paris, 1857—66).

MPL *Patrologia Latina,* ed. J. P. Migne, 217 vols., indexes 4 vols. (Paris 1878—90).

Otto *Justinus Martyr opera,* ed. J. K. T. von Otto, 3rd ed. (Jena 1876—81), 3 vols. in 5.

Basel Ed. Cyrillus, St. Patriarch of Alexandria, ca. 370—444.

Divi Cyrilli Alexandrine episcopi theologi praestantissimi Opera quae hactenus haberi potuere, in tomas quinque digesta; nam quintus hac editione accessit . . . Basileae, Joannis Hervagii. M.D.LXVI.

Finally, I wish to thank the editoral staff of CPH, and especially my devoted and talented wife Delpha for her efforts in checking references, typing the manuscript, and in encouraging me in what can sometimes be a tedious and exhausting task.

J. A. O. Preus

[Foreword]

The dean and the members of the theological faculty of the University of Jena greet the saintly reader in the Lord.

A double calamity has befallen our age in the form of an overabundance of literary production. In the first place, the frightful maliciousness of the writing wears out most readers, and the pens of many are so contentious that they scarcely understand their own writing—and yet for them to know something is to write about it. And then add to this evil a second pest, the love of novelty. For the zeal for something new has so blinded the eyes of many that they show their loathing for the writings of great men by simply referring to them as old-fashioned, and they seek out those emerging authors who must be read not on the basis of how well they have written but how recently.

From this results a twofold detriment to the state of public letters. First, the earth is buried by such a flood of useless new books that nothing has become more worthless, nothing more contemptible, nothing more despicable than the very books which were at one time of the greatest value. In fact, the same thing has most deservedly happened to this generation as befell the mad people of Athens under the tutelage of Thales. For just as he, in the brightness of the noonday sun, lit a torch in the midst of a raving mob of people and explained that he was looking for men, so today each piles up books for himself, no matter how worthless they may be.

The second detriment is that in writing new books, most of them worthless and useless, we are at the same time losing the good old ones, that is, we are objecting to these books on the ground that they are the greatest hindrances to solid learning that we can imagine. Seneca wrote of some sick people who used changes in place of remedies. And in our love of novelty and variety we have the notion that progress in doctrine has been achieved. This notion is the surest hindrance to progress. For the very process through which books are produced creates this obvious hindrance. When printers everywhere use their presses to produce these worthless modern books, they charge high prices, use the most brilliant kinds of type and even the most elegant paper, so that those books which are good, even if old, either cannot find a printer or, if one does offer his services, such books cannot find anyone to help with the cost of the edition; or if the matter proceeds most fortunately, they get scarcely anything except unreliable and worn-out type and off-color and rough paper.

If it were only a human problem underlying this evil which afflicts the minds of good men, it would be a thing of little importance. But I am persuaded that this state of affairs has come about mainly by the cunningness of the devil, so that whatever benefit has come to the Christian world through the invention of printing for the propagation of the heavenly doctrine, the evil foe by his most clever misuse has corrupted, as it enters into the heart of men. For this reason we must practice even greater vigilance in all things which are good, so that the possession of this great benefit may not be forever lost to us through the malice of Satan. And we will be able to accomplish this if the only new books published are good ones, or if at least the old books are reprinted; or to put it succinctly, if we devote as much effort to preserving the old ones as we do to writing new ones.

In keeping with this concern we wanted to fulfill our obligation by reissuing this little volume of Chemnitz. This book, in the judgment of all right-thinking and godly men, is assuredly the best and most outstanding of its kind, truly a golden book, the kind of book one would expect to come from the pen of that great and truly orthodox theologian Martin Chemnitz. This author at the very beginning dedicated his book to the church, and it was most warmly received and found a place in the library of special treasures of every orthodox theologian. It came to be regarded by very great men as the standard work on the Sacramentarian controversies. It deserved this reputation, for the church republished the book every year.

But it also experienced that most unhappy fate which befalls even the best of books. For although there were those, here and there, who might wish to buy this book, or occasionally those who opened a borrowed copy and jotted down quotations from what they had read, yet during a period of 10 years in which thousands of books of one kind or another were produced, not one printer was found who would produce a reprint of this most useful volume.

We are going to right this wrong in the face of Satan, since we are mindful that what we are doing has the approval of the author himself while he was still with us, and the result has been that this book was put into the hands of our printer. Considering the possession of this book to be a rich heritage, we brought it again to the printing press and obtained the services of M. Ambrose Chemnitz to copy and correct the book, in order that it might appear in a clearer and more accurate form in this edition. Therefore, since we have desired this sound teaching only for the benefit of the church, we have absolutely no doubt that all good men will approve of our action and will use this work with grateful mind, zealous for the pure truth, and we are confident that this desire of ours will surely be pleasing to God. Therefore we pray with heartfelt longing that He may sanctify us all in His truth, and preserve and bless us into eternity. To Him be glory and honor forever and ever. Amen.

[Dedicatory Epistle]

To the most illustrious princes and lords, the brothers Lord Henry the Younger and Lord William the Younger, Dukes of Brunswick and Lüneburg, etc. To their most clement Highnesses
Grace and peace through Christ.

The Son of God commended to His church the words of institution of the Supper in the form of a last will and testament—at a time of high emotion, with most fervent prayer, and under the most serious circumstances on the night in which He was betrayed. Therefore these words should be observed with the greatest reverence and piety and in the fear of the Lord by all people, for they are the words of the testament of the Son of God. But some evil genius has brought these most holy words into controversy like an apple of discord, so that what ought to be a bond of unity and agreement has become the cause of the most tragic differences and arguments. For the controversy concerning the true and genuine meaning of the words of the Lord's Supper has been carried on for many years now with the saddest possible contention, and the true, happy, and salutary end to this tragedy has not yet appeared. For the efforts of certain people who thought they could settle this controversy through compromise have long been doomed to failure. This cannot be done without injury to the last will and testament of the Son of God.

Yet it is possible to find scholars who do not fear to make the pronouncement that this entire controversy is merely an inane battle over words (*logomachia*). There are also those who place this controversy in the class of those disputes in which either ignorance, error, imagination, or semantic difficulties are at the root, but that there is nothing of substance or any detriment either to faith or to salvation. As a result, among these theologians there are some who very carefully explain other matters pertaining to the main points of the heavenly doctrine, but concerning this controversy the most complete silence reigns among them. And if some necessity demands that they must make some mention of this controversy, so that they cannot avoid touching

17

upon it, they handle it in a cold, aloof, detached, and perfunctory manner, as if it were a terrible burden to touch such a sore spot (as they themselves have recently said, thinking they were very wise). Some of them do not conceal the fact that they feel it is of no importance what one may fabricate or hold regarding the meaning of the words of the Lord's Supper. These profane notions are even instilled into the minds of the youth, so that they think it is useless and unnecessary to contend with anyone regarding the true and genuine meaning of the words of the Supper, so long as there is some kind of consensus concerning other dogmas. Hence many are seduced into this profane opinion, so that they take a cold and aloof attitude toward the Lord's Supper itself, and either make no use of it or attend very seldom and then not with serious purpose. Others, as if they were arrogating to themselves a privilege as a result of all this, undertake without any fear of conscience freely and with impunity to interpret and reinterpret the holy words of the last will and testament of the Son of God, to twist them into any forms they wish, to pick at them and to attack them.

Into this arena with great eagerness descend as into a gladiatorial contest the philosophers, the poets, the orators, the medical men, and even those who in the courts seem to want to claim for themselves some authority as doctors of the law. No one feels he is sufficiently learned if he cannot dream up some meaning which runs counter to the proper and natural simplicity of the words of Christ's testament, and each is audacious enough to try it. In other situations, in their own respective professions, they scrutinize the laws of nature and develop their skills on the basis of rational principles. Is this not indeed a marvelous thing? For they bring and apply to this controversy the same criteria. As Athanasius says, they measure the flesh of Christ and describe it (contrary to the Scriptures) on the basis of the principles of reason and the laws of nature as to how much it weighs and how it exists.

This is even more to be wondered at in the case of the doctors of the law. For their writings are filled with weighty statements concerning the scrupulous observance of the words of a last will and testament, which must be observed in the case of a secular will of a good man. Some hold that when the meaning of the testator is manifestly at variance, it is better to stick with the sense rather than the words, and then we must consider the thinking of the testator even if it goes counter to his words. But when the matter of a will has not been settled beforehand and under other circumstances, when there is insufficient clarity concerning the mind of the testator, and when there is anticipation of dispute and doubt, then the doctors of the law are most definite in their pronouncements: In case of doubt it is safer not to depart from the words but to insist upon them tenaciously with no extraneous interpretation, for the words are to be given greater weight and followed more closely than the fancied or uncertain mind of the testator. For we must not believe that the testator willed anything other than what he expressed in his words. If he had willed the contrary there would have been no difficulty for him to write it. Therefore they say that many people are deceived in determining what the meaning is by not weighing the words of the will, which in themselves are of paramount importance. They say, moreover, that men often err in attempting to read the mind of the testator because of the great subtlety of the subject. Therefore they advise that we must not rashly or heedlessly depart from the strict understanding of the words, since we should be content with the definitions of the words, neither adding to nor detracting from them. The emperor has added another very important reason, namely, that in an overly great concern for the subtleties of the meaning of such a matter the legal intent of the will and testament may be annulled.

If they wish to demonstrate such religious solicitude for the words of the last will and testament of some good man, what should they be demonstrating toward the words of the last will and testament of the very Son of God, a testament He made concerning the most serious matters on the night in which He was betrayed? Thus we can rightly say, even if all the professors of other disciplines hold to the opinion of the Sacramentarians, that what the doctors of the law teach should be done in the case of the will and testament of any good man should rightly and properly be done in the case of the last will and testament of the very Son of God.

This irreverent and superficial attitude, so prevalent in the discussion concerning the holy words of the last will and testament of the Son of God, is no different from what was indulged in in the schools of the sophists regarding purely material things. We can deplore it, but we cannot get rid of it. Yet repeated strong and serious reminders are useful and necessary that this controversy is not a mere dispute over idle questions or ill-defined genealogies but deals with the words of the last will and testament of the very Son of God, our Savior. If in the case of the words of the law even the least tittle is more important in the eyes of God than heaven and earth (Matt. 5:18), the godly mind should ponder what we ought to think regarding the words of Christ which He in the form of His last will and testament on the same night in which He was betrayed willed and commended to His church till the end of the age so that the church might will to repeat it after His ascension into His glory and dutifully distribute it (1 Cor. 11). And we should weigh carefully the stern words of Paul concerning the judgment which he declares has been laid upon those who violate the will and testament of Christ. For when the Son of God affirms and asserts regarding the bread of His Supper: "This is My body," he who does not discern that body is judged by Paul to be eating to his own judgment and to be guilty of the body and blood of the Lord. And this violation of Christ's will and testament brings even external penalties with it, as Paul shows not only by words but also by examples. Therefore the best and safest rule is to lead the minds of people to the very words of the last will and testament of the Son of God and to a consideration of their importance. In this way we will see more clearly that the devil is trying by various devices such as irreverent arguments or irrelevant questions to lead our minds away from the words of Christ's testament. For this reason we should pay closer attention to godly teachers, so that by means of their earnest warnings, based on the true foundation, people can turn their attention away from all these disputes and cling to the very words of the testament of the Son of God with a godly and sincere reverence for them, with the result that in this controversy they will wish to know nothing else and will endure hearing nothing else than those holy words of the Son of God, our Savior, which He commended to us in the form of His last will and testament on the night in which He was betrayed.

The importance of this method is demonstrated clearly by the very roaring of the adversaries against the literal meaning, as they call it, of these words. For they seize upon other controversies most avidly as long as they are more general, but when the point of the controversy is confined to the words of institution and limited to these four or five words, then they speak scornfully as if they are terribly burdened and loaded down under a mountain of work.

For this purpose eight years ago,[1] using a simple method and rationale, I gathered together the main points under dispute in this controversy and explained them in a simple and unaffected way, irenically and without acrimony, on the basis of the true, sure, and clear foundation of Scripture and noticed that the little volume which was published at Leipzig[2] seemed to please godly and even learned men. But after that time I began to give more serious thought to the matter and to weigh the causes and rationale of each part very carefully on the basis of the foundation. Furthermore, in considering these matters I became more and more convinced of the simple, proper, and natural sense of the words of the testament of Christ. So I began to rework those earlier notes and to add things which I had noted in the meantime and to explain and support the fundamental points carefully and at greater length.

I had no desire to bring in anything new but simply was trying to retain the old, fundamental, and simple teaching and to repeat it out of Luther's writings, namely, that the dogma of the Lord's Supper has its own proper and peculiar setting (sedes doctrinae) in the words of institution and that in these words its true meaning must be sought. Moreover, those words, because they are the words of the last will and testament of the very Son of God, must not be treated in a frivolous or light manner but must be pondered with reverence and great devotion. Since "Scripture is not of private interpretation" (2 Peter 1:20), I have shown on the basis of the sure and continuous analogy of the interpretation of Scripture and by a comparison of those passages in which the doctrine of the Lord's Supper is treated and repeated in Scripture the compelling, sure, certain, and clear reasons why the simple, proper, and natural meaning of the words of institution of the Supper must not be given up or rejected but rather must continue to be held and adhered to in the simple obedience of faith. On the other hand, I have shown on the basis of all the arguments of the adversaries that it is impossible to produce such sure, certain, and compelling arguments to prove that we should give up, repudiate, and condemn the proper and natural meaning of Christ's testament as those words read concerning the substantial presence, distribution, and reception of the body and blood of the Lord in the Supper.

I have explained these matters simply and calmly without ambiguity or acrimony. For I hoped that all could be led to this consideration so that they might note, ponder, and accept the words of institution as the words of the last will and testament not merely of some holy person but of the Son of God Himself, with reverence, with fear of the Lord, and with a truly religious heart, and not in a frivolous or unthinking way permit themselves to be drawn away from these words, much less to attack them with impious thoughts and statements. For if this is the case they will judge more fairly and equitably not only my writing but the subject itself.

Now this treatise is written concerning the foundations of the simple, proper, and natural meaning of the words of Christ's testament concerning the true and substantial presence of His body and blood in the Supper, which is dealt with and explained in the Augsburg Confession and the Apology; and since it should be published with the counsel and encouragement of good men, I was anxious to publish it under both the imprint and auspices of your most illustrious name. For to the family of your illustrious Highnesses belongs, as a legacy by right of inheritance, a heritage of sound doctrine, a summary of which, drawn from the Word of God, is contained in the Augsburg Confession, to which at the Diet of Augsburg in 1530, in the presence of Emperor Charles, in a time when it was dangerous even to make a confession, the father and the uncle of your Highnesses made solemn and public subscription. What a significant and special badge of distinction for your family! A reverent and grateful posterity will honor you forever.

Because in that Confession the sound doctrine is expounded in such a way that it is coupled with a clear antithesis and distinguished from the errors of the papal church and from all opinions of the fanatics, such as the Anabaptists and the Sacramentarians, therefore your Highnesses have inherited this concern that no enemy inject leaven or tares into the sound doctrine. This is true both in regard to other articles of faith and particularly with reference to the doctrines of Baptism and the Lord's Supper. For God Himself has shown with clear testimony that He has given your Highnesses the possession of this special inheritance together with the rest of your paternal heritage and wishes you to preserve it.

Even during the time of your Highnesses' minority, when that insidious formula of the Augsburg Interim was thrust upon the churches with threats and terror, and when many people began either to yield or at least to be less zealous, the counselors and officers in your Highnesses' domain, under the singular blessing of God, steadfastly refused that union of Christ and Belial and clung to the form of pure doctrine and sound words contained in the Augsburg Confession. Afterwards, when your Highnesses had reached maturity and had undertaken the reins of public office, you showed yourselves both in your judgment and in the matter itself not only to be willing to enter into government but particularly into the possession of your wonderful paternal inheritance, both in confessing and defending the sound doctrine, the sum of which, drawn from the Word of God, is contained in the Augsburg Confession. For your Highnesses gave place in your churches to no fanatic opinions or corruptions in doctrine but always with the same vigor were careful to retain the form of sound doctrine and correct words.

Nor do I have this information only on the basis of common rumor and popular opinion. Not so long ago I was invited by your Highnesses to some very important meetings of your theologians regarding the Sacramentarian controversy. Before them all I heard your Highnesses express your opinion and judgment in a reverent and correct way regarding the disputes of these times. Indeed, I saw your Highnesses with your own hand signify that you most vehemently disapproved of the subterfuges of those involved in the Sacramentarian controversy, whereby they tempered their words and hid their meanings so that they were neither hot nor cold. But the judgment: "These are the words of the true and almighty Christ," which your Highnesses made concerning the words of the testament of the Son of God, was not only brief and to the point but also pious and Christian and was also particularly pleasing to me.

For this reason I felt that your Highnesses would not be ungrateful for this writing of mine, in which I have repeated and explained the fundamentals of the correct teaching regarding the true and substantial presence of the body and blood of the Lord in the Holy Supper and have done so in a simple and calm way without any bitterness. And I have no doubt that because of your name the reading of this volume will be more pleasing to many people. Therefore I reverently and humbly pray that your Highnesses will kindly deign to accept the patronage of this writing.

I truly desire to declare before your Highnesses my devotion to you in as significant a way as I can. I pray the Son of God, our Lord Jesus Christ, that He will lead your Highnesses by His Spirit and be present with His benediction over your reign.

Brunswick
In the year of our Lord 1569
With reverent devotion toward your Highnesses
D. Martin Chemnitz

Chapter I

The words of the Lord's Supper are not to be treated in a light or frivolous way, but with great reverence and respect and in the fear of the Lord, because they are the words of the last will and testament of the Son of God.

The sad and horrendous irreverence and diversity of opinions concerning the holy will and testament of the Son of God has arisen primarily from the fact that certain men either have devised ideas out of their own heads or presumed from irrelevant passages of Scripture what they want to believe regarding the Lord's Supper, and have not exercised sufficient care as to whether and how these presumptuous opinions square and agree with the words of institution. A case in point is Schwenkfeld, who argued that the words should be ignored and kept out of sight, as it were, until a decision could be made as to what each person wanted to believe regarding the Lord's Supper. For other people, however, it is certainly not in keeping with religious conviction to apply to the holy words of the last will and testament of the Son of God any number of different interpretations or to change those words into different forms in order that they might be able to accommodate or rather twist them in some way to fit their notions, which are either preconceived or picked up from some other source. Thus the words of the testament of the Son of God in this present controversy are actually used to confuse the issue.

This irreverent desire to invent various interpretations for the last will and testament of the Son of God is confirmed by the proposal that there be a kind of immunity to criticism in this area, so long as one retains the fundamentals of the other articles of faith, since there is no danger to faith or loss of salvation no matter how a person wishes to treat, interpret, or understand the words of the Supper—so long as one accepts an interpretation which is in keeping with some passages of Scripture. Long ago Pelagius argued the same way—that it had nothing to do with the essence of religion how a person understood and interpreted the words of Scripture dealing with original sin in Rom.

5:12 ff.; Eph. 2:1 ff.; or Ps. 51:5. Thus it was said that the essence of the question was not a matter of faith.

By this kind of sloganeering insolence is aroused, increased, and strengthened in profane minds, so that now there are many people who treat the words of the last will and testament of the Son of God with no more reverence than if they were arguing about which stars are mentioned in Job 9:9 or Amos 5:8, or what kind of jewels were placed in the breastplate of the high priest of which Moses wrote in Ex. 39:10-13, or what kind of plant is mentioned in Jonah 4:6-7. To be sure, there is the case of those who were envious of Jerome and were condemned by law at Rome for charging him with the crime of sacrilege for having translated "vine" in the passage in Jonah instead of "gourd"; and in Africa some people started a controversy over the gourd as if it were an article of faith, in order to put the word "gourd" back into the Bible in place of "vine." But now in our time many people feel that no one should be condemned regardless of how he treats, understands, and interprets the very words of the Supper—and that even if you cannot or will not approve of these interpretations or opinions, yet they should not be condemned. Indeed, they say no one should be afraid to label as a mere superstition even in his public writings any concern for the words in this controversy regarding the last will and testament of the Son of God.

Therefore, first and foremost in this whole argument, we must set forth and impress on hearts and minds by constant consideration the true, clear, and compelling reasons, affecting not only the ears and minds but also including dangers to conscience, in regard to the words of the Supper. They are the words of the last will and testament of the very Son of God and not a game or place for exercising the mind by dreaming up unending interpretations that depart from the simplicity and proper meaning of the words. The mind should treat and consider these words with neither temerity nor frivolity but with reverence and piety and in great fear of the Lord.

In the first place, it is certain and cannot be denied that the words of the Supper are not to be classified in the category of points in Scripture which can either be ignored or variously explained or even incorrectly understood and still have no bearing on faith or salvation. For these are the words of the last will and testament not of a mere man but of the very Son of God. He instituted it on the night in which He was betrayed, and it concerned the most important matter of all. He did so with most serious emotions, words, and actions. Even in glory He repeated these words to Paul, thereby showing it was His will that this be the giving of a new and special dogma that should remain in the church to the end of time.

Therefore there is no doubt that to these words pertains the teaching of Scripture which says: "You shall not go aside, neither to the right nor to the left" (Deut. 5:32) . . . "neither by adding or taking away" (Deut. 4:2). Likewise, John 8:31: "If you continue in My Word, and My words continue in you, you shall be My disciples indeed" (cf. John 15:7). Here doubtlessly also apply those very stern warnings of Deut. 18:19: "If anyone will not hear the words of this prophet, I will be his avenger." And Rev. 22:19: "God will take away his share in the book of life." Cyprian in a correct and beautiful way applies the statement of Matt. 5:18 to the controversies regarding the Lord's Supper, saying: "For if 'one jot or one tittle of the Law is of greater weight than heaven or earth,' so that 'whoever shall break the least of these commandments and shall so teach men shall be the least' or the rejected 'in the kingdom of heaven,'" then what reverence and care for pious minds must be our concern that in the handling of these words we do not arouse the anger of Him who by these words made His last will and testament for our salvation in the night in which He was betrayed? And this is especially important with the addition of the threat of judgment and guilt for anyone who judges and handles these mysteries in any other way than He Himself who instituted it has willed.

In the second place, when the last will and testament of a man has been executed, we are required under the law to observe the words with special care so that nothing be done which is either beside or contrary to the final will of the testator. Even the civil laws regard such a will as so sacred that they have determined that those who have made any profit at all from the will for themselves shall be deprived of it, and their inheritance through the provision of the laws themselves shall be taken away from them as being unworthy, on the grounds that they have departed from the will of the testator as it is stipulated in the words of the testament. Now, because the Son of God in His last will and testament has not permitted His heirs the liberty of believing or doing whatever seems good to them, but has willed that we believe what He has spoken in His words of institution and do what He has commanded, therefore we should give very careful thought that we do not thrust anything upon these words of the last will and testament of the Son of God, lest we deprive ourselves of the benefit of eternal happiness conveyed to us by His will or our inheritance itself be taken from us as being unworthy because we have departed from the will of the Testator as it has been given to us in the words of His last testament. There is no doubt that all too many will come under this judgment, sad to say, because of their shameful contentiousness.

In the third place, after citing the words of the testament of the Son of God, Paul adds an extremely severe threat of judgment and guilt if anyone judges or treats these mysteries in any other way than Christ the Testator has willed and determined in the words of His last will and testament. For he says: "He who does not discern the body of the Lord eats judgment to himself and is guilty of the body of the Lord" (1 Cor. 11:29). Moreover, he is not speaking of the discerning of the human nature in Christ per se or in an absolute sense, but of the fact that what we eat in the Supper the Son of God calls His body. This Paul wants us to discern, not in accord with anyone's private conjectures but according to and on the basis of the words of Christ's testament, which Paul asserts he received by the revelation of the Son of God (1 Cor. 11:23). Therefore if anyone departs from the true and genuine sense of those words, it is certain that he is not able to discern what he is eating in the Supper. But would this not simply be an innocent lapse? By no means, for he is eating to his own judgment and becomes guilty of the body of Christ, says Paul.

When we have given serious consideration to those points, we will see that they furnish the best antidote against the willfulness and inpudence of human reason and create true reverence and piety in our handling of the words of the testament of the Son of God. At the same time they show how tragic and abhorrent is the mutilation to which the Sacramentarians have subjected these holy words of the last will and testament of the Son of God, tearing them limb from limb and picking them into small pieces by their various radical interpretations, so that there is scarcely anything left from the proper and true meaning of these words which is sound, inviolate, or untouched. No one would endure this patiently if it occurred in the secular realm in the case of the will and testament of a good man.

1. *HOC* [this].   Some contend that the particle "this" (*hoc* [τοῦτο]) does not prove that what is distributed with the hand and received with the mouth in the Lord's Supper is the body of Christ in an absolute sense. Others interpret the "this is" in the sense of "this action." There are those who explain the τοῦτο to mean that the bread is a spiritual nourishment.

2. *EST* [is].   Some interpret the "is" (*est* [ἐστίν]) as meaning "it signifies," and others "it represents," or that the term is used symbolically. Some even understand it as a remembrance of something absent.

3. *CORPUS* [body]. With regard to the word "body" some people understand it not in the sense of the very substance of Christ's body but as a figure or sign of an absent body. Others understand it as not being a true and substantial body but as a symbolic and sacramental one. There are those who interpret "body" not in the sense of the very substance but in some abstract sense, perhaps with reference to the power, strength, or efficacy of Christ's absent body or with reference to the fact of our communion in the absent body of Christ.

4. *QUOD* [which]. With regard to the word "which" some interpret it in the sense of "what kind," others interpret it "to what extent."

5. *TRADITUR ET EFFUNDITUR* [given and shed]. With reference to the words "given and shed" some contend that because they are in the present tense they must not be understood as referring to the giving of His body and shedding of His blood on the cross but rather to the distribution of the bread and the drinking of the wine.

6. *PERVERTITUR TOTA PROPOSITIO* [The entire statement is perverted]. Others simply pervert the words "that which is given for you, that is, My body" or "My body which is given for you" to refer to a spiritual food.

7. *SPIRITUS SANCTUS* ΣΟΛΟΙΚΙΖΕΙ [The Holy Spirit is in error]. Finally, someone has come forward who does not hesitate to suggest that there is a grammatical fault in the words of the last will and testament of the Son of God, or if this is not sufficient, that the text of the will has been corrupted because in Luke 22:20 the participle ἐκχυν-νόμενον [poured out] by its use of the article τό [that which] refers to the cup, so that according to the proper meaning of the Greek word He is simply emphasizing that what is present in the cup of the Lord's Supper and distributed and received orally was poured out for us on the cross. But this is really not an interpretation but a perversion of the words which make up the last will and testament of the very Son of God, as Peter says (2 Peter 3:16). Peter pronounces a terrible sentence on those who pervert the Scriptures, namely, that this twisting results in the eternal perdition of those who thus corrupt the words.

If these points do not move a person, I have no doubt that he is completely void of true fear of God and true piety.

And yet these strange and violent corruptions of the words of the Supper [are taught] by our adversaries, while they strenuously oppose the substantial presence which the words teach, and openly and earnestly condemn it even though they could never approve such impudence in the case of the civil will and testament of a good man.

Chapter II

The doctrine of the Lord's Supper has its true and proper foundation in the words of institution, where the reverent mind ought to search and seek what we ought to believe concerning this mystery.

Just as all the dogmas of the church and the individual articles of faith have their own foundation in certain passages of Scripture where they are clearly treated and explained, so also the true and genuine meaning of the doctrines themselves should rightly be sought and developed accurately on the basis of these passages. Likewise, it is beyond controversy that the correct belief concerning the Lord's Supper has its own particular foundation and its own basis in the words of institution.

But who does not know this, you say, or what sane man would deny it? My reply is that all do admit it and concede it in their words, but when we come to the matter itself, there is a clear diversity. For all the Sacramentarians, no matter who they are, derive some of what they want to believe and understand regarding the Lord's Supper not from the words of institution in the proper and simple sense clearly conveyed to our understanding, but they come with preconceptions on the basis of other passages of Scripture, most of which say nothing about the Lord's Supper. Each prefers certain passages which he interprets for himself according to his own analogy. And when they have gone through this process, they decide on the basis of other passages whatever they want to believe regarding the Lord's Supper. Finally they approach the words of institution, and at this point it becomes necessary for them to force upon the words of institution their preconceived meaning brought in from elsewhere on the basis of some distorted and twisted interpretation.

Thus, among the arguments the Sacramentarians pile up in order to establish and strengthen their opinion regarding the Lord's Supper, the words of institution ("This is My body") properly do not have any place at all. But when in a refutation we suggest that those passages which seem to oppose their established opinion should be removed, then at that precise point they insist upon the words: "This is My body" (1 Cor. 11:24), not, to be sure, that they might be compelled to use them in the sense they actually possess, but to serve their preconceived opinion brought in from elsewhere.

It is perfectly clear that this is the method of the Sacramentarians, and no one can deny it; as Victorinus says, with his right eye he is looking at the religion of all times and with his left at the words of the Supper. I am fully aware that this method and way of interpreting is proper and even necessary in many passages of Scripture. But we must note and bear in mind the manifest, true, and absolutely necessary difference among the passages of Scripture. For in some passages the dogmas are not clearly set forth but are either repeated briefly or are only touched on in passing. Therefore, if we are to interpret passages of this kind correctly, we must seek an analogy from other passages in which the dogmas have their own proper foundation and deal with them according to this explanation.

In other passages the dogmas are set forth under a kind of cover of rather obscure words or are presented in the polished form of figures of speech. In interpreting such passages it is sufficient to hold to the meaning which is in keeping with the other clear and appropriate passages of Scripture, as Augustine teaches in his *De doctrina Christiana,* Bk. 3, ch. 7,[1] and in his *De Genesi ad literam,* Bk. 1, ch. 21.[2]

But in certain passages of Scripture dogmas are dealt with and explained in their own proper setting. If even in these passages we permit and give license to a departure from the genuine and simple meaning of the words, and if it is sufficient that there be some kind of meaning which is in agreement with other passages of Scripture, then no dogma will be certain or remain firm. For all dogmas can be overturned and destroyed if in the case of passages of this kind we permit some opinion counter to the proper and natural sense of the words as long as it is so astutely developed and explained that it seems to be in agreement in some way with certain other passages of Scripture.

By this device Pelagius in dealing with Rom. 5:12 departed from its proper and natural meaning and asserted an interpretation which was not in itself entirely false and was entirely in agreement with many other passages of Scripture, as for instance that many people are corrupted by the example of other people's sins as by a disease and are led to imitate these examples. But if this method of interpretation is useful and correct in the case of many passages of Scripture, why do we not concede to Pelagius that he is correct in his interpretation of Rom. 5:12? For very good reasons, namely, because in the passage in Rom. 5

the dogma of original sin is treated and expounded in its own proper setting. Therefore its natural meaning must not be sought elsewhere but be derived from the proper and genuine meaning of the words in this passage.

The papalists also try to evade the perfectly clear passages in regard to justification in the Epistles to the Romans and the Galatians, where the doctrine of justification has its foundation, by making an analogy between the true and genuine meaning of these words and other passages, which seem to speak of works. In this way they develop an interpretation which leads to the creation of the *fides formata.*

But the correct answer to this is that in those passages the article of justification is plainly treated in its own true and proper setting and therefore on the basis of a simple and proper understanding of these passages we must establish the true and natural understanding of this article. We must not on the basis of preconceived notions drawn from elsewhere disturb or overturn it, but rather expound these other passages on the basis of this analogy.

The Son of God Himself gives us an example of this rule. When in Matt. 19:7 the Pharisees, in disputing about whether there was any cause for divorce, offered as a plausible case in point not their own ideas but the passage in Deut. 24:1-4, about the bill of divorcement, Christ brought the whole discussion back to the sources and foundations of the institution of marriage. He was so anxious to retain their original meaning that He did not even yield to any other passages of Scripture, but pointed out that the later passages must be interpreted in such a way that they do not conflict with the earlier institution of marriage. These points are completely clear.

Therefore, because the proof passage and the proper setting for the doctrine of the Lord's Supper are in the words of institution, an opinion must not be drawn in from somewhere else by which the proper and original meaning of the words of institution is later overturned, destroyed, or evaded. But this very excellent rule of Hilary is of value at this point: "He reads best who looks for the meaning of the words on the basis of what is said rather than imposing his own ideas; who draws from the material rather than adding to it; who does not force the material to contain what seems best to him because he has, even before reading it, had a preconceived notion as to how it should be understood."

Not that we should remove and reject the other passages of Scripture in which the dogma of the Lord's Supper is explicitly and expressly repeated and explained, for we use them ourselves as definite arguments by which we cast light on and corroborate the proper and literal meaning of the words of institution, but we have reference here to irrelevant passages which do not speak of the Lord's Supper.

This point is much more weighty in this controversy than in the case of other dogmas. For other other dogmas, although they have their foundation in definite passages of Scripture, as though to highlight them, yet have been treated and repeated in Scripture at all times. Thus we can seek explanation and enlightenment concerning them by a comparison with other passages where the same dogmas are dealt with.

But the dogma of the Lord's Supper did not exist in the church before its institution, and only on the night in which Christ was betrayed was the Lord's Supper dealt with for the first time with a definite form of institution and with definite words in the actual last will and testament of the Son of God. Therefore we must not look for the true meaning of this dogma anywhere else but in these words. For what is more out of place than to seek the meaning of the Lord's Supper in other portions of Scripture when the dogma itself had not yet been dealt with in the church and to give up the distinctive foundation of this doctrine in order that we might try to overturn and destroy the very foundation of this doctrine because of a preconceived notion brought in from someplace else?

For the Son of God in the same night in which He was betrayed instituted His Supper with a definite form and at that time first delivered this dogma with definite words, so that He might show His will that His Supper be celebrated and this dogma be handed down and judged in the church according to this rule even to the end of the age.

Therefore after His ascension He also repeated to Paul these words by which He had instituted His Supper, so that by these words and according to this rule he might hand down the doctrine of the Lord's Supper among the Gentiles. And when certain arguments arose in the church of Corinth concerning this doctrine, Paul wanted the judgment of the matter to be based not on other Scripture passages but on the very words by which Christ on the night in which He was betrayed instituted His Supper, words he dutifully quotes as having been received from the Lord.

I must confess that I am so much impressed by this argument concerning the setting of the dogma of the Lord's Supper that I can in no way follow or approve of the methodology of the adversaries whereby they take from other passages of Scripture whatever they want to believe regarding the Lord's Supper and for this reason depart from the natural meaning of the words of institution. And I do not think the adversaries, if they thought over the matter, would deny that we have extremely cogent reasons for our position, since we must realize that the last will and testament of the Son of God has to be treated with great reverence and piety in the fear of the Lord lest we call down upon ourselves the wrath of the Testator.

We shall demonstrate later that it is vain to pretend that the proper and natural meaning of the words of institution conflicts with other articles of faith. Among other rules for preserving purity of doctrine Paul hands down this final warning to Timothy, that he not permit himself to be moved from the simplicity of his faith by the arguments and oppositions which present themselves under the appearance of a great name: "O Timothy, keep that which is committed to your trust, avoiding the opposition of what is falsely called knowledge, by the professing of which some have erred from the faith." (1 Tim. 6:20-21)

On the basis of this point pertaining to the setting of the doctrine in its context we can reach many conclusions in a simple and correct way. For example, the specious statement Beza makes: "On the one hand it is agreed that the Lord's Supper consists not only of the symbols of bread and wine but also of the substance of the body and blood of Christ; likewise, it is agreed that in the Lord's Supper not only the symbols are communicated but also the true body and blood of Christ; but on the other hand the question concerns the mode of presence." For he says that his followers define the Lord's Supper on the basis of other passages of Scripture—that the body and blood of Christ, even though they are very far away, yet are spiritually present to faith and are communicated spiritually through faith. He goes on to say that this presence and communication are truer, more efficacious, and more significant than if the body and blood are received orally.

But Christ in the institution of His Supper does not teach the dogma of the presence and communication of His body and blood in such a way that He has permitted us to speculate or to draw our definition from other Scripture passages and thus believe or hold whatever kind of presence or communication in the Supper we wish. For He Himself defined it this way in the words of institution when He speaks of our oral reception of the Sacrament: "Take, eat; this is My body." Thus we are not permitted to argue about which presence and communication are more significant and fitting, but we should reverently believe and hold that presence which the Son of God has given us in the words of His last will and testament, even though it may seem absurd to our human reason. For we must not take only certain points from the words of institution and then bring in from elsewhere the rest of the points as they seem good to us, but rather we must judge and teach the whole dogma of the Lord's Supper on the basis of that passage in which we find the true and proper setting for the doctrine.

Chapter III

The true question at issue in the controversy concerning the presence, distribution, and reception of the body and blood of the Lord in the Supper.

In this controversy the various questions are so completely intermingled that the minds of the readers are confused by arguments, some relevant and others irrelevant; thus they are kept from a true understanding of the real issues under dispute. Therefore it is useful to establish the true and proper question at issue in the controversy on the basis of the words of institution and to keep this always in view in the whole controversy as a kind of guideline. Further, it will be most helpful if we first separate the relevant points from those which are irrelevant.

The question does not have to do with transubstantiation or a change of the elements, or with an absolute and unchanging presence in the elements outside of their use, or with the reservation, carrying about, offering, or adoration of the elements; both parties reject and disapprove of these practices on the basis of Scripture.

Nor is it a question of the local enclosing of the body of Christ in the bread, or of a crass physical commingling of the body of Christ with the elements, or of a Capernaitic chewing, swallowing, and guzzling of the body and blood of Christ, or of a crass physical mixing of the substances such as takes place in the case of other kinds of bodily food which go into the stomach. All these ideas we reject and disapprove.

Nor is it a controversy about the spiritual indwelling of Christ in us through His Word, through faith and the Spirit. For this we both believe and teach, as it is described in John 14:23; Rom. 8:9-11; Eph. 3:16-19, etc.

Nor is there any argument over whether we deny the spiritual eating of Christ's body and blood in the Supper through faith, as described in John 6. For we clearly teach and expressly affirm that those who in the Lord's Supper eat and drink the body and blood of Christ only sacramentally and not also spiritually eat to their own judgment and render themselves guilty of the body and blood of the Lord.

Now when these points have been separated in this way from the present controversy, then we must see how we can establish the true question at issue in the controversy. For we must not permit each person either by his own notions or on the basis of some extraneous passages of Scripture to establish whatever he desires as the question at issue. But only on the basis of the words of institution and in accord with those words in which the heart of the matter is really dealt with can and must the question at issue in the controversy be established with real exactness and certainty.

Moreover, there are two points in the words of institution which should be dealt with one at a time and distinctly. The first has to do with the essence or substance of the Lord's Supper, namely: What is present in the Lord's Supper, distributed and received orally by the communicants? This subject is dealt with in the words of institution: "He took bread, gave thanks, broke it, and gave it to His disciples, saying, 'Take, eat; this is My body which is given for you.' . . . Likewise He also took the cup, and when He had given thanks, gave it to them saying, 'This is My blood.' . . ." (1 Cor. 11:23 ff.)

The second point is this: For what purpose and use did Christ in His Supper distribute these elements to be received by the communicants and what is the salutary use or what is the spiritual benefit of those things we receive in the Supper from Christ, who distributes them? This point is treated in these words of the institution: "This do in remembrance of Me," that is, remember that My body which you are receiving was given for you, and the blood which you are drinking was shed for you for the remission of sins; and also in these words: "This cup is the New Testament in My blood." These words do not speak of some historical, cold, or idle memory, but of true faith, which lays hold of and applies to itself Christ with all His merits and benefits for reconciliation, salvation, and eternal life. This is the spiritual eating of Christ or the benefits of Christ.

These two points, dealt with separately in the words of institution, must not be confused, as if in the Lord's Supper there were only spiritual eating or the benefit of the body of Christ which comes only by faith. But just as we make a proper distinction between the substance of the Lord's Supper and its power or purpose, so also in the words of institution those words which describe the substance of the Lord's Supper ought to have special consideration and be distinguished from the other words of the institution, which describe the salutary power and efficacy, the purpose and benefit of the substance of the Sacrament.

Therefore in regard to the second or latter part of the institution, namely, the power, efficacy, purpose, and benefit of the Sacrament, there is no controversy. On this point we are in agreement. But the entire argument centers on the first part. The question at issue in this controversy neither can nor ought to be established as anything other than this: What do the actual words of institution clearly and openly present and offer to those who seek the Sacrament?

It is clear from these words that something is present in the Lord's Supper, that by an external distribution it is given or offered, and that the Son of God has commanded that we receive it. When He says: "Eat, drink," He is prescribing the mode of reception, namely, that we receive orally what is present and distributed in the Lord's Supper. For we have to understand that the words "eating and drinking" apply to this kind of reception, and no one can deny it unless at the same time he is presumptuous enough to abolish and destroy the entire external action of the Lord's Supper.

Now right here is the heart of the whole controversy: What is it which is present in the Lord's Supper which is distributed to those who eat, which we are commanded to take and receive, not just in the way it seems best to each individual, but by eating and drinking? That is: What is it which we are commanded to receive into our mouths in the Lord's Supper? The evangelists in the words of institution teach us that Christ took bread and that in the cup was the fruit of the vine. And even after the blessing or the giving of thanks Paul affirms that there was bread (1 Cor. 10 and 11). But the question is: What is present in the Lord's Supper, what is distributed to those who eat, what do we receive into our mouths? Is it only common bread or has it been sanctified? Likewise, regarding the fruit of the vine.

The real truth of the matter is that Christ gave His last will and testament in these words by which He instituted this Supper and by which He gave to the church till the end of time the correct faith concerning this dogma. For in regard to what is present in the Lord's Supper, what is distributed, what those who eat receive orally, He has pronounced and affirmed: "This is My body, which is given for you. This is My blood, which is shed for you for the remission of sins."

These words of the last will and testament of the Son of God must be taken as they read, in that true and simple understanding of them which the natural, sure, and common understanding of Scripture reflects and demonstrates. For it is sure that in the Lord's Supper not only bread and wine are present, distributed, and received orally by the communicants, but at the same time also the body of Christ which is given for us and His blood which is shed for us.

Thus the very heart of the controversy and argument will be precisely at this point. It will be our purpose to demonstrate to the earnest heart which remembers that the words of the last will and testament of the Son of God must be treated and considered with reverence and devotion and in the fear of the Lord, that there are not sufficiently serious, weighty, definite, and firm reasons to compel a person to reject that sense which the words of the testament of the Son of God convey and demonstrate by their proper and natural meaning. It will also be our purpose to show that there are many clear, convincing, sure, and certain testimonies and arguments both in the actual words of Christ's testament and in other passages of Scripture in which, after the institution, this dogma is repeated and developed; therefore that it is simplest, safest, and surest to hold and retain the meaning which the words of the testament reflect, convey, demonstrate, and show us in their natural, proper, and definite sense.

These points are simple but sure, firm, and useful for determining and retaining the correct belief regarding the Lord's Supper. But when the opinions of the adversaries are compared with this simple understanding, the reader can judge with what varied and marvelous devices they conceal, complicate, change, pervert, and evade the real heart of this controversy; then he will be able to determine from this consideration what weak and unsure foundations they have for their opinions.

In the early stages of the controversy they contended that in the Lord's Supper through the simple figure of bread and wine there was and took place only a reminder or a kind of theatrical reenactment of the giving of Christ's body for us and the shedding of His blood for us, or that it was only a kind of symbol which taught us that just as bread nourishes the body so Christ is food for our soul. Many to this very day hold and cling to this notion in their public writings. In playing with the words of the last will and testament of the Son of God they use the analogy of a betrothed or married man who plans to go to a foreign country and gives a ring to his fiancee or wife and says to her: "This is your betrothed or your husband. Every time you look at this ring, or wear it, or kiss it, do it in memory of me."

There are others who do not want to identify with such profane notions and teach that only the divine nature in Christ is present and communicated in the Supper. And because in the hypostatic union of Christ the deity is united with the humanity, in this way as in a kind of secondary manner the body of Christ is also distributed and received in the Supper, even though it is far away.

Others refer the same idea to the Holy Spirit, who is present in the Lord's Supper and joins Himself to the believers. In this way a communication of the body of Christ can be said to have occurred in the Supper because the same Spirit is present in the flesh of Christ and in the believers. There is a geometric rule that says: "Those parts of one entity which are joined to a third may be said to have made a union between them." By this line of reasoning we may finally be said to have fed on all the saints when we partake of the Lord's Supper, because the same Spirit is in all the saints and our communion with Christ is no different from our communion with the other saints. But the Son of God does not say regarding the bread of the Supper: "This is the Holy Spirit," or "This bread is the communion of My divine nature," but rather: "This is My body," and "This bread is the communion of the body of Christ."

Others interpret these words not with reference to the substance itself but to the merit and benefits of Christ's body which is given for us or with reference to the righteousness and fellowship we possess in the blood of Christ which is shed for us. They want only these things to be communicated in the Supper to the believers but not the substance itself. However, Calvin, because he saw that the words of institution speak so expressly concerning the very substance of the body of Christ, so that to deny it would be not only great impertinence but also blasphemy, therefore spoke emphatically to his followers and said that he understood the words of institution to refer to the very substance of Christ's body. And they cried out that a great injustice had been done them—as if they would deny that there is a true presence and a true communication of the very substance of Christ's body in the Lord's Supper. God forbid, they said, that we should think that the body and blood of Christ are absent from the Supper! And they added that they would be in serious error if they believed that the Lord's Supper consisted only of the external signs of bread and wine and not also of the very substance of the body and blood of Christ.

But let the reader note how carefully they present their evidence regarding the actual substance of Christ's body. Note that they are unwilling to appear to remove it from the Lord's Supper because they see that the words of the last will and testament of the Son of God teach and affirm it with such conspicuous and resounding vehemence that they fear the judgment of their own hearers among dvout people if they were to say less. And the reader should also carefully note this argument in favor of the natural and proper meaning of the words of institution.

But beware of traps. You hear the terms and you hear the agreement that there is a substantial presence of the body of Christ in the Lord's Supper. But then the deception is immediately added, namely, that the body of Christ is present in the Supper, that is, in the fiery heaven outside this world. In this way they alter the Supper and its observance (*actio*). Thus Peter Martyr says: "If anyone by the term 'presence' understands the grasping by faith whereby we ourselves ascend into heaven and lay hold on Christ in His majesty with our mind and our spirit, then I am in agreement with him." They use the same tricks when they say that in the Lord's Supper a substantial communication of the body and blood of Christ takes place. In the end they finally reveal themselves, when they say that we receive orally only the signs of bread and wine but that the actual substance of the body and blood of Christ is as far distant from the symbols which are present with us here on earth and received orally as the earth is from the highest heaven. For just as these symbols are on earth and nowhere else, so Christ according to His flesh is in heaven and nowhere else—thus Beza says.

Calvin in his *Formula of Agreement* expressly says that he rejects the substantial presence of the body of Christ on earth, because according to His body He is absent from us. But if you ask what then do the communicants here on earth where they still live in the flesh receive in the Lord's Supper, which according to Paul is to be celebrated in the gathering of the church here on earth, Calvin will reply: "I have said that the body of Christ is distributed efficaciously, but not naturally; according to its power, but not according to its substance." Likewise in his *Defense of the Agreement* he says the same thing: "The body of Christ is given to us and it nourishes us to the extent that while remaining in heaven He descends to us with His power." Likewise: "He pours out the life-giving power of His flesh upon us and we are nourished through its rays no less than by the vital warmth of the sun." As a rationale for the agreement he says: "This power and ability of giving life cannot properly be called something that is separated from its substance."

They subsequently departed so far from the words of the last will and testament of the Son of God that they have nothing sure or certain and cannot determine where they stand. For because of the evidence of the words of institution they have to concede that the Lord's Supper consists not only of the bare signs and external symbols of bread and wine but also of the body and blood of Christ and that there is communicated in the Supper not only the efficacy but also the very substance of the body of Christ. But after they have kept the hearer in suspense for a long time with all these magnificent words, then finally, when they come to the heart of the matter, they leave only the external signs and symbols which are received orally in the celebration of the

Supper when it is administered in the church here on earth. But the actual substance of Christ's body they remove as far from this celebration as heaven is from earth—and in its place, so that the signs might not be completely bare, they substitute some abstract power and efficacy. Indeed, they state expressly that in no way can there be a true union between the bread and Christ's body, since they are separated by an enormous interval of space, and they magnificently declaim that the substance of Christ's body can be communicated to us by the Spirit and by faith, even though it is absent from us and remains as far away from us as heaven is from earth; yet by the power of the Spirit there is a true and efficacious communion.

But the question is not what the power of God can do and what kind of presence and communication seems more outstanding and effective to us, but the question concerns the words of the last will and testament of the Son of God, which words, as we have shown, in their proper and natural meaning speak clearly and explicitly of the substantial presence of the body of Christ in the celebration of the Supper which is observed among us here on earth. For concerning what is distributed and received in the Supper, the Son of God pronounces: "This is My body." And these words describe the communion of the body of Christ in the Supper by the use of the term "reception," which takes place orally, for this is the simple meaning of the words: "Take, eat; this is My body," as we shall later explain.

Therefore, among these many and marvelous concealments and subterfuges and among the specious and magnificent orations of the adversaries, it is safest and simplest always to bring the question at issue in the controversy back to the words of the testament of the Son of God and to keep it within those bounds and not permit the subject to be moved from this fundamental and simple base. Further, for laying bare the hidden tricks of the adversaries these criteria of Luther are most useful against those who practice them: 1. Are the words of the last will and testament of the Son of God to be understood in their proper and natural sense, as they read? 2. What is present in the Lord's Supper which is celebrated among us here on earth; what is distributed and received orally? 3. Is the body of Christ only in heaven, so that it cannot also at the same time be present when His Supper is celebrated here on earth according to His institution? 4. What do the unworthy receive when to them the Son of God also says: "Take, eat; this is My body?" For by this line of thinking that which they are hiding is brought into the light so that even simple people can understand it.

I have gone to some length on these points, for I know that many people are disturbed, misled, and deceived precisely by this confusion over the question at issue. But when the question at issue in the controversy has been properly established, then we have the clearest possible way to a correct explanation, if only we are willing to do so on the basis of the words of institution, as we must be.

Chapter IV

What kind of descriptive terminology it is when it is asserted that the bread of the Supper is the body of Christ and that the wine of the Lord's Supper is the blood of Christ.

Because the most important aspect of this controversy lies in the question whether we must accept and understand the words of institution in their proper and natural sense, as they read, it is useful to note that there is a point which has not been rightly explained or considered and which disturbs many people, namely, that one question concerns the individual words in a statement, as to whether they have to retain their proper and natural meaning, and a second question concerns our descriptive terminology regarding mysteries which do not pertain to our natural human reason but to heavenly and divine wisdom and power. These are therefore not to be judged according to the common rules of nature but according to the word and ordinance of divine wisdom and power. For example, the statements: "God is man," and "The Son of Man is the Son of God," at one time were the subject of great controversy as to whether they were figures of speech. And when it became evident that these statements did not agree with the common and usual formulas of description because "God" and "man" are two separate and distinct entities and terms which are not predicated of one another interchangeably, the heretics contended that we absolutely must introduce a figure of speech into these words. The Manichaeans placed it in the word "man" and the Arians in the word "God." Others put the figure of speech in the connective verb in order to say: "The son of Mary is God," that is, in a nominal sense.

But the church on the basis of the Word of God correctly defended the fact that in the words of this statement we must retain the proper and natural meaning, namely, that the term "man" refers to an entity made up of the true substance of human nature, "like His brothers in all respects except for sin" [Heb. 4:15], and that the term "God" means the hypostasis of the Son of God truly subsisting in the very essence of the deity. But the copulative verb "is" (*est*) explains what actually obtains, namely, that that person is not only man, as He appeared to be, but also true God. When there was a dispute, as we are now pointing out, concerning the mode of predication, the fathers did not concede to Arius the right to use the term "deity" in a metaphorical sense or to Eutyches the right to abolish the humanity so that these two separate and distinct entities, God and man, could be predicated of one another interchangeably in accord with commonly used formulas of predication. Rather they taught, in accord with Scripture, that God is man by the hypostatic assumption of the human nature and that that man is God by the hypostatic union with the deity.

This form of description of the union of the two separate entities, since it does not agree with the usual modes of predication, is correctly called an unusual mode. The words of the proposition have and retain their own proper and natural meaning, to be sure, but such a mode of description of the two separate and distinct entities does not follow the regular and commonly used rules of the logicians regarding figurative language.

Thus when we predicate concerning the bread of the Lord's Supper that it is the body of Christ, the word "bread" has and retains its own proper meaning. And we should add the note regarding the word "body" that because it was given for us we are absolutely compelled to understand it in no other way than in its proper and natural sense—as the substance of the human nature, conceived by the Holy Ghost, born of the Virgin Mary, and nailed to the cross. The copulative verb "is" (*est*) denotes what obtains, what is present, what is distributed and received, namely, that this bread here present, after receiving its name from God, is not only bread but at the same time also the body of Christ. Thus the words of this expression possess and retain their own proper and natural meaning without being changed by a figure of speech.

The other question concerns the mode or form of predication, because this bread is described as being the body of Christ. Now the true solution to this question should not be handed over to the schools in such a way that the answer is given and defined only according to the rules, precepts, or preconceptions of grammarians, dialecticians, rhetoricians, or some profession of this type, as to what kind of predication this is and who should judge it. Many people already have done this, as if divine mysteries can be made subject to the rules of human sciences. But the simplest, safest, and surest way is this, that the answer and definition of this question be sought in and judged by the clear teaching of the Word of God regarding this mystery and by examples which are in agreement with this clear teaching. No one can condemn or deny this method. Moreover, we can do this most expeditiously and correctly by the use of antithesis or through a comparison of the descriptive terminology, of which examples are given us in Scripture.

In the first place the dialecticians have descriptive terms which they call the regular or proper type—those which are in agreement with one of the five modes of predication. Scripture is replete with examples of these. I am aware of the fact that certain people argue with great subtlety that we have instances of regular and proper predication when we say of Christ: "This man is God," or "The dove John the Baptist saw is the Holy Spirit." For they maintain that it can regularly and properly be predicated of the minotaur: "This man is a bull." But it is certain that such predications do not agree with any of the five modes of predication, for they refer to the union of two entities. These statements must be understood in this sense: "This man is not only a man but also at the same time God," for the deity and the humanity have been united into the one hypostasis. Likewise: "That dove was not only a dove, but at the same time the Holy Spirit was also present," united to the dove by a very special mode of presence. Therefore these cannot be called instances of regular or ordinary predication. Thus we correctly state and admit that the regular type of predication does not agree with the modes used of exalted things, when we say regarding the bread of the Supper: "This is the body of Christ." For according to the ordinary rules of predication an entirely false meaning would follow, namely, that it was not the true substance of the human nature which was given for us but only a mass of dough baked in the oven.

In the second place, the dialecticians, in addition to the regular descriptive terms, also have figures of speech or tropes. There is no doubt that many of these are found in Scripture. Moreover, it is not difficult to show fully and clearly and in keeping with the rules of the grammarians, dialecticians, and rhetoricians themselves that this predication by which we say of the bread of the Supper that it is the body of Christ cannot be put in the category of figurative predications in the sense that the dialecticians use the term. For in these instances either the subject or the predicate or both have been changed from their proper and natural meaning into something else, as "The lion of the tribe of Judah has prevailed" [Rev. 5:5; cf. Gen. 49:9], or "Herod is a fox" [Luke 13:31–32], or "The wolf lies down with the lamb" [Is. 11:6], that is, in the one church are gathered together people from both Jews and Gentiles. But in our proposition both the subject and the predicate, that is, the word "bread" and the word "body," retain their proper and natural meaning, as even the adversaries admit.

Therefore I often am amazed with the followers of Calvin who want to appear learned, at how boldly they assert (as if they were dealing with a very minor matter) that in the words of institution when we predicate concerning the bread of the Supper that it is the body of Christ we are using the common figure of speech called metonymy, in which by the use of a symbolic word a name is given to the thing designated. For it is absolutely certain that metonymy is not used for any kind of complete statement, but only in the case of a change of one of the words, and there is no metonymy in the copula or the verb of the statement but it is only in either the subject or the predicate or in both at the same time. For example, when I mention the word "scepter" metonymically, it is understood as though I were really saying the word "rule." Or if I use the word "right hand" in a metonymic sense, it is not necessary in the same statement, in the place of a predicate, to use the word "faithfulness," because by the use of the word "right hand" the same idea is understood through the figure of speech, just as if I had used the word "faithfulness" in its simple and proper sense.

Moreover, it is unheard-of among all the authors who speak correctly that there is a use of metonymy which would consist of a complete statement which by name expresses both the sign and the thing signified through the copula "is" (est), so that we would attribute to the symbolic word in the subject the actual thing signified in the predicate, like saying that the scepter is the rule, the right hand is faithfulness, the fasces are the power of Rome, the toga is peace, etc. I am certain that it is impossible to bring forth such an example of metonymy from any recognized author. And yet this very kind of metonymy is so constantly taught in the case of the words of the Supper and is accepted by so many people that they are not even afraid of perverting the proper and natural meaning of the last will and testament of the Son of God, even though it is absolutely certain that the words in the institution of the Supper, which are the point under dispute, do possess and retain their own proper and natural meaning, as the adversaries themselves admit.

But in a metonymic figure of speech the words either in the subject or the predicate are changed from their proper and natural meaning, as that example in the letter of Cicero to Piso so clearly demonstrates. Piso had interpreted the statement of Cicero ("Arms shall surrender to the toga") thus: "You say the imperial power is going to yield to your toga." But Cicero replies: "I did not say this toga that I am wearing, nor the arms, shield, and sword of this emperor, but the toga is a symbol of peace and quiet, and on the other hand, following the example of the poets, we use the word 'arms' as a symbol of tumult and war. I wanted this to be understood, that war and tumult would give way to peace and rest.''

Therefore, because the words both in the subject and the predicate have and retain their own proper and natural meaning in the statement in which the body of Christ is predicated of the bread of the Supper, it cannot be rightly said that there is a figure of speech in this statement or that the proposition is figurative because of some kind of trope. For this conflicts with the definition of a trope, namely, that it is a change of meaning of a word from its proper and natural meaning into something else.

In the third place, there is still another kind of predication in Scripture about which the dialecticians themselves argue as to how they can refer it to their rules as a clear and sufficient antithesis to us and our position. For when in Scripture a parable occurs, it is customary to interpret it under this kind of predication: "The field is the world" [Matt. 13:38]; "The seed is the Word of God" [Luke 8:11], etc. The interpretations of visions are also handled under this kind of predication, e.g., Ezek. 37:11: "These bones are the whole house of Israel"; Zech. 4:11: "What are these two olive branches?" Rev. 1:20: "The seven candlesticks are the seven churches." The interpretation of dreams also comes under this kind of predication in Scripture; for example, Gen. 41:26: "The seven cows are seven years."

Zwingli, Schwenkfeld, and others argue that the kind of predication in the words of the Supper: "This is My body," is exactly the same as this. But both among themselves and among the majority of the adversaries the difference and diversity is so plain and manifest that there is no need of argument to prove it. For in the words of the Supper there is neither a story, a parable, or a vision, the explanation of which lies in the words: "This is My body." But on the contrary, in these words is instituted a certain kind of distribution and communion or participation. It is horrendous to realize that there are still some people who in their public writings do not fear to compare this statement with the interpretation of the dream in Gen. 41:1 ff. For certainly the things which Christ performed in His Supper were not done in a dream, as if we can interpret the words: "This is My body," as some kind of dream.

In the fourth place, the papalists, in order to strengthen their false concept of transubstantiation, by which the substance of the bread is annihilated, argue concerning the bread in the Supper that the body of

Christ is predicated of it in a twofold sense. First through conversion, as in Ex. 4 and 7, where the staff is changed into a serpent, and John 2, where the water in the water pots is turned into wine, that is, just as what before was a staff and water now through conversion becomes a serpent and wine, so in the Supper the substance of the bread through annihilation is changed into the body of Christ. Second, after the transubstantiation has occurred there is a predication of identity, so that in answer to the question in Ex. 4:2, "What do you have in your hand?" Moses replies, "What I have in my hand is a rod." And the servants at Cana after the conversion would have said to the master of the feast, "This is the wine which Jesus made."

But these examples are entirely diverse and different. For in Ex. 4 and 7 it is written that a rod is changed into or becomes a serpent; and in John 2 that water is made wine (cf. John 4:46: "He had made the water wine"). But the words of the Supper do not speak of the bread and wine this way. On the contrary, in the very act of blessing, Christ in the place of the subject does not indicate some vague entity, but He takes the cup in His hand (Luke 22:17; 1 Cor. 11:25). And after the blessing Paul, just as he had received it from the Lord, still mentions the bread and says of that bread that it is the body of Christ. Thus this figment of transubstantiation, because it is a late development and unknown both to Scripture and the faithful ancient church, is properly and correctly exploded. And transubstantiation brings with it the carrying about, the reservation, and the adoration of the bread (ἀρτολατρεία), all of which are beyond the usage instituted by Christ.

Finally, because the body is predicated of the bread and the blood of the wine, but not in any of those ways we have discussed, the question arises: Are there in Scripture any other modes of predication by which we could make a comparison with the words of the Supper so that thereby we could determine what kind of predication it is when we say of the bread of the Supper that it is the body of Christ?

Moreover, this kind of predication must not be derived from our conjectures but from the actual points themselves, as they are treated and explained in the words of the Supper. Now the words of the Supper teach, just as the most ancient doctors of the church have always understood (which even the adversaries themselves admit), that the Lord's Supper or the Eucharist consists of two things, the bread and the body of Christ, the wine and His blood. And Paul, as we shall later demonstrate, affirms in 1 Cor. 10 that the distribution and reception of this bread is the distribution of and participation in the body of Christ.

When two things or substances are joined together without

confusion or mixing but in such a way that they are and remain distinct and yet at the same time are both present and the one is distributed at the same time the other is, Scripture explains and describes this communion or union, this presence and distribution, with its own special kind of predication. This is particularly the case when one of the substances or entities is visible, subject to the senses, and serves as a kind of medium through which the other substance is shown to be truly present, to be sure, but at the same time invisible. Likewise, when one substance is a visible and external instrument, perceptible to the senses, through which the other substance is distributed in a way not perceptible to the senses, then Scripture with its own method of predication puts this visible entity, perceptible to the senses, in the position of the subject; the other entity, truly present and distributed at the same time but in an invisible and imperceptible way, it places in the attributive or predicate position. Scripture joins these two different entities together through the use of the copulative verb "is" (est), which means nothing else than that there is a union or communion of these two entities. Thus, together with the perceptible thing, that other entity, described in the predicate, is also at the same time truly present and distributed. Or, to say it in other words, Scripture puts in the position of the subject the entire entity, which by reason of the union now consists of two things, and in the position of the predicate it mentions the second thing, which is the chief thing and something that does not appear to the senses or is not obvious to them.

This mode of predication is very common in popular language, as when we say of a vessel which is on display, "This is wine," or of a bag, "Look, you have money." It is as if the master of the feast had shown the water jugs and said, "This is the wine Jesus has made." Or as if the priest in Num. 5:17-19 should say of the earthen vessel, "These are the bitter waters which cause the curse." Or as if John the Baptist should say of the dove, "This is the Holy Spirit" (Matt. 3:13 ff.). Or as if Elisha should say of the fiery horses, "These are the angels of God." (2 Kings 2:11-12)

To be sure, among the Latins and the more polished authors I have not noticed that such a mode of predication is frequently used or in common practice. But dialecticians do teach that when two different things are mutually predicated of one another, out of necessity from the proper and natural meaning of the words, one must be made into the subject and the other into the attributive or predicate.

But in Scripture there is a mode of predication which is both frequent and common, whereby the different words remain in the subject and the predicate with their own natural meaning and through a copulative verb are joined in one proposition so that the subject indicates something visible or perceptible but the predicate indicates that, together with that perceptible thing, there is present another entity which is expressed by the attributive word.

Thus in regard to the dove which John the Baptist saw, the Holy Spirit is predicated of it in this way, that when the dove descended the Baptist asserts that through the dove he saw the Holy Spirit descending (John 1:32; Luke 3:22). Concerning the appearance of the cloven tongues in the mouths of the apostles or the flames over their heads the Holy Spirit is predicated in such a way that Scripture affirms that with these external manifestations the Holy Spirit whom the apostles received is at the same time truly present and sent through this medium (cf. Acts 1:8; 2:3-4; John 7:39). Christ with His external breath breathed on the faces of the apostles (John 20:22). As a result of this breathing, which was perceptible to the senses and which the apostles received, Christ then proclaimed; "Receive the Holy Spirit." Thus the flaming horses in 2 Kings 6:17 are the angels of God, for "He makes His messengers spirits and His ministers a flaming fire" (Ps. 104:4). How this statement regarding the angelic spirits is to be understood is expressly shown in Heb. 1:7; in Judg. 13:6 ff., where the man of God is the angel of the Lord; and in Gen. 19:1 ff., where the two men are angels of the Lord. The youths or men who appeared in shining white garments at the tomb of the Lord in Mark 16:5 and Luke 24:4 are angels of the Lord; the serpent in Gen. 3:1 ff. is Satan or the devil (cf. Rev. 12:9 and 20:2). The man who wrestled with Jacob in Gen. 32:24 ff. was God. In regard to the appearance of the burning bush there is this predication: "I am the God of your father" (Ex. 3:6). The pillar of cloud and the pillar of fire in Ex. 13:21[1] is connected with the angel of the Lord in Ex. 14:19. When the cloud and the fire descend to Mt. Sinai, it is asserted that God Himself has descended (Ex. 19:18). The glory of God is predicated of the appearance of the cloud and the burning fire (Ex. 24:16-17). Likewise the glory of the Lord (cf. Ex. 40:34) is predicated of the cloud and the fire in Num. 9:15 ff.

When the ark was lifted up in Num. 10:35-36, Moses said: "Rise up, O Lord, and let Your enemies be scattered," and when it was set down he said: "Return, O Lord, to the multitude of Israel." That is to say, God had promised His presence with the ark by means of a special kind of grace (cf. Ex. 25:22; 1 Kings 8:1-11). The Branch of David is called Jehovah in Jer. 23:5-6. The Child is called "the everlasting Father" in Is. 9:6. The Son of Man is "the Son of the living God" (Matt. 16:16). "The Word was made flesh" (John 1:14), that is, by taking on the seed of Abraham (cf. Heb. 2:16). When God breathed the breath of life into the body of Adam, which had been formed from the earth, Scripture says that man was made a living soul (Gen. 2:7). Thus the second Adam was made a life-giving spirit (1 Cor. 15:45), which is understood simply because of the union of the deity and the humanity.

Similar to predications of this kind are also these: "The washing of water in the Word" (Eph. 5:26) is the washing of regeneration and the renewing of the Holy Spirit, in the sense that the Holy Spirit is present in this act [of baptism], and through this means He is given to us, works among us, and gives the seal of regeneration. The Gospel which is proclaimed with our mouths is the power of God unto salvation, in the sense that Christ, who is the power of God (1 Cor. 1:24), is present in this means and instrument (Matt. 28:18, 20), and through this means He shows and exercises His power. Circumcision was a covenant because it was a means through which God conferred His covenant upon those who were circumcised, and sanctified and strengthened them.

I have given these examples in order that I might demonstrate that this method of predication concerning the union, presence, and distribution of two distinct things through the uniting of the subject and the predicate by the copulative verb is common and well known in Scripture, even though the kind of union is not the same in all cases. For example, in Christ there is the hypostatic or personal union, which is not the case with the dove of John the Baptist or the bread of the Supper, which is another kind of union but yet is a true and substantial union.

Because the institution of the Lord's Supper demonstrates that the Eucharist consists of two things, the bread and the body of Christ, and because Paul points out that the distribution and reception of this bread is the distribution of and participation in the body of Christ (1 Cor. 10:16), therefore these statements in the words of the Supper about which contention has arisen are rightly and correctly to be compared with those points we have already touched on. As a result of this we can correctly determine what kind of predication it is when we predicate of the bread that it is the body of Christ, and likewise that the matter itself must be drawn from and judged by the simple and basic words of the institution of the Supper. The idea of comparing these statements is so manifest and evident that even Calvin recognized its validity and approved of it.

Much light is shed on this whole controversy by a careful examination of these statements, for although in these propositions which we have cited from Scripture two different things are joined together by the copula, and thus they are not regular predications, yet it is not necessary that the words in either the subject or the predicate give up their proper and natural meaning on the grounds of being figures of speech. Rather they possess and retain their proper and natural meaning both in the subject as well as in the predicate. But the mode of predication is peculiar in that a union, communion, or presence of this kind between two things is notable for the fact that along with a subject which is visible and perceptible to the senses there is a second element which is mentioned in the predicate which is understood to be present and distributed at the same time.

In the words of the Supper, since the body of Christ can be predicated of the bread, the papalists in the subject devise a transubstantiation of the bread; the Sacramentarians in place of the substance of the body of Christ substitute in the predicate either a symbol of the absent body or something efficacious which is separate from the substance, which is not present where the bread is. When the Holy Spirit is predicated of the dove, it is not necessary that the dove be transubstantiated or that it be substituted for the substance of the Holy Spirit or made only a sign or the efficacy of the absent Spirit so that the Holy Spirit could be predicated of the dove. Rather, by reason of a union or communion the one can be predicated of the other.

To be sure, the dove is called the symbol of the Holy Spirit, but not in such a way that it symbolizes either the absent substance of the Spirit or the presence of only His power and efficacy while His substance is actually absent, but because with that visible symbol the actual substance of the Spirit is understood to be truly, really, and substantially present. As I have said, by reason of a union or communion the one can be predicated of the other.

By this communion and presence we do not mean a hypostatic or inseparable union, or a local inclusion, or a mixture of substances, or some physical and crass union devised by the reasoning of this world. In an invisible, heavenly manner, which is impossible for us to understand, we believe that the dove and the Holy Spirit are truly and substantially joined together for this occasion; for the Spirit desired to show and confirm the peculiar and invisible presence of His essence and power through this visible symbol.

These concepts in a simple and beautiful way are exactly parallel to the predication by which in the words of institution the body of Christ is predicated of the bread of the Supper and the blood of Christ is predicted of the wine. Hence the whole mode of predication can be properly evaluated in all these cases. This mode of predication which occurs in Scripture and our daily speech is so simple, common, and ordinary that the meaning offers itself without being asked. For the words are understood just as they read, in their proper and natural meaning.

Luther calls this method of predication synecdoche in his *Contra Carlstadium,* p. 49, and in his *Maior confessio,*[2] p. 222. But this is not the usual synecdoche of the rhetoricians, for it does not agree with the descriptions or examples treated in the rules of the rhetoricians and thus cannot be judged on this basis. However, what Luther calls synecdoche is the union of two things which are understood as being present and distributed at the same time, one of which is predicated of the other, either as part of the part, as when the dove is the Spirit, or as part of the whole, as when Adam says of Eve: "This is my flesh and bone." (Gen. 2:23)

Some call it a sacramental predication because of the sacramental union, to indicate that the Sacrament consists of two parts. It is commonly called an irregular predication, because it does not fit the usual rules of predication. But it does not matter by what name it is called as long as we correctly understand the method of predication and as long as the heart of the matter as it is taught in Scripture remains unimpaired.

But if someone, because of the regular rules and preconceptions, tries to discredit, overturn, pervert, and destroy this idea, we will answer him in the words of Hilary, who in speaking of the mystery of the Lord's Supper made this significant assertion: "We must not speak of the things of God in a human or secular fashion, nor must we allow our perversity to twist the purity of the heavenly words into an alien and irreverent meaning by a violent and improper predication."[3]

From this comparison of statements or predications much light is shed on all aspects of this controversy, many strictures are removed, and the true sources of the ways of speaking are made evident. For we are speaking in harmony with the whole ancient church when we say that the body of Christ is present, distributed, and received in the Lord's Supper in the bread, with the bread, and under the bread.

But these ways of speaking are criticized in amazing ways by the adversaries. They cry that we are departing from the words of institution and are ipso facto demonstrating that the proper and natural meaning of these words cannot be retained, because it is far different to *be* something than to be *in* something.

We agree that this is true in normal predications. But we have shown that this predication does not agree with the modes used of exalted things; still it does not thereby follow that the words are figurative or that we must read a figure of speech into these words whereby they can be deprived of their proper and natural meaning. For we have demonstrated that it is one thing when we are affirming regarding individual words in a statement that they possess and retain their proper and natural meaning, and it is a different question as to what kind of predication it is when according to the statement of Scripture there is a union of two things, as we have indicated, whereby the one is predicated of the other.

In this latter type of predication Scripture itself shows these predications in its own statements, e.g., Ex. 3:2: "The Lord appeared in a flame of fire"; Num. 12:5: "The Lord descended in a pillar of cloud"; Ex. 14:19: "The angel of the Lord removed Himself and went behind them, and with Him went the pillar of cloud"; Deut. 12:23: "The blood is the life itself"; Lev. 17:11: "The life of the flesh is in the blood"; Luke 3:22: "The Holy Spirit descended in bodily form as a dove." Even the statement regarding the hypostatic union—that the Son of Man is the Son of God—is demonstrated in this way in Scripture, e.g., "God was in Christ" [2 Cor. 5:19]; "In Him dwells the whole fulness of the Godhead" [Col. 1:19; 2:9]; "He was in the form of God" [Phil. 2:6]; "Immanuel, God with us" [Matt. 1:23]; "God was with Him." [Acts 10:38]

Therefore in the matter of the Lord's Supper we retain and are determined to use that particular form of language with which the Son of God instituted His own last will and testament, whereby He predicated of the bread that it is the body of Christ. On account of the communion of the bread and the body Paul also spoke of the distribution and reception of this bread as the distribution of and participation in the body of Christ. Therefore we, following his example and authority, regularly thus explain this statement of Scripture whenever the body and blood of Christ are present, distributed, and received in the Lord's Supper in the bread or the wine. We thereby bear witness by these modes of speaking that we do not approve either of the transubstantiation of the elements or of the absence of the body and blood of Christ in the Supper. But in accord with the words of institution we believe that the Eucharist consists of two entities—the bread and the body, the wine and the blood of Christ.

These ways of speaking also have clear precedents from the entire ancient church, as we have already fully explained in our previous discussion of the doctrine of the Lord's Supper in regard to the question of the modes of speaking.

Chapter V

Concerning the physical eating of the bread and concerning the twofold eating of the body of Christ, the sacramental and the spiritual, in the Supper.

The argument regarding the eating, if it is not correctly, simply, and distinctly taught and explained on the basis of the very foundations of its institution, has disturbed many people in this controversy. The adversaries contend that the body of Christ in the Supper is eaten only by faith and in a spiritual way, that is, faith turns itself from the celebration of the Supper which takes place in our midst here on earth and by meditation ascends into heaven and there in mind and spirit embraces Christ in His majesty. These are the words of Peter Martyr. And if one does not agree with them, they immediately let loose with some blasphemous slanders about Capernaitic eating of the body of Christ or about the cyclops who ate human flesh or the Scythian slurping of the blood of Christ. For human reason neither knows nor understands any other kind of eating except the physical and gross eating by which the flesh of cattle is eaten or a cow eats hay.

But because this kind of eating cannot and must not be attributed to or believed of the body of Christ without danger to our faith, they think that it follows from this that there is only a spiritual eating of the body of Christ in the Supper, because they are unwilling to grant any third kind of eating between the physical and the spiritual. But there is no doubt that a great deal of light will be shed on this controversy if we can show in a brief way the difference between the kinds of eating which take place in the Supper. However, this discussion must take place on no other basis than the very words of institution which are the basis of this doctrine, and here we will seek and draw our conclusion with the greatest certainty and safety.

Now it is certain that in the Lord's Supper we eat bread. For "Jesus took bread, broke it, blessed it, and gave it to the disciples, saying: 'Take and eat'" [Matt. 26:26]. And Paul also, after the blessing, says: "As often as you eat this bread . . . ." (1 Cor. 11:26)

But it is also certain that we do not eat only bread in the Lord's Supper, for in regard to what is received and eaten in the Supper, Christ says: "This is My body" [Matt. 26:26]. Thus in the Supper we eat also the body of Christ, but not only with our minds and spirit through faith alone. For if the eating in these words of the Supper means that faith by its meditations ascends above all heavens and there embraces Christ in His majesty, the Supper can then be celebrated without any external reception into the mouth, something which no one has ever dared even to suggest. Thus the word "to eat" possesses and retains in this passage its proper and natural meaning. For Christ commanded us to receive something in His Supper when He said: "Take," and He defined the mode of receiving, namely, that it take place orally, when He added: "Eat." But regarding what is thus received orally and eaten, the Son of God Himself affirms: "This is My body." But it is impossible that one and the same word in the same statement at the same time possesses both its own proper meaning and a figurative meaning. Therefore there is not ony the spiritual eating of the body of Christ in the Supper, for many by eating that which Christ affirms is His body eat judgment to themselves, according to Paul, something which does not happen by a spiritual eating.

The spiritual eating is not described in these words: "Take, eat," but in the other words of the Supper which follow. That is to say, the sacramental eating is done in memory of Christ because His body is given for us, which by being distributed to us in the Supper sanctifies the new covenant to us. In these words, I say, the spiritual eating is also described, and this absolutely must happen in order that the eating of the Sacrament may become salutary for us and that we may not do it to our judgment.

Therefore it is manifest on the basis of the words of institution that there is a threefold eating in the Lord's Supper.

First, there is the eating of the bread, which is rightly and properly called a physical eating.

Second, there is the eating of the body of Christ, which although it does not take place in a physical or gross way, yet (according to the words of Christ) takes place orally, for He says: "Take, eat; this is My body." This is called a sacramental eating in the old method of designation.

Third, there is the spiritual eating of the body of Christ. Likewise the things which I say regarding the word "eating" and regarding the body of Christ I want to apply with equal force to the word "drinking" and to the blood of Christ.

But now let us speak clearly and simply in regard to each of the individual terms, according to the analogy of the words of institution.

The physical eating is well known and manifest. The bread is taken in the mouth and chewed with the teeth, masticated in the mouth, swallowed by the throat, and taken into the stomach. There it is changed into chyle and then changed into nutrient in the liver and then turned into flesh and blood. But part as waste is ejected from the body by the digestive process. It is beyond all controversy that the substance of the bread in the Eucharist is eaten in this natural way. Thus Origin, on Matt. 15, writes: "The sanctified bread according to its material aspects goes out with the waste and is ejected by the digestive process." And Augustine says, *De Trinitate,* Bk. 5, ch. 10: "The bread which is used for the purpose of receiving the Sacrament is consumed. With regard to this physical eating of the substance of the bread, because it is evident, known, and manifest to our senses and our experience, it is unnecessary to say more. But because of the union, the body of Christ is predicated of that bread which is eaten physically, so that according to the words of Christ those who eat it are rightly and properly said to be eating not only the bread but also the body of Christ. For He says: 'Take, eat; this is My body.'"[1]

Therefore the question is whether the body of Christ in the Supper is eaten in this kind of physical, outward, bodily way through the process of mastication, swallowing, and digestion. Augustine[2] and Cyril wrote, to be sure, that the people of Capernaum were of the opinion that it was as if the body of Christ were going to be cut into small pieces and given to us to be eaten, just as the flesh of cattle is sold in a meat market and cooked and eaten [John 6:52]. But Christ criticizes these people sharply, and Augustine often rejects the Scythian concept of cannibalism (ἀνθρωποφαγία), and Chrysostom says, *De encoeniis:*[3] "Does the rest of the food go out through the digestive process? God forbid!" And Paschasius in a long sermon[4] rejects this concept of Capernaitic flesh eating (σαρκοφαγία).

Likewise Luther always and everywhere, and particularly in the book on the Word, declared that when he taught that the body of Christ was eaten in the Supper he did not understand this to mean that it took place in a visible or perceptible way, so that the actual substance of the body of Christ would be torn with the teeth, chewed up or butchered, masticated in the mouth, swallowed, digested, and changed into the substance of our flesh and blood, in the way other food is. For death has no more dominion over us. (Rom. 6:9)

But immediately the Zwinglians cry out: "If you agree that the eating of the body of Christ which takes place in the Supper is not physical and does not take place in the way of other natural foods, whereby they are food in our stomach, then it will be only a spiritual eating which takes place only by faith, that is, our physical mouth receives nothing but the bread and meanwhile our soul by faith applies to itself the benefits of Christ which He merited for us by the giving of His body. Meanwhile faith extends its thoughts into the fiery heaven and there in mind and spirit embraces Christ in His majesty."

But the words of Christ in the institution, concerning what those who eat in the Supper receive orally, clearly and expressly state: "This is My body." Therefore, according to these words of the last will and testament of the Son of God, we must rightly and necessarily acknowledge and believe that in the Supper there is more than a spiritual eating; there is also a sacramental eating of the body of Christ, as the ancient church so correctly called it. Nor is it true, as certain people imagine, that our physical mouths do not receive the actual substance of the body of Christ but only a kind of sacramental body to which, because of a symbolic designation, we attribute the name "the body of Christ." Added to this consideration is the sure and evident point that we must understand no other body than that which was given for us.

Now some will ask: "What is the nature of this sacramental eating of the body of Christ in the Supper and how does it take place?" And if the union or presence of the body of Christ with the bread is physical, consistent with some kind of natural or rational or secular mode of presence, then it is right to demand that we show the evident and manifest meaning of sacramental eating. For as is the union or presence of the body of Christ in the Supper, so is also the eating.

But the union or presence is not physical in the sense of our secular reasoning. Therefore we can more easily show what the sacramental eating of the Supper of the body of Christ is *not* rather than what it *is*. That is to say, it is not physical in the sense that it consists of the chewing, mastication, swallowing, and digesting of the substance of what is eaten, because the presence of Christ's body in the Supper is not a natural presence in the sense consistent with the ordinary use of this term.

And yet it is not something merely figurative or imaginary but true and substantial, even though it occurs through a supernatural, heavenly, and unsearchable mystery. Thus we must not doubt as true and sure what the Son of God Himself affirms in the words of His last will and testament, that those who eat in the Supper receive and eat with their physical mouths not only the bread but at the same time also that body which was given for us, even though this does not take place in a physical way as when we eat ordinary bread.

Although we are not able to demonstrate or understand how this takes place, it suffices for faith simply to believe what the words of Christ teach us in their proper and natural sense—that the physical mouths of those who eat in the Lord's Supper are not eating common or plain bread when they receive the bread, but the bread which now has been given its name by God, that is, the body of Christ. That is to say, it is bread with which the body of Christ is truly and substantially (although in a supernatural way) present and distributed. The very Son of God by this distribution and reception, which He willed with His own counsel and wisdom, determined to employ the service and work of our mouths. He did this not only by His Spirit or by the efficacy of His humanity, but rather with the very substance of His body and blood He joins as closely as possible to Himself not only the soul but also the very bodies of those who eat. And He accomplishes this not by some physical and outward mixing of the substances or by joining something to the food in our stomachs, but in a way whereby it becomes a heavenly and spiritual nourishment for both the body and soul of the believers unto eternal life.

He accomplishes this in a manner which is known to Him alone who is the Author of this tremendous mystery, but it is incomprehensible and ineffable to us who can only believe it for our salvation according to the words of the last will and testament of the Son of God. We can never understand it with our thoughts and we ought in no way investigate it with our minds.

However, some light can be shed on these matters by a comparison with the ways in which two substances are described as being joined together in a peculiar and heavenly manner. We have referred to this in the preceding chapter [p. 55] in connection with Luther's explanation in his *Maior confessio*. For by reason of this union the dove which John the Baptist saw is called the Holy Spirit, and when the dove descended it is correct to say that the Holy Spirit also descended. Moreover, the descent of the dove is physical and consistent with the normal manner of nature, that is, by a movement from a higher place to a lower one, where the dove had not been before. But the descent of the Spirit did not take place in this physical way, because the Spirit fills all things with His substance and therefore in the proper sense of the word does not move from one place to another. Yet not only the dove but at the same time also the Spirit Himself is described as truly having descended, and we believe it is so.

Nor was this descent of the Spirit merely fictitious or imaginary, but a true event, even though it was not one in keeping with nature or the manner of this physical world. Nor was it merely a spiritual event, as when God is described as arising, ascending or descending, or as when by some action He demonstrates His power. But because the actual substance of the Holy Spirit willed to join itself to the dove with a peculiar kind of presence and to show itself to the Baptist in this way—therefore where the dove was, there also it can rightly and truly be said that the very substance of the Spirit was also present at the same time with that peculiar kind of presence. For this reason, when the dove descended it is equally correct to say that the very substance of the Spirit also descended, although the descent as it applies to the Spirit did not take place by physical movement.

Likewise, in regard to the flaming cloven tongues in the mouths of the apostles [Acts 2:3], the Holy Spirit is predicated of them in such a way that we believe that He was truly present in the mouths of the apostles with these visible flames, not only with His efficacy but with His actual substance. Indeed, these flames were locally limited to the mouths of the apostles, but the substance of the Spirit was not in their mouths by any such local limitation or circumscription. Yet we believe that He was truly and substantially present no less than the flames themselves, although in a different manner than the way the flames were sitting on the heads of the apostles. For Scripture says that the Holy Spirit sat on each of them.

To be sure, these flames were sitting on the heads of the apostles in a physical way but the substance of the Spirit did not thereby take on the physical localization of each individual flame. And yet, because the substance of the Spirit was also at the same time present with the flames with its own peculiar kind of union, therefore it can truly be said that through these visible flames the Holy Spirit sat upon the apostles. For, says Luther, that which can rightly be attributed to the one part can because of the union also be attributed to the other which is present at the same time and united with it.

Isaiah saw the Lord of Hosts in visible form sitting on His throne [Is. 6:1]. By this act of sitting in a visible form there was, to be sure, a manifest physical localization of His members which cannot be attributed to the actual essence of the deity. Yet, because of this peculiar kind of union and presence, the essence of the deity itself was present in this visible form and it can truly be said that by means of this manifestation and through this manifestation God [actually] sat—not as elsewhere in a figurative sense, as when God is said to sit [in judgment], for example, when He shows the power of His judgments by performing an act of judgment.

Likewise John the Baptist affirms that he saw the Holy Spirit when he saw the dove [John 1:32]. Now the physical pupils of the eyes of John the Baptist could not see the very substance of the Spirit, because it is invisible. But because the Holy Spirit Himself was at the same time not merely figuratively but truly and substantially present with the outward appearance of the dove through which He desired to show His own presence, therefore the dove which was seen can actually be said to have been the Spirit Himself. He was seen through this outward manifestation and not as in other cases, where God can be said to be seen outside of such an outward appearance, by faith, in our minds and spirits.

Thus the sacramental eating of the body of Christ in the Supper is not what the adversaries imagine, namely, that we orally eat only a symbol of the absent body of Christ, or that somewhere else beyond the observance of the Supper (which according to Paul is celebrated in the gathering of the congregation) faith should seek and embrace the humanity of Christ. But because the body of Christ is truly and substantially present and distributed with this bread, therefore, when our physical mouth receives this bread and eats it, we can truly say and believe that our mouth at the same time also receives and eats the body of Christ, although this does not take place in the same kind of physical way in which the bread is eaten. We can very simply understand and judge this on the basis of the examples and similes we have indicated.

On the basis of what we have said up to this point we can draw the sure, firm, and correct conclusion that in addition to the physical eating and spiritual eating there is a third kind of eating, namely, the sacramental eating of the body of Christ which of necessity must take place in the Supper if we do not want to reject the proper and natural meaning of the words of the testament of Christ.

But the spiritual eating of the flesh and blood of Christ can take place either outside of or within the celebration of the Lord's Supper. For when, even outside of the celebration of the Lord's Supper, faith embraces and lays hold of Christ, who is both God and man, who is brought to us and offered to us in the Word—when faith does this in such a way that it applies to itself His benefits which He merited for us by the giving of His body and the shedding of His blood—then we can say that we are eating the body of Christ spiritually (John 6). But in the Lord's Supper the spiritual eating must not so turn our mind and faith away from this celebration of the Supper which is taking place in the gathering of the congregation that in our meditations we are carried beyond the heaven of heavens, as our adversaries imagine.

Because faith, however, in accordance with the words of the testament, believes that with the visible elements a communion (κοινωνία) of the presence of the body and blood of Christ is also distributed to those who eat, it has been firmly established that the Son of God Himself in this distribution and reception of His body and blood is also giving, applying, and sealing to you all those benefits He gained for us by the giving of His body and the shedding of His blood. Moreover, His new testament of grace sanctifies, confirms, and seals these benefits to you. Furthermore, He bestows His whole being in so intimate a union that He joins Himself to you with that nature with which He is our brother and consubstantial with us, and through which He accomplished the work of our redemption and propitiation. Thus my faith may hold that the most certain and most precious pledge pertains to me and that I possess and will possess as sure, sealed, and immovable those blessings which God in His general promise has assured to all believers.

Later on, when we speak about the benefits of the Lord's Supper, we shall explain these matters more fully. At this point I have only wanted to show the different kinds of eating which take place in the Supper, on the basis of the words of institution. There is no argument about physical or spiritual eating. The argument clearly has to do with the sacramental eating, and this we must admit. For the spiritual eating is the enjoyment of Christ and of all His benefits, but the Lord's Supper was instituted as the seal of His benefits. And how is the spiritual benefit of Christ sealed to us? Surely not with only a little morsel of bread and a few drops of wine, but with the very substance of the body which was given for us and the blood which was shed for us. For this is what the Son of God Himself affirms. Therefore, just as there is one thing which is sealed and another thing by which the sealing is done, so also the spiritual eating of Christ which is sealed is one thing and the sacramental eating of the body of Christ by which the sealing is done is another.

Chapter VI

The sources and the manner of gathering the principal arguments against departing from the proper and natural meaning of the words of the last will and testament of the Son of God and how these arguments can be most simply arranged.

The point of this whole controversy revolves around the question, as we have said, of whether the words of the last will and testament of the Son of God (by which He predicates with strong affirmation in regard to the bread of the Supper: "This is My body," and of the wine of the Supper: "This is My blood") are to be taken in the sense which the simple, proper, natural, sure, and common meaning of the words requires.

Therefore it is useful and absolutely necessary that we always keep in mind the sure, clear, and well-established arguments which are drawn from and based on the solid foundations of Scripture, so that our minds may be instructed and fortified against all specious and seemingly plausible opinions but rather can take refuge in the simple, proper, and natural meaning of the words of the last will and testament of the Son of God, who Himself will enlighten and guide our minds.

These arguments have certainly been learnedly demonstrated and confirmed with ample documentation in the many writings of our theologians and particularly in the writings of Dr. Luther. I therefore, in order that that ancient saying of Irenaeus, "the same things about the same things" may be observed, do not wish to assert anything new. I have merely gathered material from those earlier extensive writings and will attempt to note with simple and plain brevity the principal points as to why we must not depart from the simple and natural meaning of the words of the last will and testament of the Son of God.

Furthermore, I will show how these arguments can be arranged in a simple and expeditious way so that when they are placed in order as in battle formation they will have more clarity and force. Moreover, I think arranging them in proper order will aid in teaching the subject with simplicity.

In the first line of battle we shall place those arguments which are drawn from the clear and continuous analogy of interpretation which the Holy Spirit has taught us to observe in those passages where dogmas or articles of faith are established.

In the second line we shall gather the arguments based on the words of institution, wherein lies the foundation of this doctrine, as they are found repeated in passages of Scripture.

In the third line we shall add the arguments taken from other places in Scripture in which the dogma of the Lord's Supper is expressly treated, for example, 1 Cor. 10 and 11.

In the fourth line we shall bring in the opinions of the ancient church, demonstrating by a clear, sure, and definite line of reasoning what the agreed-upon confession of the older, purer church was in regard to this dogma.

Finally we shall show how useful and how consoling the teaching which is based on the proper and natural meaning of the words is for troubled consciences. In this order we shall deal with the main arguments with simple clarity and brevity.

Chapter VII

The arguments from the clear and continuous analogy of interpretation which the Holy Spirit has taught us to observe in those passages where dogmas or articles of faith are treated and established.

Peter has correctly said that "no Scripture is of private interpretation" (2 Peter 1:20), for we are not given the license, freely and without peril to dream up and contrive any kind of interpretation we may wish on the basis of our own thinking or personal conjectures, particularly in the case of those passages where dogmas are treated and established. But in order that our faith may be sure, the Holy Spirit has shown in Scripture itself that there is a definite method or analogy which must be followed in the interpretation of such passages. As a result many clear, firm, and very weighty arguments have been developed which compel us not to depart from the proper, simple, and natural meaning of the words of the last will and testament of the Son of God.

On the basis of only these arguments which appear particularly important and clear, and without the lengthy and rhetorical amplification which has been undertaken by others, we have determined with simple and plain brevity to note only the main headings and, as it were, to indicate the main points of the arguments.

[A. In which passages we may permit figures of speech and in which not.]

There is no doubt that there are many figures of speech in Scripture, but it is also certain that not all the figures of speech or tropes are in veiled language. Many in Scripture are very clear and can be treated and interpreted on their own terms or with the simple and natural meaning of the words. But is there not such a thing as freedom in the interpretation of a particular passage of Scripture to the degree that seems good to each individual so that we may either retain the proper meaning of the words or through the use of a figure of speech depart from the simple, proper, and natural meaning of the words according to each person's own notions?

The answer is a categorical no! For if this were the case, all dogmas and all articles of faith could be so completely overturned and bypassed that all assurance of faith would be snatched away from consciences. Therefore it is necessary that there be a definite rule or analogy of interpretation as to which passages of Scripture are to be treated as figures of speech and which are to be taken in their simple, proper, natural, sure, and usual sense, so that conscience can rest safely and securely in the interpretation which has been given.

Augustine, in his *De doctrina Christiana,* Bk. 3, ch. 10, gives us this rule: "Whatever in the divine Word can properly be applied to neither the uprightness of morals nor the truthfulness of the faith may be taken in a figurative sense."[1] And in ch. 16 he says: "If a precept seems to command an evil deed or something disgraceful or to forbid something useful or beneficial, it is figurative."[2]

Others state the rule in this way: When the literal interpretation forces an absurdity on other, clearer passages of Scripture or on articles of faith, then we must correct it by treating it as figurative.

These rules are correct because they are developed on the basis of Scripture itself, but in controversies and disputes they are corrupted in various ways in their application. For when the minds of certain people are preoccupied with a different opinion, they can easily dream up certain conflicts in the rules, as we say in popular speech, or "contraditions," as Paul puts it [1 Tim. 6:20], and they devise and pile up various absurd notions which are either contrary to good morals or against the faith. The result is that under a pretext of this kind they can depart from the simple, proper, and natural sense and thus no longer hold to it.

This line of reasoning is simpler and surer, something which can neither be denied nor easily bypassed, if one's explanation or application of this rule or analogy regarding the interpretation of Scripture is derived from examples out of Scripture itself. For Scripture, especially when it treats of dogmas, because it is not of private interpretation, interprets itself either in the same passage or in other passages where the same dogma is touched on. Because of this, the same dogma is fully treated and repeated in various passages of Scripture in such a way that no one can dream up his own personal interpretation but must derive it from Scripture itself. For the same dogma is repeated on the basis of either the same or similar words which have the same meaning and set forth the same teaching, so that the simple, proper, and natural meaning of the passage may be confirmed, as St. Paul says in Phil. 3:1: "To write the same things to you makes you safe." Or if something in one passage is too brief or obscure because of the puzzling nature of the figures of speech, Scripture will explain and interpret it in other passages where the same doctrine is repeated more fully, clearly, and openly, using proper, clear, natural, and commonly understood words. Along this same line, Jerome in his comments on Isaiah 19 lays down this principle: "It is the custom of the Scriptures to add clearer passages to those that are obscure and to add a clear explanation to those things which have been spoken in veiled language."[3]

The Son of God Himself observed this rule with the greatest diligence and solicitude in order that all obscurity and ambiguity might be removed from all dogmas which might disturb consciences. For when He had said something obscure in His parables, "He explained everything privately to His disciples," as Mark says in 4:34, either when they asked or even when they did not ask, in order that Scripture might not be "of private interpretation." [2 Peter 1:20]

When, as He does occasionally, He sets forth dogmas in figurative language, for example, in John 3:3 ff. regarding regeneration, or John 4:14 ff. regarding the Holy Spirit and eternal life, or John 6:27 ff. in regard to the benefits of Christ, or Matt. 16:5 ff. regarding fleeing from hypocrisy and false doctrine, He does not leave His disciples in suspense, so that one of them might think the statement is literal and another might contend that it is figurative and that therefore each is free to determine what the figure of speech means. But lest the disciples be carried about by some kind of figurative wind, He Himself sought and used occasions when He might clearly and expressly demonstrate that the words dealing with regeneration by water, with bread or with leaven, for example, are not to be taken in the common, literal sense as they usually are. Moreover, He would add a definite statement with literal, well-known, and commonly understood words in order to show what He meant by the use of the figure of speech involving regeneration, water, bread, leaven, etc.

If what is said in the statements of Christ still is not explained clearly enough, then the Holy Spirit through the apostles has interpreted it for us even more clearly. Matt. 10:26-27 and Luke 8:17; 12:2-3:[4] "Nothing is hidden which shall not be made manifest, and nothing is secret which shall not be known and come to light," or: "The things which I have said in the darkness you shall say in the light." These matters are clear, sure, and firm.

Therefore it is beyond all doubt that the Son of God was concerned about the same thing in the teaching of the new dogma of the Lord's Supper, since it is very important that one judge it rightly, as Paul declares [1 Cor. 11:29] that the guilt which brings judgment is involved. For this very reason He is anxious to repeat the same thing regarding this dogma in different places in Scripture, through different writers and at different times, so that there we may seek the correct meaning and understanding. Therefore, if faith in dealing with this controversy desires to proceed safely, so that it may place its confidence not on sand but on solid rock, it must not dream up an interpretation of the words of the last will and testament of the Son of God either out of its own speculations or by the use of some obscure passage of Scripture which does not deal with the Lord's Supper. For this reason this dogma is repeated in several passages of Scripture, that there one should seek a correct interpretation and it not be brought in from elsewhere.

Therefore whoever feels and contends that the words of the Lord's Supper must be understood differently than they read must be able to show in a clear, sure, and comprehensible way that in these passages where admittedly the Holy Spirit treats and repeats the dogma of the Lord's Supper He has demonstrated, in clear and manifest terms, these two things: 1. That the words must not be taken literally; and 2. In what sense they are to be understood if not taken literally.

Moreover it is manifest, as we shall demonstrate later on, that this dogma is repeated in Scripture in part with the exact words and in part with words of the same meaning and that there have been added to it such explanations as do not permit the words to be understood in any other way than literally. Nor is it valid to set in opposition to these passages statements drawn from other places in Scripture which do not deal with the Lord's Supper and to use them as the correct interpretation. Therefore this same dogma which is repeated in the Word of God at different times and in different places and by different writers exists and is derived from these passages both as the words of the last will and testament of the Son of God and as the true interpretation of those words in the places where these repetitions occur.

Thus my conscience can safely rest on this foundation and resist all temptations with this assurance. This will be my constant defense before the Testator Himself, the Son of God: "I stand on the words of Your last will and testament with great care and solicitude, so that I might not discern Your Supper wrongly and thus incur judgment. But because Scripture is not of private interpretation, I see that You have done in the case of this dogma the same thing that You have established in other dogmas, namely, that what is repeated from time to time in the passages of Scripture contains within it the correct interpretation so that it is not necessary either to seek it elsewhere or to add something drawn in from somewhere else. Moreover, in these repetitions I have not found that You desire that the words of institution are to be understood in any way differently than their literal sense, but rather I have observed that the proper and natural meaning of the words is confirmed by these repetitions. Therefore I have simply concurred with this interpretation because if You had willed that these words be taken in any other way than they sound, just as You have done in the case of other dogmas, You would have showed it, since You have seen to it that this dogma is repeated seven times in Your Word." This line of argumentation is patently clear.

[B. How human reason attempts through figures of speech to evade the things which are spoken in the proper sense.]

It is nothing new that human reason in the case of those passages where dogmas are treated, even when the words are entirely clear, should devise for itself unlawful interpretations which are absurd, unconvincing, and contradictory. It thinks it can rightfully depart from the proper and natural meaning of the words, and it judges that it is a sign of great learning to be able to escape the proper and clear meaning by the use of some special interpretation of the words. However, Scripture itself in some places uses such examples and adds its own refutations, so that it may rightly direct our conscience as to what it may safely do and follow in serious controversies in order not to be deceived when there is discussion about the passages of Scripture in which certain dogmas are treated.

For example, God gave to Abraham the promise concerning the seed (Gen. 12 and 15). But because he was incapacitated by reason of age and Sarah was barren, he reasoned that perhaps the words of the promise were not to be understood in their literal sense but in the sense of an adopted seed. However, he did not immediately concur with these ideas but rather placed them into the lap of God and besought His instruction. But God only repeated His promise and in such a way that He added the statement: "You will have an heir who will come from your own loins" (Gen. 15:4). These words are clear.

But still Sarah tries by some special kind of interpretation to escape the literal and natural meaning of the words and says (Gen. 16:2): "Go in to my maid; it may be I shall obtain children by her." By this departure from the literal word she seemed in her own eyes to possess a perfect understanding of the promise. Indeed she did not wish to appear to be making this assumption on the basis of worldly considerations drawn from reason, much less to be doing so out of contempt for the divine Word. But "because the Lord has closed me up so that I do not conceive" (Gen. 16:2), she therefore assumed that there must of necessity be another meaning to the promise than the words themselves indicate in the literal sense.

But the Lord (Gen. 17:19) made a clear restatement and explanation of the promise: "I will give you a son by Sarah." But what happened? Abraham "laughing, said to himself, 'Shall a child be born to a man who is a hundred years old? Shall Sarah, who is ninety years old, bear a child?'" [v. 17]. So deeply was imbedded the notion that it could not happen in the way the words described it! Therefore God came with a fourth restatement and explanation of the promise (Gen. 18:10). But because they were both old, Sarah laughed to herself [v. 12]. Therefore God finally said as if from His emotions [His stomach]: "Why did Sarah your wife laugh? . . . Is anything too hard or impossible for God?" [Vv. 13–14]

This example is especially significant because Abraham is the father of believers (Rom. 4:11, 16). Moreover, Scripture wanted to depict in him a warning to all posterity that human reason, in the area of interpretation of dogmas of the faith, must not force its way in even when the proper and natural sense seems absurd and in conflict with certain facts. At the same time it demonstrates a true analogy and a sure rule which one's conscience can safely follow and ought to follow in controversies of this kind. For at different times Abraham attempted, on the basis of the words of the promise, to devise a different meaning than the proper and natural sense of the words conveyed. Yet he did not believe or rest his faith in these notions, for his assurance of faith rested only on the divine voice. He sought the mouth of the Lord.

The Lord repeated the promise, partly with the same words, partly with equivalent words, partly with clearer words, and He added certain explanations so that He might show that one must not depart from the proper and natural meaning of the words. And although He gave so many repetitions of the same promise, yet the minds of men because of their presumptuous lawlessness (ἀντινομία) and contrariness (ἀντίθεσις) still did not acquiesce, since they still did not understand the manner in which it could take place. Finally God, as if in anger, replied: "Is anything impossible with God?" [Gen. 18:14]

At last, therefore, assured by so many repetitions of the same promise, Abraham ceased to be moved by absurd objections: "For he did not consider his own body, now as good as dead . . . and no distrust made him waver concerning the promise of God, for he was strengthened in faith and gave glory to God, fully convinced that God was able to do what He had promised" (Rom. 4:19-21). Paul shows that in this way Abraham had come to the full assurance (πληροφορία) of faith, for he uses the word πληροφορεῖσθαι.

In the great confusion because of the debates regarding the Lord's Supper, the frightened conscience can safely lean on God, following in the footsteps of the father of believers. For the words of institution give this meaning if they are taken in their proper and natural sense, as even our adversaries admit and confess. But the human mind seems to inject into this proper and natural meaning all kinds of illegitimate and contradictory notions which are absurd, incredible, and inexpedient, so that it may meditate on and invent other strange and varied interpretations.

But is the genuine, constant, and solid assurance of faith going to desert the natural sense and immediately accept some bizarre interpretation which has been dreamed up by someone? By no means. For Abraham sought the mouth of God, and the Lord by repeating the promise revealed His mind. Although Abraham later sought various subterfuges whereby he might escape the proper and natural meaning of the words, God always opposed this by a repetition of the promise.

Likewise, in this controversy regarding the Lord's Supper we must refer the whole matter to the Originator of this Supper and pour the deceptions of our minds into His bosom, namely, those arguments that the proper and natural meaning of the words of institution is to be set aside and cannot stand and that we can adopt any novel and expedient interpretation which pleases us. But do not immediately accede to these arguments of ours and give them preference. Because Scripture is not of private interpretation, and particularly because if this controversy is not rightly evaluated there is attached to it the guilt of judgment, let us seek the mind of the Testator who invited us to this Supper and is our Host.

We must not seek or expect new and special revelations, nor look for an explanation based on other passages of Scripture, which do not deal with the Lord's Supper. For just as God revealed His mind to Abraham when he was in doubt by repeating the same promise to him, so the Son of God has taken care to have the words of His last will and testament or the dogma of His Supper repeated several times in Scripture. But even though these repetitions clearly prove and confirm the natural and proper meaning of the words, yet our lawlessness and contrariness always get in our way. But when we have proceeded from one repetition to the next and no firm or clear objection has been raised against our accepting the words in any other way than their literal sense, if then the Sarah in our heart still does not yield to them but still keeps wondering, arguing, laughing, more inclined toward a different understanding, even when she cannot extricate herself from her illegitimate objections, then let us remember that the Lord in wrath will finally answer: "Why are you laughing in your heart? Is anything too difficult or impossible for God?"

Therefore, in the same way, Abraham finally, after so many restatements of the same promise, when he could no longer, as he had wanted to from time to time, clearly and definitely conclude that the words should be understood differently from their literal sense, did not consider what seemed to stand in the way or could be raised as an objection. Rather he joined together the certainty of the oft-repeated promise with the power of God and thus came at last to the full assurance of faith. (Rom. 4:21)

Likewise, when from all those passages in which the dogma of the Lord's Supper is repeated we could not clearly and firmly conclude that the Son of God wills that we should depart from the proper and literal meaning, it does not suffice for the true assurance of faith that for various illegal and contradictory reasons we should bring in other interpretations. For if the Son of God had wanted this, He doubtless would have shown it in this large number of repetitions, which He by His own wisdom caused to be written so that we can discover both the words of His last will and testament and their correct interpretation in these restatements.

But how can this assurance of faith stand firm when so many objections are raised which cannot be resolved? Paul shows us the answer to this in the instance of Abraham, the father of believers (Rom. 4:11, 16), as we have indicated above. Likewise in this controversy, even if we cannot resolve all the objections, we can bring to bear divine truth, divine wisdom, and divine power. We can draw the truth from the large number of repetitions of the same dogma, all of which agree with one another. Nor is it permissible to argue that the same thing can take place in some other and even more convincing way, namely, by a spiritual eating. For His divine wisdom knows best of all what is most useful and necessary for our salvation. But if there seems to be an objection that this could not take place with the true quality of the human nature left intact, the answer is: His omnipotence. Whatever He has said, this He can perform. But do you ask how He does it? His wisdom knows and has the way by which He can accomplish what His words say, far beyond what we can understand or imagine. This way Abraham, the father of believers, received assurance (πληροφορία).

It is noteworthy how carefully Abraham, after receiving this assurance (πληροφορία), observed this method. In Gen. 22:2 God commands Abraham: "Take your son and sacrifice him. . . ." The proper and naural meaning of this statement is perfectly clear. But some very basic conflicts (ἀντινομίαι) and contradictions (ἀντιθέσεις) seem to stand in the way. The first is that of the Law: "Thou shalt not kill" (Gen. 9:6). In the second place there is the Gospel promise: "In Isaac shall your seed be called" [Gen. 21:12], so that the proper and natural meaning of this precept seems to be in diametric opposition to both the Law and the Gospel, that is, contrary to the analogy of the entire Word of God. The Sacramentarians pile up as many objections as they can, but they will never be equal to these contradictions.

But what did Abraham, the father of believers, do? Did he, because of these contradictions, depart from the proper and natural meaning of this precept? It is absolutely true that many thoughts doubtlessly went through his mind because it was his only son, whom he dearly loved, and especially because it was the son of the promise. But he had already learned that the Word of God is not of private interpretation and that interpretations must not be drawn from other statements of the Word of God which do not address themselves to this precept. Therefore, because God Himself with His own voice did not indicate that the words of this precept were to be interpreted in any other way than in their literal sense, even though various conflicting and contradictory interpretations seemed to stand in the way, he did not dare to depart from the proper and natural meaning.

The Epistle to the Hebrews in ch. 11 beautifully demonstrates how Abraham, who was tossed about by various deceptions, finally found full assurance (πληροφορία). For "he considered" [Heb. 11:19]: "Both expressions are the Word of God, 'In Isaac will your seed be called' [Gen. 21:12], and 'Sacrifice your son Isaac' [Gen. 22:2]. Therefore I must do both and in some way believe both. Moreover, although the two seem to conflict with one another and the one to annul the other, yet I believe God, who has spoken them both, even though He has not shown with His voice how the one interpretation can stand and not conflict with the other. But He is able even to raise my son from the dead, so both statements are true because they are the Word of God." God Himself has wonderfully ascribed to Abraham this simplicity and obedience of faith.

Therefore, if Abraham in the face of this most powerful opposition did not dare to depart from the proper and natural meaning of this precept which he had heard only one time (and he did so for the one reason that God had not spoken to indicate that His precept was to be understood in any other way than literally), with what kind of conscience will we dare in this present controversy, in the face of much more insignificant objections, to depart from the proper and natural meaning of this dogma which has been repeated in several places in Scripture with consentient and equivalent words? Especially is this the case when in all these repetitions it cannot be clearly and consistently demonstrated that the Son of God wills that we should depart from the proper and natural meaning of the words.

Obviously there is never a time when sharp minds are lacking a pretext for finding Scripture passages which are in conflict with one another; as when the Pharisees in Matt. 19:3 ff. place in opposition to the institution of marriage the passage from Moses regarding the bill of divorcement. In Matt. 22:23 ff. the Sadducees, when they deny the resurrection of the dead, pretend that they are not doing this at all by rationalistic arguments but because of the law of the brother's wife. But Christ answers the Pharisees that the basis of the doctrine of marriage is in the words of its institution and that therefore the other passages of Scripture must be interpreted according to these words and not vice versa. And to the Sadducees He says: "You err because you know neither the Scriptures nor the power of God" [Matt 22:29], namely, that Scripture is able to stand and God knows the way, so that things are not in conflict that seem so to us.

Therefore we must retain with the greatest diligence the precept of Paul in 1 Tim. 6:20 f.: "Guard the sound doctrine which has been entrusted to you. Avoid the contradictions of what is falsely called knowledge, for those who profess it and hope in it have missed the mark of faith." And we should give thought to the warning of Augustine in *De doctrina Christiana,* 3:10, where he says: "It often happens that if the Scriptures prescribe something which is contrary to the practice of those who hear it, they treat it as a figurative expression. Likewise, if some erroneous notion has gotten into our minds first, regardless of what Scripture has asserted, men will think it is figurative." Thus Augustine.[5] But we must studiously avoid this practice in this controversy, since Paul states that attached to it is the guilt of judgment if one does not rightly discern the Lord's body, of which the words of the Supper speak.

[C. The analogy of interpretation of the passages in which dogmas have their proper foundation.]

Previously, in ch. II, I have pointed out that Scripture uses a peculiar and specific method or analogy of interpretation in those places in which the dogma or the articles of faith have their particular location, where the fundamentals of the dogma are treated or explained. In other, more obscure and difficult passages the words need not be so meticulously noted nor their natural force and meaning so rigidly or strictly adhered to, but rather it suffices if a meaning which is in accord with other, clearer passages of Scripture be drawn from it. But if, neglecting or rejecting the natural and proper force of the words, this same notion is attempted and permitted even in those passages wherein the foundation of the dogma is laid down, there will be nothing certain in the dogmas or in all of Scripture. Everything can be evaded, torn down, and corrupted by this methodology. Therefore it is necessary that the meaning of these passages whence dogmas or articles are derived be sure, proper, and natural, consisting of the proper and genuine force and true sense of the words, so that the sense of these words can in no way be twisted with respect to other passages so as to make them appear to be in conflict. Rather, the interpretation of the other passages ought to be so tempered as to be accommodated to the analogy of those passages in which the dogmas have their source.

We have shown above that the source of the dogma of the Lord's Supper is in the words of institution. Therefore the nature, force, and genuine meaning of these words must be carefully weighed and firmly retained so that from them we can determine the true, proper, and natural meaning of this dogma. Furthermore, in no way is it sufficient to pass over or reject the proper and natural meaning and to adopt a different opinion, even if it is in agreement with certain other passages of Scripture. If certain other passages seem to conflict with the proper and natural meaning of the words of institution, they must be accommodated by interpretation to the analogy of the words of institution. For we must not twist or distort the true and natural meaning of the institution to fit other passages, which do not speak of this dogma, as we have discussed at length in ch. II.

[D. The doctrine of the Lord's Supper is taught primarily in the words of institution.]

Those points in the Word of God which have been delivered to the church and noted by it are often repeated in the Scriptures and illustrated with figurative language and various kinds of pictures. The true and natural meaning, however, can be gathered from other passages, where the dogmas are touched upon in simple, proper, and clear words. As Augustine says, *De doctrina Christiana*, Bk. 2, ch. 6: "We must draw nothing from obscure passages which is not found written elsewhere in clear language."[6] And in his *Contra epistolam Petiliani*, ch. 16, he says that the things which are spoken in an obscure, ambiguous, or figurative way cannot be rightly understood or interpreted unless we first hold with firm faith to the things which are spoken clearly.[7]

In the institution of the Supper, Christ did not want anything to be delivered to the church before it had been used in the church, nor did He want it repeated with various kinds of pictures and figurative language or ornamented with flowery words. For it was the night on which He knew that He was going to be delivered over to the most bitter sufferings, and at this very time He instituted this new observance, a new mystery, a new dogma, which had not been known in the church before.

To be sure, He had spoken clearly about spiritual eating, which is an act of faith alone without any external distribution or eating (John 6). This is a metaphor which also is used in the writings of the prophets. But in the Supper Christ instituted the external distribution and the external reception which He willed should take place orally, when He said: "Take, eat." And concerning that which is distributed in the Lord's Supper and received orally He willed that we believe: "This is My body; this is My blood." Such an action and such a dogma had not been delivered, known, or used in the church prior to that time. Thus it was not done either previously or at some other time, but as Paul says, He instituted this ceremony and delivered this dogma "on the night in which He was betrayed" [1 Cor. 11:23]. And He handed down this dogma thus at that time because He willed by this act of delivering that at all times in the church until the end of the age this dogma should be judged and controversies which might arise be settled on the basis of this delivering. (1 Cor. 10 and 11)

Thus it is necessary that the words be used in their simple, proper, natural, commonly known, and commonly understood sense and meaning. For since the ceremony undertaken at that time was new and since the dogma which was handed down was new, and since this mystery had not been revealed before, but rather was given to us by the words of institution in the way that it was revealed by this tradition for the knowledge of the church, therefore one is led to ask the question: "How could a new ceremony and a new dogma not previously given to us, not known, not used in the church be understood if an unknown matter is delivered to us in imprecise, figurative, and obscure language?"

Further, there is no doubt that Christ willed that both this ceremony and this dogma be correctly understood, not only by the erudite who by reason of the gift of interpretation are able to penetrate into the depths of obscure points which are hidden in Scripture, but also by the whole church, the greater part of which are those who need to be fed on the milk of the Word. Therefore He is undoubtedly speaking about this new dogma, not previously known, so that it can be understood by all; for He fully realized that attached to it is the guilt of judgment if the proper discernment does not take place.

Also in other disciplines there is the common rule that one must set forth the known (τὰ κοινά) in new ways (καινῶς), but that the new (τὰ καινά) must be treated in a known way (κοινῶς) so that these matters can be perceived and understood. But if the institution of the Lord's Supper had been delivered to us in figurative language, with improper words and obscure and ambiguous terminology, where could we seek a firm and sure interpretation of it on the basis of which to draw a definite conclusion, since the dogma had not been previously given to us in the Word of God? And there is clear and convincing evidence for this very point in the many and various interpretations of the adversaries, namely, that if one departs from the proper and natural meaning of the words of institution it is impossible to render a consistent argument or a firm demonstration that there is one particular and definite interpretation of the words. But the fact is that there is one natural and proper meaning of the words and one definite understanding of them.

[E. Doctrine cannot be established solely on the basis of figurative passages.]

There is a rule which is correct and of long standing which Jerome deals with, namely, that dogmas cannot be established or corroborated purely on the basis of figures of speech and allegories. For not just any kind of meaning ought to be derived from figures of speech, nor ought one develop any kind of dogma he wishes. But whatever is developed on the basis of improper words, figures of speech, obscure and ambiguous language—that, in order that the full assurance of faith might have a sure and solid foundation, must of necessity be taught and established on the basis of words used elsewhere in Scripture which are proper, clear, and commonly known and used, as Augustine most correctly teaches.

Therefore, if the language in the words of institution is figurative, the terminology imprecise, and the words ambiguous and obscure, it will be necessary that the dogma of the Lord's Supper not be established on the basis of the words of institution but on something else. This is in clear conflict with Paul, who affirms that the Son of God on the night in which He was betrayed laid down the foundation on which the dogma of the Lord's Supper was to be established, proved, and evaluated.

Moreover, how could this dogma be established, proved, and evaluated on the basis of other passages of Scripture, since it was not delivered to us previously, nor at any other time than when it was given for the first time on the night in which Christ was betrayed? But, you say, it is repeated later in several passages of Scripture. However, I have shown previously that this is the very thing we have tried to get across, namely, that our adversaries contend that the actual words of institution (over which there is controversy) as repeated at different times in Matthew, Mark, Luke, and Paul, are in *all* these instances figurative and imprecise. They even attribute a figure of speech to those words in Paul: "He who eats of this bread unworthily is guilty of the body of the Lord" [1 Cor. 11:27], and likewise to the words: "He eats judgment to himself, not discerning the Lord's body" [1 Cor. 11:29]. And even if we turn to 1 Cor. 10:16-17, 21, they again argue that this passage clearly and manifestly cannot be explained or understood without a figure of speech or a trope.

And thus, if in all these passages of Scripture where the dogma of the Lord's Supper is repeated the words are improperly used and the language figurative, it necessarily follows that the dogma of the Lord's Supper either is established entirely on the basis of figurative, improper, tropological, and allegorical passages contrary to the ancient rule, indeed, contrary to the truth itself; or it follows that it is not founded at all on those passages where this dogma is obviously treated and repeated, with the result that nothing can be established, proved, or evaluated on the basis of these passages when contention arises, since in all these passages the language is figurative.

However, since it is necessary that there be in Scripture some passages in which this dogma, if it is to be certain at all, is properly and clearly taught and established, it finally comes down to this, that if we disregard the very foundation of the matter (*sedes materiae*), since we neither can nor ought to establish the dogma on the basis of figurative language, then we are trying to establish and prove the dogma on the basis of passages of Scripture which do not speak of the Lord's Supper. But what kind of assurance of faith is this—to subvert the very foundation passages of the dogma and then to seek the dogma in other passages of

Scripture which are unrelated, which do not speak of this subject? I will leave many of these passages to the meditation of the reader, since Paul pronounces: "He who does not rightly discern the Lord's body," of which the words of the Supper speak, "eats judgment to himself."

[F. The norm of judgment in matters of doctrine cannot be ambiguous or open to doubt but must be sure and certain.]

Thus the Son of God handed down to us the words of institution of the Lord's Supper on the night in which He was betrayed. Afterwards in glory He repeated to Paul the words He wished to be the norm of all doctrine and faith, of all arguments and controversies regarding this dogma, as is perfectly clear from Paul. (1 Cor. 11)

But what kind of norm and of what certainty would it be if the words were ambiguous? And that the words become ambiguous if we depart from their proper and natural meaning is manifestly clear from the varied and different interpretations of the words the adversaries treat as figurative. Furthermore, what kind of norm for faith and controversy would it be if it is a norm which cannot govern itself but must inquire elsewhere for something to govern it and seek from elsewhere that which has to be present if we depart from the proper and natural meaning and turn the simple words of institution into a tropological and figurative expression?

Therefore, in order that this norm may be certain, sure, and constant, we must above all retain the simple, proper, and natural meaning of the words, as Augustine in his book *Contra Petiliani epistolam* argues at great length as to what kind of Scripture passages ought to be the ones from which dogmas are to be established and proved and what ought to be the norm for the judging of controversy. "We should not gather and take note," he says, "of those passages which are obscure, ambiguous, or figurative, which each may interpret as he wishes and according to his own ideas. For points which are stated ambiguously can be used both for our side and for your side. Thus our answer is: This class of passages is mystical, hidden, and figurative. We must seek out something clear that requires no interpreter." Thus Augustine.[8]

[G. The institution of the Supper was set forth by Christ in the form of His last will and testament.]

Christ Himself in the institution makes mention of a new testament which is a treaty or a covenant of grace. And the Epistle to the Hebrews (ch. 9) applies the meaning of this testament to the fact that it is confirmed by the death of the Testator: that among all people covenants or treaties are expressed and explained in proper, clear, and plain words, so that the true, sure, and natural meaning may be obvious to all. Thus when strife or dissensions arise, they may be obviated and no one can twist the words to another meaning.

It is the sin of sycophants to practice evil and deceit by inserting obscure and ambiguous words into covenants and treaties. In the preparation of wills no one is so hardhearted and godless that when the information has been given to him he would speak in such imprecise, obscure, and ambiguous language as to cause the minds of the heirs, after the death of the testator, to be led astray by various arguments over the meaning of the words of the will. For no testator would allow such a will to be prepared that would thrust upon his heirs litigation over the matters or be a cause of strife. Rather he would see to it that litigation or deception would be avoided and removed, so that what he desired to take place after his death would be accomplished without error or mistake. If this sometimes does occur in secular wills because sufficient care and wisdom have not been exercised to assure correct language, this takes place either because of the weakness or the inexperience, thoughtlessness, or misunderstanding of the testator.

But these are qualities which cannot be attributed to the Son of God without terrible blasphemy. We have been most correct in stating that as the Sponsor of a new covenant and the Testator of a new will He has spoken in simple, proper, clear, and normal words, in order that the true, sure, and genuine meaning of the covenant and will can be understood, established, confirmed, and judged without any deception or ambiguity by all the heirs because the words have their simple and proper meaning, since the Testator Himself knew full well He was later going to pronounce through Paul what kind of guilt a person encountered if he did not rightly carry out the will.

Moreover, the various and different interpretations of these words which are proposed by our adversaries clearly show what happens if we depart from the simple, proper, and natural meaning of the words of institution. There are hardly two who agree as to what kind of figure of speech it is and into what category of figures it belongs. Moreover, it is not sufficient that we believe that something, whatever it may be, took place in the Lord's Supper. Rather we must carefully consider that we neither do nor decide anything in regard to the last will and testament of the Son of God which is alongside of or contrary to the will of the Testator lest as heirs we fall under the penalties of the will or, having violated the will, be legally deprived of the inheritance and all its benefits.

Scripture itself uses this argument, that the comparison of a secular will with the last will and testament of God shows that what is legitimate and God-pleasing in the case of a man's will ought to be observed with even more piety in the case of the will and testament of the Son of God. Lawyers have many weighty, serious, and honorable statements to show that the will of the testator or whatever person is making the disposition must be observed and carried out on the basis of the precise words of the testament. Therefore, when the words are clear and sure, we must in no wise depart from them but rather take them in their proper, natural, and preferred meaning.

The words of the law are: "When there is no ambiguity in the words, no questioning of the will should be allowed." Likewise: "We must not depart from the meaning of the words in one direction, when it is perfectly clear that the testator held to another. For to what purpose are the words used except to demonstrate the will of the speaker?" Again: "If he had wished to say the contrary, there would have been no difficulty in so indicating." There are also these words of the law: "The force of a will can be drawn from the words."

The imperial law says that the words of a last will and testament must be carefully considered, and if we depart from them we must give the reason lest we exercise too great subtlety over the meaning and thus the will of the testator is neglected. The words in the Greek constitution are most significant: "Therefore watch carefully over the words of the testament." The word "watch" (ἐπισκήτειν) means to say something with religious significance, as to confirm something with an oath, and on this basis it is applied to commands given at the time of death by which something is entrusted to friends or an heir, entrusted under a religious duty, with the addition of a curse if the injunction is not obeyed. There are examples of this in Herodotus, Demosthenes, Lysias, and Aeschines. And it is because of this that the imperial law warns that the words of a last will and testament must be weighed and considered with great care, diligence, and precision. This emphasis applies very beautifully to the last will and testament of the Son of God.

Many similar statements are found among the learned men which testify as to how religiously the words in the testaments or the last wills of men must be observed and weighed. For they teach that we must in no way depart from the words of a testament, indeed, from the strict construction of the words of a testament, but we must weigh each word. It is not permissible to add to them or take anything from them.

They often reiterate a very trenchant saying: "In cases of doubt it is safer not to depart from the words but to cling to them tenaciously, with no outside interpretation." They define "clinging to the words" as meaning that "they are not to be interpreted in any other way than as the words literally read." Again: "We should weigh the words and follow them rather than an imaginary and uncertain opinion."

They add as their reason for not departing from the words of the testator the axiom that we must presume that the intention of the testator was what the proper meaning of the words requires, and we must not believe that the testator willed what he did not say. Again: "We must not presume that the testator willed something different than what he expressed by his words. For if he had wished to say something contrary, it would not have been difficult for him to write it. Therefore we do not believe that the testator willed anything other than what he expressed."

In favor of this position we have been given the maxim that "the directions of the will are to be carried out at once" and that "the words are the indication of what is going on in the mind." Therefore: "What is omitted from the writing of the testator or not committed to words must be treated as an omission, and therefore what the written text of the will does not say we should not say. Thus nothing should be inquired about except what is written in the instrument of the will. We ought to be content with the boundaries laid down by the words, for no disposition should go beyond what the words permit. Thus, the one who reads the instrument has the answer to the question." Again: "What the testator does not say, he may be presumed not to have willed. We must consider that the will is such as the words indicate, for there is no greater or surer testimony to our thinking than the kind of words we use. The mind of the speaker is determined by what his clearly spoken words demonstrate." All these statements are citations from the doctors of the law.

Here are some more very important statements from the doctors: "We err greatly if we imagine that we will arrive at the reason for the law by conjecture." Likewise: "Men often err in trying to guess at the mind of a testator, because they use too much imagination." And Baldus asserts that many are deceived because they do not weigh the words of wills, which have great weight in themselves for understanding what the meaning is.

Accordingly they teach that words which can be understood both in a natural and a judicial way, both as true and fictitious, both properly and improperly ought to be used in dispositions in a natural rather than a judicial way, in a true rather than a fictitious way, and in a proper rather than an improper or doubtful way; because in a matter of disposing of something the words should be used in their preferred meaning.

They also add that it is one and the same whether something be done contrary to or alongside of the wording of the testament or the will of the testator. Baldus cites Boethius: "Truth is ignorant of that which can be understood in several different ways."

Likewise they teach that an interpretation or explanation, even in those cases in which such a thing is permitted, ought to be of such a kind as is in keeping with the words and we ought not depart from them, since the words are clear. For otherwise we would be rejecting the principle that an interpretation or explanation of clear words which is not in agreement with those words cannot be the correct explanation of a prior disposition but rather is a new and different disposition. This statement must be carefully noted lest we be tempted to interpret the testament of the Son as a different testament which we have devised for ourselves.

To this can nicely[9] be accommodated what the rhetoricians teach regarding the literal meaning, as when, for example, Cicero says: "When it is written clearly, then we must obey the judgment of the law and not interpret the law. For it is most shameful to alter a matter by your judgment which you actually cannot change according to its words or its letters." Again: "It is not right or possible for us to argue about the will of a person who has left us his judgment concerning his own will. For the writer lacked neither the understanding nor the ability nor the opportunity to prescribe clearly what he was thinking." Again: "Judges know that they will have nothing certain which they can follow if once they begin to depart from what is written down." And thus both for the judges themselves and their judging and for the rest of the citizenry in their living there are good reasons for confusion if once they depart from the laws. For the judges also know that they will have nothing which they can adhere to, nor will they be able to convict others of wrongdoing on the basis of any kind of mutually understood law, if they depart from what has been written.

This is what happened to our adversaries when they pretended that they could refute those who claimed to hold to the bare words in the Lord's Supper. But they could not refute them correctly or definitively once they had established and permitted the principle that the words of the last will and testament of Christ are not to be understood in their natural meaning and according to their proper definition.

Therefore Quintilian's words are important: "What is the difference between no laws and uncertain ones?" This principle can be rightly applied also to this controversy: "What is the difference between no testament of the Son of God or an uncertain one?" And the many varied and different interpretations of our adversaries show that it is rendered uncertain if we depart from the proper and natural meaning of the words.

Now I have cited these statements not because I have wanted to borrow ideas from the orators or the lawyers as the assurance of our faith in this most serious controversy, but because Scripture itself applies this argument drawn from the testaments of men to the last will and testament of God Himself. Therefore if the words in the last will and testament of a man are to be observed and weighed with such great diligence, care, and sense of duty lest the will of the testator be negated and lest something be done against or alongside the will of the testator, then the reader should consider what must be done in the case of that will which belongs to the Son of God, our Savior, which He established on the night in which He was betrayed. He did so with earnest gestures, words, and emotions which pertained to the greatest of all legacies— our salvation. To the improper discernment of this legacy, Paul pronounces, there is attached the guilt of judgment. This argument contains a great warning for us.

[H. It is impossible to derive one sure and certain meaning from the words of the Supper if one departs from the proper meaning of the words.]

When the words of the Supper are taken in their proper and natural sense, then we have the one sure meaning regarding the substantial presence, distribution, and reception of the body and blood of the Lord. For the arguments concerning the mode are easily eliminated. But when we depart from the simple, proper, and natural meaning of the words, then these words are subject to many varied and dissimilar interpretations and opinions, as is manifest. Then each person argues for his own opinion and the mind is left in a state of doubt and uncertainty. For up to this point it has not been possible for them to agree among themselves as to what category the figure of speech should be placed in, or what kind of figure it is, or what the correct and sure interpretation of these words is. Rather, there are as many interpretations as there are authors. Each queen appears most beautiful to her own king. In the midst of such a great variety of interpretations and opinions what can we have for our assurance of faith, since there always remains the element of ambiguity and uncertainty that perhaps the words can be explained and understood differently?

Therefore Luther is correct in saying that before the very judgment seat of the Son of God he would bring this defense: "Lord Jesus Christ, a controversy has arisen and an argument has come up regarding the words of Your last will and testament. Some are contending that these words must be understood differently from the meaning indicated by their proper and natural sense. But because among these people there is no agreement as to what kind of figure it is or into what category it must be placed, they cannot with consistency or consensus demonstrate one sure interpretation of the words but rather drag the words of Your testament into many different and dissimilar interpretations. Thus I have not been able, nor have I wanted to, commit my faith in this serious controversy to these uncertain, varied, and differing waves of interpretations and opinions. But on the contrary, I have seen that if Your words are taken as they stand in their simple, proper, and natural sense, then we can have one constant and certain understanding. Therefore, because I have determined that You have willed that there be one definite understanding of Your last will and testament, I rest on that interpretation which the words in their simple, proper, and natural meaning demonstrate and drive us to accept as the one, sure, and certain interpretation. For if You had willed that the words should be understood in a way other than in their literal sense, You would undoubtedly have given a clear and open declaration of this fact, just as You have done in those passages in which we may exercise our imaginations without any peril, as is not the case in the words of Your last will and testament."[10]

This is our sure, certain, constant, and solid assurance of faith. For also Irenaeus, in *Adversus haereses,* Bk. 2, ch. 46, where he deals with certain rules for the interpretation of Scripture on the basis of the apostolic tradition, says: "It is a sound and safe principle that a statement which occurs in Scripture is expressed in clear and unambiguous language."[11] We have already said previously that in cases of doubt it is safer not to depart from the words but to hold tenaciously to them.

[I. Mysteries are to be judged only from the revealed Word.]

The sacraments are mysteries that are unknown to human reason and hidden from our sense perceptions. They are made manifest and revealed by the Word alone. Therefore we must come to a proper understanding and correct judgment on the basis of the words by which the sacraments are revealed and given to us. Moreover, each individual sacrament has its own proper and peculiar word or definition, which in a sense is its form. There the sacrament or mystery of the Lord's Supper is safely, rightly, and in fact understood and evaluated on no other basis than that word or definition and according to that word which is its own proper and peculiar form. Nor should we be moved by some absurd notions to depart from these words, for they are mysteries which far surpass our senses and reason and which cannot be grasped by our thoughts. But the Son of God has put His Word by which He has given us the sacraments into opposition to our thoughts and has willed to do so in such a way so that we must learn from His Word whatever we need to know about these mysteries and must oppose all the absurdities that can be raised in objection to His Word, because He who is true, wise, and powerful has spoken it.

Chrysostom in various writings repeats this necessary warning: "Let us believe God," he says, "whenever He speaks and not contradict Him, even if what He says seems absurd to our senses and minds, for He is above our reason and our ideas. In all things and especially in the case of these mysteries let us not do those things which might destroy us, but looking only at His words, hold firmly to them. For we cannot be deceived by His words. But our senses are easily deceived. His words cannot be false, but our senses are very often deceived. Therefore when He has spoken ('This is My body') let us no longer be hung up with any kind of doubt, but let us understand it with the eyes of our minds. . . ."

I will not pile up more arguments of this kind, nor will I seek more corroboration from the great writers, but I do want to point out these simple, clear, sure, and dependable points set forth in a plain and brief manner for the conscience that is looking for a simple, certain, solid, and sufficient assurance of faith. For these statements have been drawn from the true, certain, and continuous analogy of interpretation which the Holy Spirit Himself has preserved for us and has commanded us to preserve. Especially is this the case in those passages where the dogmas or articles of faith are dealt with and set up, as it were, on their own foundation.

The adversaries make a great noise that in the interpretation of these words we must preserve the analogy of the sacraments, but each has decided for himself, and not on the basis of the clear foundations of Scripture but rather on the basis of his own understanding, the analogy which he judges is best accommodated to his own presumptuous opinion. But this analogy I have cited is the true, sure, clear, and certain analogy of interpretation which is based on the foundation of Scripture itself.

I am happy to confess that I have been greatly instructed and strengthened by a study of these arguments, for I do not deny that I have been moved by the many specious arguments which have been raised in opposition. But when I hear that Scripture is not of private interpretation, I determine that there is only one sure analogy of interpretation which is given and shown to us in Scripture itself, as I have demonstrated it in its simplicity, and to this analogy I submit in safety, certainty, and confidence. For I believe that Paul is always clearly speaking to me the words: "He who does not discern the body of the Lord eats judgment to himself."

In summary let me add some very significant words of Dr. Philip Melanchthon: "It can happen," he says, "that a certain statement which is quite in harmony with human reason may be pleasing to a lazy mind, especially if the statement is constructed and supplied with learned arguments and concepts. But what will happen in a time of temptation, when our conscience is troubled as to what reason it has to depart from the long accepted position of the church? Then the words ('This is My body') will be thunderbolts. What will the terrified mind put in opposition? With what Scriptures, with what word of God will it fortify itself and persuade itself that this statement must be interpreted as a metaphor? Then these points of controversy, which have so delighted the mind that they have been more admired for their cleverly thought-out reasoning than the very words of Scripture, will not seem so clever. I know how easy it is for us to stir up notions that disagree with Scripture, notions that previously seemed so plausible." Again he says: "When I do not find a passage in Scripture that denies that the body of Christ is present in the Supper or interprets the words of the Supper in a different way than they stand, I do not have a sufficiently strong reason to teach a new idea, especially one that arouses so great a scandal and one that I know cannot be preferred if we do not have clear and definite proof from Scripture." Thus Dr. Philip.

Chapter VIII

Arguments from the comparison, consensus, and mutual exposition of the four Scripture passages in which the institution of the Lord's Supper is described and repeated: Matt. 26, Mark 14, Luke 22, and 1 Cor. 11.

In the preceding chapter we have demonstrated that Scripture is not of private interpretation (2 Peter 1:20) but that there is one sure interpretation particularly of those passages in which dogmas or articles of faith are treated as established on their own foundation, when Scripture explains itself by clear interpretation either in that particular passage or in other passages in which the same dogma is repeated. We have already shown this in preceding arguments and examples.

It is very good to note with what care and by what rule Scripture shows its own interpretation, as to when it wishes a certain passage to be understood in a way that is different than the words read in their proper and natural sense. Many among the Sacramentarians use this argument: Just as John the Baptist is said to be Elijah [Matt. 11:14; Mark 9:13] and yet it is not precisely true that he was Elijah the Tishbite, so also, although the bread of the Supper is said to be the body of Christ, yet it does not follow that it is the true and substantial body of Christ.

There is, however, an easy explanation which sheds light on this whole controversy. Scripture affirms that John is Elijah. But should we, without some clear and express statement of Scripture itself respond out of our imagination: "He is not Elijah; he cannot be; there is no way"? Scripture is not of private interpretation; these matters must be sought in Scripture and solicited from Scripture. But where and how? Surely not on the basis of odd passages, but in the place where the same dogma is clearly and professedly taught and repeated. For in Matt. 11:14, where it teaches that John is Elijah, these words are added: "If you are willing to accept it, this is Elijah who is to come." From these words of the text Chrysostom has learnedly noted that Christ was willing that something other then the literal meaning of the expression (John is Elijah) could properly be understood. However, He immediately denies to us the right of attaching to these words any kind of interpretation that we might want to give them; rather we should be very careful that it be the same meaning which has been repeated in other passages of Scripture. Now we find that in John 1:21 the negative is clearly and expressly used: "I am not Elijah," that is, properly speaking, he is not the Tishbite. Then in what sense is the name "Elijah" attributed to the Baptist? Scripture clearly and expressly explains this in Luke 1:17, where Gabriel says: "He will go before Him in the spirit and power of Elijah."

Thus in Matt. 16:6, when Christ said: "Beware of the leaven of the Pharisees," the apostles tried to understand these words in a literal sense. But because Christ did not want the term "leaven" in this statement to be understood in its proper sense but in a figurative way, so that the prophecy might not be of private interpretation He immediately added the words: "I did not speak to you about bread" (Matt. 16:11). And yet the interpretation of this figure of speech is not a matter of individual freedom but is clearly taught in the particular passage under discussion, namely, that it is the doctrine of the Pharisees which must be understood. And in another passage, where the same words are used (Luke 12:1), He immediately adds an explanatory expression: "Beware of the leaven of the Pharisees, which is hypocrisy."

Thus all the canonical writers deal with problems of this kind; they repeat the same concepts and the same dogmas, so that if something is stated in a brief and unclear way in one place, it is explained more fully in another. So from a comparison of the passages where the same dogmas are repeated, brought together, and established we may reach a final determination as to whether to take the words in their proper sense, as they stand, or whether they are to be understood otherwise, and what is the true and correct interpretation. Thus the statement will always stand: "Scripture is not of private interpretation," but the assurance of faith rests only on the divine voice expressed in Scripture.

Therefore, because the dogma of the Lord's Supper is treated not only in one passage of Scripture but by different writers and repeated at different times in different places in Scripture, there is no doubt that the Holy Spirit wished to indicate by these repetitions that in this dogma we must preserve the same rationale and method for the analogy of interpretation that He Himself has preserved and prescribed for us to preserve in other passages. That is, we must draw our conclusions and make our decisions as to how the words are to be understood not on the basis of irrelevant passages which do not speak of the dogma in question but on the basis of those passages in which the dogma is treated and repeated, in order to give a sure and firm explanation of it. For if the Holy Spirit did this and wanted it to be done in other passages and dogmas, in the case of which it is not so dangerous to allow our imagination to roam, there is no doubt that He did this and willed that it be done in the case of this dogma, an incorrect discernment of which, Paul tells us, brings with it the guilt of judgment. And the very repetitions of the institution of the Supper clearly demonstrate the reason why and the thinking with which these things are set forth in Scripture by the Holy Spirit in the way they are. For the words are used in the way they are so that they may show that either by repetition or by the nuances of meaning or by the addition of material the Holy Spirit has wished by these very repetitions to demonstrate, teach, and confirm the true, sure, and genuine interpretation and meaning.

Therefore, because the words of institution are the proper basis and norm of this dogma and because they are the words of the last will and testament of the Son of God, let us weigh and ponder them as they are dealt with and repeated in four places in Scripture. Thus we will not derive our ideas and make our decisions on the basis of irrelevant passages but on these repeated statements, as to whether these words of the testament of the Son of God are to be understood in a figurative way which is different from their literal meaning or, on the other hand, whether we must accept and understand them in their proper and natural meaning, as they stand, and on this basis determine the true and genuine meaning of the words.

If these repetitions clearly show, as we have demonstrated to be the fact in the examples in Matt. 11 and 16, that the words there are not to be taken in their proper sense, as they stand, and if they have shown and taught us that another definite interpretation is proper, then we could safely depart from the proper and natural meaning of the words and adopt that interpretation, if by these repetitions they can be clearly demonstrated and definitely taught as having some other meaning. But if these repetitions do not clearly and definitely demonstrate this, but rather corroborate and confirm the proper and natural meaning of the words, then it would surely be the height of temerity coupled with great impiety to depart from the proper meaning of the words and to bring in a figurative interpretation. If the Holy Spirit had wanted this, there is no doubt that amidst all these repetitions, which He made for the sake of explanation and confirmation, He would have indicated this in a clear and definite way, as He did in the case of other passages and dogmas. Therefore, if in these repetitions the proper and natural meaning is explained and confirmed, then our true assurance of faith can rest quietly, safely, and simply in this meaning and even overcome any contradiction or objection. For He in whose words and assurances we trust is true, wise, and powerful.

This fundamental principle is so evident, sure, and certain that no one can overthrow or destroy it. And yet our adversaries, because they realize how difficult it is to repress it because of its absolutely clear simplicity, have tried by various sophistic subterfuges to lead men away from this citadel of truth and destroy it.

But we for our part, who believe that this dogma must be sought in its own proper setting, shall evaluate these repetitions in the order in which they have been written. For these repeated statements of the dogma have not been written by only one special author, but by Matthew, Mark, Luke, and Paul, not only at one particular time, but at various times. And although the exact number of years during which they were written cannot be computed with precision (for the notes of Irenaeus, Eusebius, Theophylact, and Nicephorus differ), yet this much is certain—Matthew wrote first, then Mark, thirdly Luke, and last of all Paul repeated the words of the institution of the Supper in his Epistle to the Corinthians.

This consideration of the order will demonstrate with what care those who wrote later whether by repetition or interpretation of the words of institution demonstrated and confirmed the proper and natural meaning. What other assurance of faith can the earnest mind desire?

A. The description of the institution as it is recorded in Matt. 26.

Matthew is the first who gave to the church in writing the institution of the Lord's Supper as it was delivered to him by Christ on the night in which He was betrayed. He gave it to all posterity in written form so that it might be a norm, a foundation, and a pillar for our faith in regard to this dogma, as Irenaeus says about the entire apostolic Scripture. Moreover, Matthew did not receive this tradition by having it handed down to him from others, but he himself was present at the first institution and saw what was done, heard what was said, and received the command that he should teach all to observe those things which Christ had commanded (cf. Matt. 28:20). He doubtless knew as well as any of them what was distributed by Christ in that first Supper and what was received by the apostles when they ate. Likewise, the apostles understood with what faith and in what sense the words of Christ were used.

Thus Matthew has delivered to us the description of the institution of the Supper in this way and in these words: "While they were eating, Jesus took bread, and when He had given thanks, He broke it and gave it to the disciples and said, 'Take, eat; this is My body.' And taking the cup, when He had given thanks, He gave it to them saying, 'Drink of this, all of you, for this is My blood of the New Testament, which is shed for many for the remission of sins.'" (Matt. 26:26-28)

These words, if they are first considered individually and by themselves, are proper and simple in their natural and common meaning. At the hour when the Supper was celebrated the tables had not yet been cleared. Therefore the bread Jesus used was ordinary, common bread taken from the supply left over after they had eaten. Nor is there any figure of speech in the word "to give thanks" (εὐχαριστεῖν), since the form of the Eucharist was accommodated to what was going on at that moment. It is manifest that the taking of the bread was an external act which was performed by the hands, for He took the bread which had been broken and distributed it, so that He gave to each of them a portion or a fragment of that bread and commanded that they should take what He had given them with this external distribution. He gave them the reason for this act of receiving by adding the word "eat," which in this passage cannot be understood in any other way than by taking it with the mouth.

In regard to the demonstrative particle "this," in the early stages of this controversy Carlstadt stirred up argument trying to demonstrate that this which is distributed, received, and eaten in the Supper is not the same thing, because the gender does not agree with the preceding word "bread." But everyone now rejects this notion; for it is common for a demonstrative particle to agree in gender with the substantive that follows, but it is impossible to demonstrate that there is always this reference to the preceding. For example in Gen. 2:22-23 when God from the rib of Adam had created a woman, He brought her (αὐτήν) to Adam; and Adam said: "This (τοῦτο) is now bone of my bone." And Scripture clearly shows what this demonstrative particle of the words of the Supper refers to when Luke says: "This cup" [Luke 22:20]. And Paul speaks of "the bread which we break" [1 Cor. 10:16]. Therefore the particle "this" points out what is distributed, received, and eaten in the Lord's Supper.

The word "is" (est) explains what it is which is distributed and received. And the word "body" is clearly explained, for Christ affirms that it is His body, and by the use of the article "the" (τό)

He strongly confirms the proper meaning of the word which is dealt with so clearly both in Luke and Paul.

Thus in the case of all the words, if we consider them individually, they possess and retain, without any figure of speech, their own proper and natural meaning. Moreover, the words which pertain to distributing and receiving are in a sense declarative of what is offered and received. Thus on the basis of these words, if we consider them together, we can come to no other meaning than the proper and natural one, that is, that they pertain to the substance of the Lord's Supper—that first common bread is taken, that then it is blessed with the giving of thanks by the words of Christ, as Mark and Paul point out. Finally after the giving of thanks it is externally exhibited, distributed, received, and eaten, that is, taken orally. Moreover, concerning that bread which becomes the Eucharist or the blessing in the Lord's Supper and is distributed, received, and eaten, if the question is asked what it is, the Son of God has affirmed with a clear declaration that it is His body.

And we should consider the antithesis: Previously He would have said of the biscuit dipped in the wine: "He who eats My bread." But of the Eucharistic bread He says: "This is My body." Therefore it is not merely bread which after the giving of thanks is distributed to those who eat the Lord's Supper and is received orally, but at the same time the body of Christ is distributed and received to be eaten, as we have shown in ch. IV, which dealt with the terminology.

This is the description of the substance of the Lord's Supper— what pertains to the first part of it. In the case of all these words, whether they are considered individually or in connection with one another, there is nothing to compel us to interpret them in any other way than literally. For all these words, both individually and collectively, teach and confirm the simple and natural meaning which these words indicate to any ordinary reader or hearer freely and of themselves—that the substance of the Lord's Supper in the first portion consists not only of bread but at the same time also of the body of Christ, so that in the external distribution there is offered to us and received orally not only the bread but also at the same time the body of Christ. For concerning this bread which is offered in the external distribution of the Supper and received orally, the Son of God says: "This is My body." No other meaning can be given to these words for any good reason, unless they are separated from their proper meaning either by mischief or by force.

Thus Matthew in his description has given to the church for all posterity at one and the same time both the tradition of Christ and the faith of the apostles in regard to this dogma. For if the apostles had understood these words in any way differently than as they stand, Matthew would have indicated this, in keeping with his practice. For in 16:12, after he has cited the words of Christ regarding the leaven of the Pharisees, he goes on to say: "Then the apostles understood that He was not speaking of the leaven of bread, but of the teaching of the Pharisees."

We shall see that the same thing applies to the second portion of the description. For brevity in the first part could produce ambiguity, since the church is also called the body of Christ, in Eph. 1:22-23, and the substance of the shadows is called the body of Christ in Col. 2:17. For this reason Matthew writes that Christ also took the cup.

But here the adversaries immediately raise the cry that we must admit figures of speech into the words of the Supper, namely, that in the word "cup" that which contains is used in place of that which is contained. But what kind of synecdoche is this? When, for example, the poet says: "When the savage stepmothers have poisoned the cups," then not the container but only the content is understood as being infected. But if this were the case in this instance, then Christ would have taken only the wine in His hands, without the container. But they make a point by saying that only the cup is mentioned and at the same time the wine contained in the cup is to be understood. Therefore I ask whether the word "cup" (ποτήριον) refers only to the contents or also to the outward form of a container. The etymology certainly comes from the concept of containing a drink (ἀπὸ τοῦ τὴν πόσιν τηρεῖν), referring to that which serves and contains a drink. And this is certainly the force or thrust of the term at some times. But in the Supper Christ expressly says that He did not take an empty cup, for He says: "Drink of it," and He Himself shows what kind of liquid He had in the cup He took. For He speaks of the fruit of the vine, signifying that it was real wine and not something imaginary or artificial like cidar. Therefore the word "cup" is not properly used with reference either to the material or the form, for in this case other terms would be used, but this word is used because it serves a drink and contains a drink, sometimes only potentially and sometimes actually. But in this passage a very clear explanation is added, namely, that Christ takes the cup which in actuality did contain the drink. Thus the word "cup" possesses and retains its proper and natural meaning—a vessel that contains a drink. And if anyone still stubbornly insists that it is a figure of speech, let his interpretation not be derived from elsewhere but be clearly dealt with in the words of institution themselves, which show that both are present at the same time, namely, the cup and the drink, as we shall shortly demonstrate. And this is what we are seeking, what we want, and what we are arguing for in the remaining portion of the words of institution.

Now because the liquid or the wine was not taken in His bare hands but in a vessel, Christ took the cup containing the wine, and He took the cup because of the fruit of the vine, that He might offer it to the disciples to drink. And now having taken the cup, He gave thanks, not in the way He had done it previously in connection with the five loaves in Matt. 14:19, nor as He had done earlier in the evening at this Last Supper when He had offered the common cup [Luke 22:17] or when He had poured out the holy type or the libation cup [ref. to the cup of Gethsemane, Matt. 26:39], but in order that through this Eucharist the fruit of the vine might by the word of Christ receive another and new designation, as Irenaeus says, the blood of Christ. Now when He had completed the act of giving thanks, He gave this cup to the disciples in order that from this cup they might all take some by mouth or drink it, for He says: "All of you drink of it."

Up to this point everything has been plain and simple. But now the question arises as to what is distributed to the apostles in this cup of blessing in the Supper and what they take by mouth or drink. For only the fruit of the vine was in the cup before the giving of thanks; this is certain. But because the Eucharistic words of Christ have been added, the question is whether even now only the fruit of the vine is present. Therefore the Son of God Himself demonstrates and declares, not with few or obscure words but with many clear ones, what is actually distributed in the cup of blessing and thus what is actually drunk orally. He says: "This is My blood." And only in Matthew is added the word "for," which leads our minds to the antithesis, by which the whole matter is beautifully illustrated. For earlier they had drunk the common cup to quench their thirst, and the Old Testament also had the practice of drinking cups of libation; but Christ had clearly and distinctly declared earlier that He was bringing an end to such typical meals. He had even concluded the common supper with a special ceremony in which He had said that He would no longer do this with the disciples, as we shall later show in the description of Luke's account [Luke 22:17-18]. Therefore the question could have arisen among the disciples as to what His will for them was, because now when all these things had been brought to an end He again comes to them offering a cup and does so in such a way that He commands them all to drink of it. And He shows the reason for this action by the use of the particle "for." "Drink," He says, not because it is a common cup, not because you are thirsty, nor because it is a typical or symbolical drink; for He had now put an end to all these. But "Drink, because this is My blood."

Therefore, because it has been said of the wine of blessing that it is the blood of Christ, the simple, proper, and natural meaning is that the Lord's Supper in its second portion also consists of two things, namely, the wine and the very blood of Christ—not that there is only wine present in the cup, while the blood is as far away as heaven is from earth; and not that we ourselves should imagine that there are two modes of the presence, distribution, and reception of the wine and the blood of Christ, as our adversaries do when they are compelled by the evidence of the words to admit that the Eucharist does not consist only of the external signs, the bread and the wine, but at the same time also of the very body and blood of Christ. But then they fabricate the notion that it is not therefore necessary that the body and blood of Christ be present here on earth where the bread and wine are present in the Lord's Supper. Nor is it necessary, they say, that the bread and body and the wine and blood of Christ both be present in the external offering and distribution or be received orally. For, they say, to faith the presence and the reception are no less real, sure, and efficacious. And these specious and beautifully developed speculations can be amplified and adorned, particularly when they do not come into direct conflict with other passages of Scripture. And consideration could be given to these ideas if Christ in His institution of the Supper had taught that His Supper consists only of the bread and body and the wine and blood, and had added nothing else. But the fact is that He taught not only this, but also in many clear and plain words asserted that His Supper consists of two things, so that in the present celebration which is carried on here on earth in the gathering of the church both the bread and the body and the wine and the blood are offered in external distribution to the mouth of the recipients. Not only the bread and wine but also at the same time the body and blood of Christ are received by the mouth of those who eat. For in regard to what is offered in the outward distribution and received to be eaten and drunk, Christ demonstrates and pronounces: "This is My body; this is My blood."

Not even the adversaries can deny that this is the simple,

proper, and natural meaning of the words. Therefore they look for figures of speech so they can have some pretext to depart from the natural meaning. But we have already shown that it is not permissible for us to devise figures of speech whenever it pleases our fancy. Let us therefore look to the words of institution themselves as to whether it is proper or not to take the words "This is My body; this is My blood" in a figurative sense. It is a fact that in the first part of the Supper Matthew is very brief, for he simply says: "This is My body." But in his account of the second part he uses many very clear and distinctive explanations which clearly not only point us but convince and compel us to retain the proper and natural meaning of the words. For he does not use merely the simple words "This is My blood," but he adds the words "of the New Testament": "This is My blood, which is the blood of the New Testament." Now it is absolutely certain that the blood of the New Testament is not a shadow, a figure, a symbol, a type, nor is it the blood of bulls or of goats, but it is the very blood of the Son of God (Heb. 8 and 9). This statement ought to be enough. But in order that He might demonstrate with great and special asseveration how firmly, how earnestly, and how seriously He wants it to be believed that what is distributed and received in the cup of blessing in the Supper is His own true blood, Christ affirms [Matt. 26:28] 1. demonstratively, "This is My blood"; 2. He adds the completely clear statement, "This is My blood, which is the blood of the New Testament"; 3. He repeats the same thing again and confirms it, so that we will have no doubt that this is a most serious and emphatic assertion, "This is My blood which is shed for many for the remission of sins." Surely Christ did not shed a figure, a type, a symbol, or wine for us for the remission of our sins, but "with His own blood God redeemed the church." (Acts 20:28)

The natural and proper meaning of the words is greatly confirmed and illustrated by the antithesis. For a short time earlier in that Last Supper they had partaken of the blood of the Old Testament, namely, the blood of the paschal lamb, which according to the law in Ex. 12:22 was put into a bowl and with hyssop was sprinkled on the doorposts and lintels of the house. Now by way of antithesis Christ says: "In this cup of blessing I am not giving you the blood of the Old Testament, as you had before in the bowl, which was a type; but what I am offering you in this cup is the blood of the New Testament, which is My own blood. And you will not apply this blood by sprinkling it on your doorposts, but you will apply it to yourselves." But how? "All of you drink of it." But what do we receive orally from the cup of blessing? He answers: "This is My blood, which is the blood of the New Testament."

He gives to the words such a form that He thereby leads us very clearly to this antithesis or comparison with the occasion when the covenant of the Old Testament was ratified, confirmed, and sealed with the people. In Ex. 24:8 we read the words of Moses: "Behold the blood of the covenant," which in the Greek version reads ἰδοὺ τὸ αἷμα τῆς διαθήκης. In the time of Christ and the apostles, as we know from Heb. 9:20, this read: "This is the blood of the covenant" (τοῦτο τὸ αἷμα τῆς διαθήκης). Christ imitated this covenantal form because by using these words He wanted to point out the difference between the Old and the New covenants: "This is My blood of the New Testament" (τοῦτο τὸ αἷμά μου τὸ τῆς καινῆς διαθήκης). As the old covenant was ratified both with God and with the people, with God indeed by the immolation of the victim and the sprinkling of the blood upon the altar, but with the people in such a way that the same blood which had been sacrificed to God was sprinkled on the people, in order that by one and the same blood this covenant might be both confirmed with God and ratified and sealed with the people. For there was no difference between the way this covenant of the Old Testament was confirmed with God and the way the application and sealing of the covenant took place among the people. Both were ratified by one and the same blood. In the same way in the ratification of the New Testament Christ says that He is shedding His blood for the remission of sins, that is to say, that by the shedding of His own blood He is ratifying and confirming the covenant of the New Testament with the Father. But because He wished to ratify this covenant or testament also with His disciples and to apply and seal it to them, so that they might have a guarantee as to what they might lay hold upon in this covenant of grace, He performed this ratification, application, and sealing with His disciples by that very same blood, which is the blood of the New Testament, by the shedding of which He ratifies and confirms this covenant with the eternal Father. Thus Christ is both the Mediator and the Guarantor of the new covenant, who brings together both parties to the covenant by the one means of His own blood, so that this covenant is ratified, confirmed, and sealed by both parties. And He uses the term "the blood of the New Testament" in two senses, with respect to God and with respect to us. With respect to God, through the shedding of His blood Christ brought the Father into the holy of holies, in order that before Him He might ratify and confirm this new covenant or testament. With respect to us it is called and is the blood the the New Testament because this very blood which Christ brought into the holy of holies He offered for us in order that by this act this new covenant which had been ratified and confirmed with the Father might also be ratified, confirmed, and sealed with us.

The method of this sealing God has defined with His own voice in the Old Testament, that is, when He commanded the sprinkling in Ex. 24:6, Num. 19:4, and Ps. 51:7. In the New Testament the application takes place by faith alone, outside the use of the Supper (1 Peter 1:2). But in the Supper Christ has instituted and plainly commanded a new, special, and peculiar mode, for He says: "All of you drink of it, for this which you receive orally from the cup of blessing is My blood, which is the blood of the New Testament." Our adversaries cannot deny that this is the proper and natural meaning of the words if they are taken without any figure of speech and in their simple sense. Their only objection is that it seems absurd and seems to conflict with other statements of Scripture. But this is not a sufficiently strong argument for departing from the natural meaning of the words and adopting another interpretation, which Christ in the institution with His own voice did not teach or point out, as we have shown in ch. VII.

Thus we have found nothing in Matthew's description which shows that we should depart from the literal meaning of the words. Rather, those things which corroborate and confirm the proper and natural meaning are so plain and clear that they merely bring us back to what we have said above regarding the true analogy of interpretation, so that I do not see what can be said that is plainer, clearer, or more to the point. If, as we must, we wish to take the true interpretation of this matter from the words of Christ Himself, the pious heart can ask nothing more than that we be taught and confirmed in the proper and natural meaning of the words in a way which is sure, certain, and clear, unless a person decides to depart from the clear statement of the Son of God Himself because his own speculations have led him away from the demonstrated and natural meaning of the words.

These words are filled with all kinds of teaching and sweetest comforts regarding the use and benefit of that which is distributed and received in the Lord's Supper. With what nobler guarantee and promise could the new covenant be sealed to the believers than with the very blood of Him by the shedding of whose blood the new covenant was sanctified and confirmed before the Father? But the teaching regarding the use and benefit of the Supper will have to be repeated and explained more fully later on. At this point I have wanted to treat and explain those statements which pertain particularly to the substance of the Lord's Supper. For we must always observe and keep the rule we have mentioned in the preceding chapters, namely, that in the words of institution we should distinguish and distinctly consider and explain first of all the things which pertain to the substance of the Supper; when we have done that, we shall then describe its use and benefit.

B. The description of the institution of the Supper as it is recorded in Mark 14.

The statements in Matthew's description which have fully confirmed the proper and natural meaning certainly ought to be sufficient to satisfy those who are honestly seeking the simple truth of the matter, even if there were no further explanation of the subject in Scripture. But in order that our faith might have even clearer confirmation and more certain assurance in regard to this dogma, the Holy Spirit has been concerned to repeat the account of the institution several times after Matthew, so that by the very concern for repeating it He might admonish us to seek nowhere else and to draw from nowhere else the correct interpretation, since He has been concerned for this very reason that the words of institution be repeated in these four passages of Scripture so that the true interpretation may be sought there and drawn from that source alone. Now I do not want to speak too harshly, but it takes great temerity to neglect heedlessly this counsel of the Holy Spirit.

Some years after Matthew, Mark wrote his account of the Gospel, in which he also repeated the words of institution of the Supper. Moreover, just as we have learned from Matthew both the teaching of Christ and the belief of the apostles concerning this dogma, so also Mark has shown us what meaning the apostles handed down to their disciples and hearers concerning this dogma and with what belief the apostolic church received this dogma. For Mark was not an apostle who had actually witnessed the celebration of the Supper in the upper room in Jerusalem or heard the words from Christ Himself, but he received either from Peter, as the ancients held, or from some other apostle the things he wrote in his Gospel history. And just as he received them, so also he faithfully put them in writing, giving the same meaning as he had heard the apostles give in their interpretation of them. Therefore he repeated for all time nearly everything Matthew had written, using almost the same words; but certain things, where there was need, he explained more clearly and fully, for example, concerning the sin against the Holy Spirit and why they who are rich do not enter the kingdom of heaven, etc.

Indeed, in the very repetition of the words of institution of the Supper he wanted to clarify certain points. For where Matthew has the words "after He had given thanks" (εὐχαριστήσας) Mark uses the term "after He had blessed" (εὐλογήσας), an expression which found such favor with Paul in 1 Cor. 10:16 that he followed Mark at this point. He was trying to indicate that this was not the kind of thanksgiving (εὐχαριστία) that people give when they are blessing ordinary food, as in 1 Tim. 4:3, or as in Luke 22:17, where Christ Himself when He had completed the observance of the Passover took the cup and gave thanks. Mark uses the word "to bless" (εὐλογεῖν) because it points to the special power of the divine Word, as in the account of the miracle of the five loaves which were multiplied so marvelously by the divine power that they fed five thousand people. Here Matthew, Mark, and Luke all use the word "to bless." Therefore, because the bread of the Supper receives this designation from God by the divine power of the Word of Christ whereby it is the body of Christ and the wine is the blood of Christ, Mark uses the word "to bless" in order to show that it is the same power and has the same meaning in this passage as does the word "to thank" (εὐχαριστεῖν), and he himself in the second part of the description will soon use this word.

In the second part, where Matthew has: "All of you drink of it," Mark says: "They all drank of it." Not only does he show that the apostles obediently did what they were commanded to do, but he also shows clearly what Christ had in mind in the institution of the Supper when He used the word "drink." For some people try to use this word "drink" in an ambiguous way in one and the same passage, as though it had two contradictory meanings at the same time, namely, to drink with the mouth and not to drink with the mouth but only to embrace by faith, so that they may refer it to either the wine or the blood of Christ. But Mark clearly destroys this contention. He says that all the apostles drank from this one cup when it was passed around among them, that is, they took by mouth or drank something from it. Then he adds a statement as to what they took by mouth from the cup of blessing. "This is," he says, "My blood." Thus they drank or took by mouth not only wine but at the same time the blood of Christ.

In these words of institution, however, concerning which there is now controversy, Mark changes nothing, nor does he add or substitute anything which would indicate that he wanted the words lightened in any of their meaning or understood differently than they sound. But he repeats the same words in so many syllables, as if he had religiously counted them: "This is My body; this is My blood which is the blood of the New Testament, which is shed for many." But Oecolampadius takes exception to the fact that these words which are in controversy are repeated syllable by syllable in the two passages. He says that we cannot therefore arrive at a clear conclusion, but rather the matter is equally obscure in both, as if there were only one passage. But I call on Paul as a most authoritative witness, and he says: "To write the same things to you is not irksome to me and makes you certain" (Phil. 3:1). He uses the word ἀσφαλές, which refers to an assurance which has been checked out and is certain, which is not tossed about by every wind of doctrine but in the true sense has been checked by definite criteria so that it rests secure in its certainty and will not be deceived. The word is used in this sense in Luke 1:4; Acts 21:34; 25:26. A guarantee confirmed in writing is called an ἀσφάλεια. This is therefore Paul's rule: When the same dogma is repeated with the same words in Scripture, the purpose is that by this repetition of the same words the assurance of our faith may be strengthened and confirmed, so that it can rest secure in the simple and natural meaning of the words against all the winds of objections.

Therefore, because Mark retains the same words which are used in Matthew and dutifully repeats them, by that very repetition he is proving and confirming by a very clear argument the simple, proper, and natural meaning of those words, as he does throughout his entire Gospel account where with the same words he repeats the things written by Matthew and thus confirms them. But where he wishes certain things to be interpreted, there he uses other explanatory words. Therefore we have established the fact that if the Holy Spirit had wished these words of institution to be understood in a different way than their literal sense, He would not have repeated the same words but either would have substituted or added some indication from which it would be possible to conclude that the words must be interpreted in a different way from their literal meaning.

In this repetition of Mark, however, it is useful to observe the pious simplicity of the apostolic church and the true obedience of faith, because Mark, a disciple of the apostles, so scrupulously retained and so to say counted the words just as they were taught by Christ and written down by Matthew, because they are the words of the last will and testament not of a man but of the Son of God Himself.

C. The description of the institution of the Supper as it is recorded in Luke 22.

After Matthew and Mark, Luke is the third to undertake a repetition of the words of institution of the Lord's Supper with the same intention that has now often been stated. Further, Luke was not an apostle but a traveling companion and co-worker in the ministry of Paul, and he confesses in his Gospel account that he had received material from those who were both eyewitnesses of the works and ministers of the teaching of Christ, that is, from the apostles. But in his account of the institution of the Lord's Supper he does not follow Matthew and Mark as much as he does Paul. For he almost copies Paul's words. Therefore he most probably received the form of the institution of the Supper from Paul, whose companion and associate he was. And Paul received this form and these words of institution, just as he taught them, after the ascension of the Lord—not from man but from the Son of God Himself, not while He was sitting in the midst of His infirmities in the upper room in Jerusalem but after He had been received up into glory and was seated at the right hand of the power and majesty of God. By this repetition the very Son of the God of all things wished to show in the clearest possible way that the article of His ascension into heaven and His session at the right hand of the Father in no way annuls or overturns the proper and natural meaning of the words of institution. For after the ascension, when He was now sitting at the right hand of the Father, He taught the form of the institution of the Supper to Paul in such a way that He confirmed the proper and natural meaning even more clearly and firmly than He had done in the upper room while He still walked on earth, in the words which Matthew and Mark record, as we shall soon demonstrate. This argument from the circumstance of the time when Christ transmitted to Paul the words of the Supper should receive careful study.

Paul himself in turn explains in 1 Cor. 11 how he had received this form of the words of institution from the Lord and handed it on to the churches. We shall speak of this passage shortly. And faithful Luke, his Achates, has shown with his own account how Paul explained this tradition to the churches. This is an immense benefit from the Son of God, which we ought to consider and embrace with a grateful mind, that out of fatherly concern He wished to give His church a complete understanding of this highly important dogma of the Lord's Supper, for He knew that the guilt of judgment is attached to it if His body is not rightly discerned. For in order that all obscurity and ambiguity might be removed and every occasion for error and every cause for argument be obviated, and that the church might not only have the words of institution but also at the same time the genuine meaning and proper interpretation as it was received from the mouth of Christ Himself and spoken with His own voice, He twice gave the institution of the Supper with His own voice and repeated it. The first time was in the upper room in Jerusalem on the night in which He was betrayed. And He took care that this testimony was given by His two most faithful witnesses, Matthew and Mark, and was published as it were in the public record. Then for a second time He repeated these words of institution, after the ascension, to Paul with His own voice, and in this repetition He gave an explanation if He judged anything in those words to be in need of interpretation. Moreover, He was concerned to have this repetition likewise commended in writing to the memory and instruction of all posterity in the church by the testimony of two witnesses, Paul and Luke. Therefore he who departs from these repetitions and seeks another interpretation elsewhere and approaches the subject from another point of view is surely both ungrateful and contemptuous in the face of such exacting care and fatherly concern on the part of the only-begotten Son of God, our Teacher, who alone can open the closed book and read it. [Rev. 5:5]

It is most manifest that Christ by this repetition to Paul wanted to explain whatever might seem to have been stated too briefly, obscurely, or ambiguously in the words He had used in the upper room. For example, because from the descriptions in Matthew and Mark one might not be able to determine clearly and with certainty whether this command concerning the Lord's Supper was only a personal one pertaining only to the apostles at that time, as the command to Peter by which he was ordered to walk on the waves, or whether it was a universal command pertaining to the whole church and to the whole period of the New Testament, Christ in this repetition to Paul adds these words: "This do in remembrance of

Me." And Paul explains these words thus: "As often as you eat this bread you show forth the Lord's death, till He comes" (1 Cor. 11:26). Likewise, the demonstrative particle clearly points to what He is referring when He says, "This cup," namely, that He is more exactly noting the circumstance of the time, since it says, "When supper was finished." Thus there is no doubt that in this repetition after His ascension He is giving to us the sure, genuine, and proper meaning of those words which now are called into such sharp controversy.

Therefore just as at one time in Asia, when Cerinthus twisted the writings of the other evangelists with a crafty and elegant interpretation to support his own blasphemous opinion, pious men who loved the truth went to John the apostle and besought him that, because he had reclined on the bosom of the Lord, he should by his confession and historical account put an end to this contention, so in the confusion of these dangerous controversies concerning the words of the last will and testament of the Son of God let us do the same. For because we are certain that the Son of God after His ascension transmitted to Paul the repetition of the institution of His Supper in such a way that He explained many things more clearly and openly than before, therefore let us approach this repetition as being the true mind of Christ concerning those words which are now called into controversy, not on the basis of elaborate conjectures and argumentations, but let us learn from the very voice of the Son of God. For these words are the true, unique, sole, and sure method for achieving a firm and solid assurance of faith.

Among other things, therefore, Luke retains the same words regarding the taking of the bread, the giving of thanks, the distribution, and the reception; and as if he had deliberately undertaken only to tell the facts as to what it is which is distributed and received in the Supper, he passes over the words used in Matthew and repeated by Mark, "Take and eat." But those words about which there now is a controversy he not only repeats but explains so clearly, by noting the circumstances of the Supper, by adding a very full explanation, and even by showing the difference between sacramental and spiritual eating, that there is no room left for ambiguity for the person who has seriously determined to abide by the voice of the Son of God as it has come down to us.

For it is not unimportant that he has added that the institution of the Lord's Supper took place "after supper" [Luke 22:20], that is, after the supper which preceded had been completed. Luke very carefully and clearly records the precise order of the events of the whole Last Supper. First of all Christ ate the paschal lamb with the disciples and without doubt observed the ritual prescribed by God Himself in the Law (Ex. 12:11), namely, that it be eaten swiftly in a standing position, with loins girded, with staff in hand. The evangelists do not describe these and other Jewish rituals because they were commonly known. But it is beyond controversy that this supper of the Old Testament was figurative, a type, a symbol, something that signified Christ, who accomplished its final fulfillment when He said: "With desire I have desired to eat this passover with you before I suffer. For I say to you that I will no more eat this passover with you until it is completed in the kingdom of God" [Luke 22:15-16]. Now those who are learned in Hebrew tell us on the basis of ancient Jewish commentaries that it was the custom that when the passover meal was completed in accordance with the ritual of the Law, after they had been standing, they then sat down to a common meal, with their loins ungirded and staffs laid aside. This order in the Last Supper is quite clearly gathered from John 13:4, where Christ lays aside His vestments and washes the feet of the disciples, who doubtless had taken off their sandals. Thus the eating of the passover lamb had been completed, during which procedure it was necessary for the loins to be girded and shoes to be on the feet. Yet when Christ washed the disciples' feet, the supper was still in progress. After the foot washing He again lay down at table and dipped the bread. This supper was not the passover meal, according to the ritual of the Law; therefore it was the other one, which customarily followed. Theophylact also explains this text in this way, namely, that Christ at the Last Supper lay at table in such a way that John rested his head on His bosom, which according to the Law he could not have done at the passover meal.[1] But Christ finished that second common meal in keeping with the Israelite custom, as the Hebrew commentaries have it. For having taken the cup, He gave thanks and said: "Take this and divide it among yourselves; for I say to you that I will not drink in this way from the fruit of the vine until the kingdom of God comes" (Luke 22:17-18). But afterward, when the typical meal of the passover lamb was finished, and also when that second meal was finished and completed, following the common custom, then Christ instituted that new meal which was peculiar to the new covenant, which Paul calls the Lord's Supper. And this is what Paul and Luke mean when they use the words "after supper." (Luke 22:20; 1 Cor. 11:25)

Further, Christ in His repetition to Paul so accurately describes this matter of the order of events of the Last Supper, and through Luke wants to have it so precisely described, that His dominical Supper of the New Testament is by the very order of the events distinguished from all other suppers, whether secular ones, observed by the necessity of nature, or sacred, typical, and symbolic ones such as the eating of the passover lamb as prescribed in the Old Testament. Thus the observation is vain on the part of those who contend that we must derive our interpretation of the words "This is My body" from the institution of the passover lamb. Equally vain is the contention of those who imagine that in the Lord's Supepr there is only the symbolic notion that just as bread nourishes the body so Christ is food for the soul. For this symbolic meaning can be applied to any kind of common meal, as in John 6, where the episode of the five loaves is used as an occasion for the sermon on spiritual eating. But Christ has separated His dominical Supper from other suppers, whether secular or symbolic, by the very order in which the events occurred.

But you ask: What bearing does this have on the understanding of the words "This is My body"? A great deal. For because the eating of the passover lamb had been completed and also the secular meal was finished, and Christ now takes the bread and having given thanks breaks it and offers it to the disciples, with the added command that they take it and eat it, it is manifest that Christ is adding something new and special by this order in which He is performing it. Moreover the question is asked as to what it is which Christ is offering to the disciples by means of this outward distribution, which He also commands them to take into their mouths. Is he here offering them ordinary bread for the necessity of human nature? Certainly not. For He has completed the secular dinner with the solemn promise that He will not partake of it again. But perhaps it is only something symbolic or typical which Christ is offering and the apostles are taking into their mouths, like the eating of the lamb together with unleavened bread. But just a short time before, Christ had made an end to symbolic actions. What is it then which Christ is offering and the apostles are receiving in their mouths, if it is neither common bread nor typical or symbolic? He who is the Truth, the Wisdom, and the power of God answers: What I am offering to you by this outward distribution and what you are receiving in your mouths "is My body."

Indeed, in the very first institution of the Supper Christ adds nothing more, as the account in Matthew and Mark shows. But lest the brevity give occasion for idle speculation as to how the term "body of Christ" was to be understood, since the church is also called the body of Christ, and the term could be interpreted as some kind of symbolic body of Christ, He Himself after His ascension, when He was now sitting in His glory, gave to Paul an explanation in plain and clear words. Luke took this explanation from Paul: "What is distributed in My Supper, in the gathering of the church on earth, this is that body which is given for you." This little exegetical explanation which Christ after His ascension adds by way of interpretation to the words of institution has great weight toward the settlement of this controversy. For in this way Scripture is accustomed to show its meaning, whether it wishes certain words to be taken in their proper and natural sense or in a figurative way. When the other evangelists called Christ God and the Son of God, Cerinthus called these words into doubt as to whether they were to be understood literally or metaphorically. But John through this kind of explanatory statement showed that we must retain the proper and natural meaning of the words, saying that the Logos is the God through whom "all things were made" [John 1:3]; likewise, that He is the Son who is "in the bosom of the Father" [John 1:18], "the only begotten of the Father" [John 1:14]. Thus also when Scripture wants to show that words must be interpreted differently from their literal sense, it uses explanatory expressions such as in Matt. 11:14, where John the Baptist is Elijah, "who is going to come"; or Luke 12:1, Beware of the leaven of the Pharisees, "which is hypocrisy"; or Col. 1:24, where the body of Christ "is the church."

Therefore, because the whole question at issue revolves around this pivotal point as to whether the words of the Supper are to be taken in their proper and natural sense or are by the use of a figure of speech to be turned into a symbolic meaning, and because the Son of God Himself after His ascension has added to the words of the first institution this kind of little exegetical explanation, therefore on the basis of this expression and on the basis of nothing brought in from outside we can reach a conclusion in our teaching as to how these words are to be understood. The explanatory expression is the following: "This is My body *which is given for you*" (τὸ ὑπὲρ ὑμῶν διδόμενον). There is no way in which this clause will permit the words to be understood in any other way than as they stand in their proper and natural meaning. Therefore if we claim to have a mind which wants to learn and are not willing to continue as blind men with eyes closed in the brightest light, the whole controversy can be

111

cut through and decided, not by human judgment but by the voice and explanation of the Son of God Himself.

Furthermore, in this repetition of the institution the Son of God who is now sitting at the right hand of the Father clearly sets forth and teaches first those things which pertain to the substance of the Supper, that is, what is distributed in the Supper and what is received in the mouths of the participants, namely, that very body which was given for us. Then He also teaches and demonstrates the use and benefit of what is distributed and received in the Lord's Supper. He says: "This do in remembrance of Me, that is, in memory of the fact that My body was given into death for you." He could in another passage and by another exegetical comment have described the substance of His body, but in order that at the same time He might show the use of it, He said that it "was given for you." Now this is not a mere idle recital of the facts but a true and living act of faith which lays hold on the giving of the body of Christ as it is described in the word "remembrance." Just as the recording and the memory of the name of God and His covenant throughout all of Scripture signifies a true exercise of faith, so on the contrary the loss of faith is described by the word "forgetfulness." (Cf. 2 Peter 1:9)

In this first portion, therefore, the following are distinctly dealt with and described: 1. The substance of the Supper, that it consists of the bread and body of Christ; and at the same time there is a description of the mode of distribution and reception. For with the bread which is seen, distributed, and received orally there is also present the actual substance of the body of Christ. 2. The salutary use of what is distributed in the Lord's Supper and received by the participants is dealt with and described. "This," He says, "do in remembrance of Me." But what is the "this"? Paul expressly deals with the explanation of this term, namely: "You eat this bread which is My body which is given for you, and you do this in remembrance of Me." We have already demonstrated that the salutary commemoration of Christ takes place when true faith applies to itself the giving of the body of Christ, and I do not think this is a matter under controversy which needs repeated proof. Thus in these latter words concerning the salutary use of the Supper there is a description of the spiritual eating of the body of Christ which takes place by faith. And just as the substance of the Supper and the salutary use of the same are distinguished, so it is one thing when Christ says: "Take and eat; this is My body," and another thing when He says: "This do in remembrance of Me," which takes place by spiritual eating

112

through faith. Thus the sacramental and the spiritual eating are dealt with and described separately. For there is a distinct and clear description of how the substance of the Supper, which consists of the bread and the body of Christ, is received, namely, in the mouths of the participants. This is the sacramental eating, of which we spoke in ch. V. And then there is also a distinct and clear description of how those who participate in the Supper receive it and use it in a salutary way, namely, by faith. This is the spiritual eating. Now when these points regarding the substance of the Supper and the use of it, and likewise regarding the sacramental eating of the body of Christ and the spiritual eating of it, which the Son of God has kept separate in His teaching on the subject, are not confused, then the proper and natural meaning of the words is plainly and manifestly established and confirmed.

In the second portion of the words of institution of the Supper, when the Son of God for the sake of clarification repeats to Paul the words of institution, He very carefully transfers the words in such a way that He clearly and strongly corroborates and confirms their proper and natural meaning. For the expression that He had used in the first record of the institution of the Supper: "This is My blood, which is the blood of the new covenant," He expresses thus in the explanatory repetition to Paul, after the ascension: "This cup is the new covenant in My blood." If someone wants to interpret the term "blood" metaphorically in the words of the first record of the institution, as witnessed in Matthew and Mark, the Son of God in His repetition to Paul shows that this simply cannot be done and ought not be done. For He calls it the new covenant in His blood. And in this Pauline repetition the term "new covenant" cannot be a figurative expression. The words of the first record of the institution make this impossible, because they speak of "the blood of the new covenant," and it is necessary that in both places the meaning be expressed and rendered in one and the same way, as Luther so beautifully deduced.

This is plainly a small point, yet it can alert us to the fact that Paul in his description of the first portion, as Erasmus noted, and Luke in his description of the second portion both omit the copula "is." And now there are some people, like Zwingli of days gone by, who allow the other words to be taken in their proper and natural sense and try to put the figure of speech in the word "is," which they interpret metonymically instead of "to be." But what will they do when they do not find the word "is"? To which they reply, "But

even if it is not present, yet it must be understood as being present."
I do not deny this, but I would like to expand the question by asking
whether the other words which they themselves concede do retain
their proper and natural meaning are to be changed into some other
meaning because of a word which does not occur but must be
supplied.

But they reply that the expression "This cup is the new
covenant" cannot be explained or understood without the use of
several figures of speech. Let us therefore consider this proposition.
For it is our purpose to learn and conclude from the words
themselves whether they are figurative or literal. Now in the first place,
we must take note of this fact, which cannot be denied, that the Son of
God in that Pauline repetition repeated particularly those things which
He judged to be in some need of clarification, and therefore did not repeat
those things which in themselves are perfectly plain and clear. For just as
in the first portion in Luke He passes over the words "Take and eat," so
also in the second portion He omits certain words both in Luke and in
Paul, namely: "When He had given thanks He gave it to them saying,
'Drink of it, all of you.'" However, we will not talk nonsense along with
the papalists, who say that it has not been commanded to the laity that
they should all drink of the cup, on the grounds that Paul, in writing to the
whole church at Corinth, omitted these words. For the Son of God by this
repetition to Paul did not wish either to retract or abolish anything but
only to explain and to clarify the account of the first institution, which
took place in the Jerusalem upper room. Therefore we must compare the
first institution in Matt. 26 and Mark 14 with the repetition after the
ascension in 1 Cor. 11 and Luke 22. In Luke He mentions only the cup, but
in Matthew He shows that He is not primarily understanding either the
material or the form of the cup but what is distributed in that cup and
what is drunk from that cup.

But in what sense is that which is distributed in the cup of the
Supper and drawn from it the new covenant? My answer is that the
word "new covenant" or "treaty" is sometimes used to indicate the
effect, as when it refers to the blessings for which the covenant or
treaty is ratified and which come as the result of the ratifying of the
treaty, as in Jer. 31:31 ff. But sometimes it refers to the covenant
itself or to the treaty itself, as to when or to what extent it is
ratified, confirmed, and sealed between those who are parties to it.
Often both concepts are joined or bound together, but in a certain
order. For example, in Ex. 24:8 when Moses had sacrificed the blood
to God, he said to the people: "This is the blood of the old covenant

which is ratified in order to obtain the covenant blessings—with God indeed by sacrifice, but with you by the sprinkling of this blood for the application and sealing of the covenant blessings." Even circumcision is called a treaty with God, because it was not an idle or empty act consisting only of cutting off the foreskin, but it had attached to it a promise, and by virtue of this promise it conveyed and sealed the treaty and as a consequence also the blessings promised in the covenant.

In the same way the new covenant is ratified, confirmed, and sealed over against God by the shedding of Christ's blood in order to merit and obtain the covenant blessings. But this new covenant or treaty must also be ratified, confirmed, and sealed over against us and with us because of the distribution, application, and sealing of the blessings of the covenant, in order that we individually might be certain we are included in this covenant of grace and that it together with the good things which flow from it might be sealed for each of us individually. But in what way and in what respect is the covenant ratified and sealed with us? The old covenant, to be sure, was ratified and sealed with the people in such a way that the same blood which was sacrificed to God was also sprinkled on the people [Ex. 24:8]. The new covenant is similar in that it is ratified, confirmed, and sealed to the believers by the same blood as is shed to ratify it before God. And this blood is called the blood of the covenant for two reasons: 1. because by its shedding the treaty is ratified with God in order to acquire the covenant blessings; 2. because by the imparting of the same in Holy Communion the treaty is also ratified and sealed with us, in order to confer and seal the covenant blessings. Christ therefore is called the Guarantor and Mediator of the new covenant: 1. because He brought into the holy of holies His own blood to be the sacrifice, and 2. because He brought this same blood out to us through Holy Communion, so that by the same blood He might ratify, complete, confirm, and seal with both parties this new covenant or treaty, which is not some empty thing but includes the blessings promised in the covenant.

Christ wished to indicate this meaning when He said in the first portion of the words of institution: "This is My blood of the new covenant." But because of the brevity of the statement, this meaning could not be plainly enough indicated in Matthew's account. Therefore Christ after the ascension, in the repetition to Paul, explained this meaning more precisely and fully, saying: "This cup is the new covenant," as if the words of Moses: "This is the blood of the covenant," were transposed to read: "This is the covenant in that blood." Therefore the blood of Christ, either when it was shed for the remission of sins in the passion or when it was imparted to Christ's disciples in Holy Communion, is not separate from the new covenant, for otherwise it could not rightly be called the blood of the new covenant. Nor is the new covenant separate from the blood of Christ, for this is the blood of the new covenant. The blood Moses used did not possess the quality of being the blood of the covenant because it was the blood of a bull; but because covenant blessings were acquired and distributed by it, either by reason of the sacrifice to God or by reason of the sprinkling of the people, it was called and was the blood of the covenant. So also the blood of Christ, because by it the blessings of the new covenant have been acquired over against God through its shedding and have been distributed by Holy Communion to the faithful, for this reason is and is called the blood of the new covenant. And just as when the blood of Christ was poured out in His passion it was correct to say that this is the new covenant in Christ's blood (for by the shedding of His blood the new covenant or treaty was established between God and the human race in order to obtain the covenant blessings) so, when the same blood of Christ is given to us in the cup of the Supper, it is correct to say that this is the new covenant in the blood of Christ. For by this Communion God because of the application ratifies and seals this new covenant or treaty with each individual communicant. And when it has been so ratified and sealed, either before God or before us, it is called a new covenant or treaty. But this new covenant which is ratified before God by the shedding of Christ's own blood in His suffering is ratified and sealed also with us in the Supper.

But how? Only by simple drinking of wine, as some contend? By no means. For this is obviated by what has already been said. Christ Himself in the Pauline repetition expressly says: "This cup is the new covenant," not because of the cup or its material or its form, nor because its content was the fruit of the vine, but "in My blood," Christ says. But where is this blood? Is it above the clouds totally removed from the cup of the Supper, as our adversaries contend? Then the sense would be: "The new covenant is in that blood of Mine which was once shed and now is far removed from the cup of the Supper and is contained only in heaven." But if this ought to be the sense, it would be necessary, as Luther learnedly noted, to add the article after the word "covenant," in this way: "This cup is the new covenant which is in My blood" (ἡ καινὴ διαθήκη ἡ ἐν τῷ αἵματί μου). But Christ says, without the article: "This is the new covenant in My blood," where the Hebraism in a sense is saying "for the sake of My blood."

But a matter so important and so serious must not be given over only to the consideration of grammatical points. Therefore we should give heed to a surer Interpreter, one who is greater than any exception, who will explain both the Greek and the Hebrew to us with exactness. For because it was necessary that the words be equivalent and of the same meaning both in Matthew and Luke, the one should be explained and understood, as a matter of necessity and precision, on the basis of the other. According to Luke and Paul it reads: "This cup is the new covenant in My blood." According to Matthew: "What is distributed to you in this cup and what you drink from this cup is My blood which is the blood of the new covenant." Therefore for this reason and in this respect this cup is the new covenant. This is what Christ wanted to say when He said "in My blood." But how that new covenant is ratified with us in the Supper by His blood Christ carefully and expressly shows us in the first account of the institution as recorded in Matthew, namely, that it was not by sprinkling, as in the old covenant, but "Drink of it, all of you; this is the blood of the new covenant," and "This is the new covenant in My blood."

Luther in a brief and lovely way connects both forms, "This is the blood of the new covenant" and "This is the new covenant in My blood," comparing them to the links which make up a chain, which he calls a "golden chain." The command of Christ, he says, lays hold of the wine in the cup; the wine by virtue of the words of Christ embraces the blood of Christ; the blood lays hold of the covenant, because it is the blood of the covenant; the covenant lays hold of the forgiveness of sins. Thus the meaning is the same: "This is My blood, which is the blood of the new covenant," and "This is the new covenant in My blood, which is shed for the remission of sins."

Thus a comparison shows and offers us a very sure explanation. For the Lord's Supper in this second portion does not consist only of wine but at the same time of the blood of Christ, which in the words of institution is called "the blood of the new covenant," because by this blood the new covenant is ratified and sealed both toward God and with the believers. Toward God, indeed, by its shedding; for in the words of institution it says: "Which is shed for you." But with us it is ratified and sealed by the sharing of the same blood in Holy

Communion. The mode of this sharing or Communion is described by these words: "Drink of it, all of you; this is the blood of the new covenant." In this way the covenant blessings are at the same time distributed, applied, and sealed to the believers. Therefore in the words of institution we have the words "for the remission of sins." All of these blessings are most beautifully and sweetly included and set forth in the words of institution, in which are to be explained the mutual benefits which the first account of the Supper records and which are repeated in the second, with Christ as the witness in both cases.

There are two main questions in the covenant of Christ: 1. What is distributed to us in the Lord's Supper and received orally? 2. Why is it distributed to us, or what does Christ will or do or cause in giving us this bread and this drink? Therefore Matthew and Mark first explain this to us in a lucid way, that it is the body of Christ which is given for us and the blood of Christ which is shed for us. Then they hint at the second point, when they talk about "the blood of the covenant." But because of the brevity of their accounts this point is rather obscure. Therefore Luke and Paul, and indeed Christ Himself in the repetition of the words of institution after the ascension, explain the second point clearly and directly—that when He distributes His blood to us, so that we drink it from the cup, He wills and brings it about that He ratifies, confirms, and seals His new covenant with us. But in what way and how this ratification, confirmation, and sealing take place in the Lord's Supper is clearly explained by Matthew in these words: "Drink of it, all of you; this is My blood, which is the blood of the new covenant." And in order that this reception might be salutary, Christ adds, as recorded by Paul: "This do, as often as you drink it, in remembrance of Me," which is to say: "This is My blood which is shed for you, and is now given or shared with you, that it may be a new covenant for you." In these words the spiritual drinking which takes place by faith is postulated and described. Thus the proper and natural meaning concerning the substantial presence, distribution, and reception of the body and blood of Christ in the Supper is fully, clearly, and powerfully established and confirmed by this repetition of the words of institution, received from the Son of God Himself after His ascension, which Luke put in writing exactly as he heard them explained and expounded by Paul.

Further, Luke still has one more peculiar and particularly illustrative argument by which he proves and establishes the proper and natural meaning in a very clear way. He uses the words "shed for you" (τὸ ὑπὲϱ ὑμῶν ἐϰχυννόμενον [Luke 22:20]) in such a way that according to the natural and proper sense of the Greek language they cannot be referred to anything but the cup, as all who are acquainted with Greek understand. So the sense is: That which is distributed in the cup of blessing, which the communicants also drink orally from the cup, is shed for you for the remission of sins. Therefore it is not only wine, but the true blood of Christ is substantially present at the same time and is distributed and received in this cup in the Supper. This point presses so heavily on our adversaries that Beza can find no other way of escape except to suggest that either the text is incorrect, although he is unable to show any manuscript which has it differently, or that we have here some kind of solecism, as if Luke were so inept in the Greek language that he was ignorant of matters which are known to boys in school. But these are clear indications that the simple truth is so powerful that it cannot be overturned except by crass and violent devices. But this merely confirms the pious in the simple and natural meaning of the words.

D. The description of the institution of the Lord's Supper as it is recorded in Paul, 1 Cor 11.

The account of the institution of the Lord's Supper, after Matthew, Mark, and Luke, was put in writing for the fourth time by the apostle Paul. And quite properly the authority of Paul's testimony should be great in this controversy. For he is the apostle to the Gentiles and confesses in his writings that he is a debtor equally to the learned and to the unlearned (Rom. 1:14). Thus it was particularly the case that those who were converted from among the Jews, because they were accustomed to figures of speech involving the Law, were also among the learned who possessed those outstanding gifts of prophecy and tongues, and they could have seen and understood a figure of speech in the words of the Supper without anyone to show them. But it is also certain that Paul was concerned about the Gentiles, who were less learned and were not so accustomed to these figures of speech. He could not ignore the fact that they were in danger of being deceived and might wander away from the true meaning of the words if in the case of the last will and testament of Christ they were left with figurative and obscure language without any clear and sure interpretation of it. For in the

119

case of other dogmas Paul was studious to explain properly, clearly, and precisely any parabolic, obscure, or ambiguous language. This is also the case with Augustine in his *De opere monachorum,* ch. 7—8, where he says: "Our Lord, to be sure, did speak in parables and similes, as the evangelists have recorded. But the apostle, in keeping with apostolic custom, tended to speak more openly and properly rather than in figures. This is the case with nearly everything in the letters of the apostles." Thus Augustine.[2] Therefore if Paul had wanted us to understand something that was absent or something else than, as the words sound, the substantial presence of the body and blood of the Lord in the Supper, he would doubtlessly have clearly said so, and there would not have been lacking plain and clear words to express and render this meaning. In other instances he clearly sets forth such explanations, as for example in 1 Cor. 5:3: "I indeed being absent in the body but present in the spirit have judged already as though I were present," and Col. 2:5: "For though I am absent in the flesh, yet I am with you in spirit."

But the highest authority of Paul's testimony lies in the fact that he did not receive his description of the institution from the other apostles, so that by his own apostolic authority he might change, transpose, or interpret certain of the words. Rather the Son of God Himself after His ascension in glory so repeated and taught the institution of His Supper to Paul that at the same time, both by repetition of the same words as well as by the change, transposition, and explanation of certain words, He might show in what way He wished the institution to be explained and understood. Paul himself describes how he received this repetition of the words of institution from the Son of God (1 Cor. 11:23). Luke, as we have shown, noted how Paul taught this to the churches. Moreover, Paul did not merely recite the words of institution of the Supper historically, as the evangelists did. For when advice was sought regarding certain disputes which had arisen in the church at Corinth concerning this sacrament, Paul set forth this form of the words of institution as a most certain rule and norm according to which all such controversies ought and rightly can be settled. And because within a few years, while the apostles themselves were still alive, the doctrine of the Lord's Supper had begun to be corrupted, and since under the guidance of the Spirit he foresaw that in later times much sadder controversies were going to arise over this mystery, without doubt he positioned the words and explained their meaning in such a way that in his description all posterity might have a sure norm and rule of correct faith and of certain judgment for settling all questions and controversies concerning this dogma.

But in the discussion of Luke's account we have called attention to and explained nearly all the points which need to be considered in proving and confirming the proper and natural meaning of the words as they stand in Paul's repetition. We shall therefore briefly note only the few things which are peculiar to Paul in his repetition.

First, we should carefully note that Paul says that the Lord's Supper is celebrated in those places or meetings where the faithful gather in the church in order to eat it. This is what Paul is saying by the words "when you come together in church" (1 Cor. 11:18, 20). But, you say, what is the use of this observation, since the matter is obvious in itself? The answer is that the adversaries are compelled to yield to the clear evidence of the words that the Lord's Supper consists not only of symbolic elements such as bread and wine, but at the same time also of the body and blood of Christ. But they immediately add that these elements must be separated from one another, by a very great distance, farther than the visible heaven is from the earth. For the symbols are on earth and nowhere else; but the body and blood of Christ, they say, are in one particular place in heaven and nowhere else, and yet not only the symbols but also the very body and blood of Christ are present, distributed, and received in the Lord's Supper, because this Supper is celebrated not only on earth but at the same time also in the fiery heaven. So the meaning would be: In the Lord's Supper, that is, in the third heaven, the body and blood of the Lord are present, and again in the Lord's Supper, that is, on earth, the bread and wine are present—so that the Lord's Supper sometimes refers to heaven and sometimes to the earth, and finally includes both heaven and earth and everything therein.

But Paul in his description of the mystery of the Lord's Supper is not trying to suspend us between heaven and earth or to investigate the secrets of the heavens when we go to the Lord's Supper and seek the things which are present and distributed there. But he explicitly and expressly shows where the Supper is and where it is celebrated (which thus consists of bread and the body and wine and the blood of Christ, so that in this Supper are present and distributed not only the bread and wine but also the very body and blood of Christ), that is to say, where any of Christ's disciples are gathered or come together in one place or meeting, in the church which is still struggling here on earth, for the purpose of eating the Supper, as he says later, "when you come together to eat"

[1 Cor. 11:33]. In that place, therefore, where the disciples of Christ on this earth come together and congregate for the observance of the Lord's Supper by external eating according to the words of institution, there, I say, those things of which the words of the Supper speak are present and distributed. For Paul clearly describes where the observance of the Lord's Supper takes place and is celebrated, when he says, "when you come together in church to eat." [1 Cor. 11:18, 20, 33]

Second, in the first portion of the account the words are repeated precisely as they occur elsewhere: "He took bread, gave thanks, and said, 'Take and eat.'" But when we come to those words which are presently called into controversy, Paul not only repeats the same words but he also puts them in such an order that by this special emphasis he points out the true body of Christ. For where the other evangelists have: "This is My body" (τοῦτό ἐστιν τὸ σῶμά μου), Paul has: "This of Me is the body" (τοῦτό μού ἐστιν τὸ σῶμα). To be sure, the meaning is the same, but the Pauline words declare and confirm the proper and natural meaning with greater emphasis.

Third, the Pauline repetition has the peculiar reading that where Luke has "which is given (διδόμενον) for you," there Paul says "which is broken (κλώμενον) for you" [1 Cor. 11:24 KJV]. Some interpret this of the passion and death of Christ, as though "broken" were being used instead of "sacrificed." And because the body of Christ was given over to torments and tortures and finally to the most bitter sufferings of death, they are trying to say that Paul used the word "broken." But the text is most clearly in opposition to this idea: The paschal lamb was sacrificed, to be sure, placed on the altar and burned, but the act of sacrificing and placing on the altar was not called a breaking. The fact is that God clearly says: "You shall not break a bone of it" [Ex. 12:46]. And in John 19:33, 36, after he has described the torments of the crucifixion and finally the suffering connected with Christ's death, John clearly adds that the suffering and death of Christ are not and are not to be called a breaking; for he says that in the suffering of Christ the Scripture in Ex. 12:46 was fulfilled: "A bone of Him shall not be broken." Thus I do not see how it is possible to say that in this passage the word "broken" is to be used in place of "sacrificed" and that it must be understood with reference to the torments of the crucifixion and the suffering and death of Christ, although Scripture itself clearly denies this notion. Therefore it remains that this passage must be understood with reference to the distribution.

At this point the adversaries immediately retort that the breaking can be referred only to the bread, which is given either in small pieces or in wafers, and therefore the body of Christ which is broken in the Supper is not the actual substance of the body of Christ but only bread. But the act of breaking is expressly attributed first to the bread when it says: "He took bread and broke it." And afterward when the bread which has now been broken is distributed, by this act of distribution the body of Christ is said also to be broken, that is, in order that it may be distributed for Holy Communion and participation. For according to Hebrew custom it was not necessary in speaking about something being broken that it actually be torn to pieces or broken into small parts, but whatever was offered, distributed, obtained, and received at a meal (even if the action took place without any crumbling or breaking) was said to be "broken." Thus in Gen. 41:56 the word *shabar* is used when Joseph distributed the grain to the Egyptians. And when foreign nations came to Egypt to procure, acquire, and receive grain from Joseph, the word used is "to break" (Gen. 41:57). And hence, because of this sharing, distributing, and offering of grain, Joseph was called a lord over the land and the one who broke grain to all the people of the earth (Gen. 42:6). Likewise in Deut. 2:6, when food was purchased, acquired, and received for silver, it is spoken of as a breaking. And in Prov. 11:26, where the comparison is made between withholding food and sharing it, the word "to break" is used. In Is. 55:1, where we read: "Come, buy and eat; come buy without money," in Hebrew the word is "to break." Thus in the words of the Supper when the broken bread is distributed it is said that at the same time the body of Christ is distributed and offered. And this is what He means when He says, "which is broken for you."

Moreover, we must remember that Paul did not by his own authority change the word "given" to "broken." For he affirms that the things he teaches regarding the Supper were received from the Son of God after His ascension, when He had already been taken up into His glory. Therefore Christ Himself, for the sake of a clearer explanation and corroboration, instead of "given" uses the word "broken." And on the basis of the record in Luke it is apparent that Paul in his explanation of this doctrine used both formulas in the churches, "which is given for you" as well as "which is broken for you," so that each might be interpreted and corroborated by the other. That is to say: It is not one body which was sacrificed for us on the cross and another which is distributed and received in the

Supper; but the same substance of the body of Christ which was given for us on the cross is broken in the Supper with the bread for those who eat, that is, it is offered and distributed; for He says: "This is My body which is given for you," and "This is My body which is broken for you." Thus the same body is given on the cross and is broken in the Supper, that is, is distributed, offered, and received; and a comparison of these phrases illustrates this point beautifully.

It is a certainty that Paul had seen Christ after He had been received into heaven in glory (Acts 9:3 ff.; 22:6 ff.; 26:12 ff.). He also had seen the very body of Christ, for he uses this as the basis for proving His resurrection (1 Cor. 15:8). But Christ, who is now in glory, had stated two points about His body with which He had ascended into heaven: 1. That it was given for us on the cross, and 2. that the same body is broken in the Lord's Supper, that is, distributed and offered. And Paul clearly and expressly shows where the Lord's Supper takes place and is celebrated when he says: "When you come together in the church to eat" [cf. 1 Cor. 11:18, 20, 33]. Furthermore, Christ very clearly describes both the distribution and the reception in the Pauline repetition, namely, that what is offered by the external distribution with broken bread in the Lord's Supper and is received by eating, that is, what is taken orally, that this is His own body. And this body of His was given for us on the cross and now after the ascension is offered and received in the Lord's Supper which is celebrated in the church here on earth. Hereby the Son of God taught that not only when He walked upon the earth in His visible presence but now when He has taken His heavenly throne and sits at the right hand of God—He taught Paul that what is offered by an outward distribution of bread in the Lord's Supper which is celebrated in the church here on earth, and is received orally by those who eat, that this, I say, is His body. Therefore He who alone knows this matter best has seen and declared that these two formulas are not in conflict with one another, namely, that Christ with His own body ascended into heaven and that the same body is present in the Lord's Supper which is celebrated in the gathering of the church here on earth, that it is distributed with the bread and received orally by those who eat it. For this is the simple, proper, and natural meaning of the words.

How this happens or can happen I will not argue, but I commend it to the wisdom and power of Him who has taught it. I do not doubt that He both knows and has the way, even though it is incomprehensible to us, by which, with the true reality of His body kept intact, both facts are true, that it is in heaven and that it is present, distributed, and received in the Lord's Supper. For when He had already been received into heaven with His body, He declared and affirmed in regard to that which is distributed, received, and eaten in the gathering of the church here on earth in the Lord's Supper: "This is My body which is broken for you." And Paul himself in 1 Cor. 10:16 interprets the breaking of the body of Christ as a κοινωνία, a communion or participation. For when in the words of institution he says in regard to the breaking of the bread of blessing that it is the body of Christ which is broken for us, he explains this statement in 1 Cor. 10:16 in this way: "The bread which we break is the communion of the body of Christ." More needs to be said shortly regarding this statement of Paul. Because the body of Christ, as well as His blood in the Supper, is not offered in some idle distribution to those who eat, but in such a way that it is prepared, ratified, preserved, and sealed with us as a treaty of grace of the new covenant, with the most sure and precious seal and guarantee, therefore he says that it is "broken for you." The other matters are explained in Luke's account.

Therefore the institution of the Lord's Supper (first given by Christ while He still walked with His visible presence here on earth, and repeated for the second time by Him when He had already ascended into heaven), an event which stands in four different places in Scripture, openly, clearly, definitely, and convincingly demonstrates, proves, and confirms the simple, proper, and natural meaning. Nor do we discover any sufficiently sure, clear, and firm testimony or argument in these words of institution which either teaches or compels us to depart from the simple, proper, and natural meaning. With what conscience, therefore, would we dare to do over against these words, which are the words of the last will and testament of the Son of God Himself, what we could not honestly do even in the case of the will and testament of a man if his words of disposition were as clear as we have shown them to be in the words of institution of the Supper? We have demonstrated this above at great length in the case of secular wills.

Let us rather with our whole heart give thanks to the Son of God, our Testator, that He Himself first gave us the words of institution and then for a second time repeated them and saw to it that they were faithfully and diligently recorded in four places in Scripture, so that by means of these explanations we can seek, find, learn, and receive from His own voice in the very words of institution which have been handed down to us the true, real, and genuine meaning of this last will and testament. In this meaning which the words of institution demonstrate and give us we can safely rest our case and surely ought to do so, in order that we may "bring into captivity every thought to the obedience of Christ" (2 Cor. 10:5). And let us pray that in this simple faith He will keep us in obedience to His Spirit, lest by some plausible kind of objection we permit ourselves to be drawn away from the voice of the Son of God, the Testator, and from the words of His last will and testament, even though Paul pronounces that judgment is attached to the one who does not properly recognize the Lord's body.

Chapter IX

Arguments from other Scripture passages which expressly refer to the dogma of the Lord's Supper, 1 Cor. 10 and 11.

The points we have noted up to this time in the repetitions of the words of institution of the Supper offer arguments which are very clear and convincing to establish and confirm the simple and natural meaning of the words. But let us also take a look at other Scripture passages, not indeed unrelated ones which do not speak of this dogma, but those in which express mention is made of the dogma of the Lord's Supper. For a consideration of them will prove and confirm the simple and natural meaning of the words of institution. And great is the power of these passages for deciding this controversy. For Paul in these passages not only makes mention of this dogma as an event which took place, but on the basis of the words of institution he develops and formulates very weighty arguments to serve as earnest warnings and exhortations. And in these arguments he sheds a great deal of light on what the genuine force, the proper meaning, and the sense of these words is from which he derives his arguments. For it is necessary that the passages from which he derives his arguments to prove a certain point not be obscure, ambiguous, or uncertain but rather clear, certain, and firm. Therefore it can clearly be determined from these passages in what sense and with what meaning Paul understood and transmitted the words of institution. Now let us first take up the passages in 1 Cor. 11, because here the words of institution are part of the unbroken context.

A. The passage of Paul, 1 Cor. 11:27:
   "Whoever therefore shall eat this bread
   and drink this cup of the Lord unworthily
   shall be guilty of the body and blood of the Lord."

Paul does not write this statement in isolation, but through the use of a subordinate particle [ὥστε, therefore] he joins it to the account of the institution in such a way that he can show that those things which he treats concerning guilt logically follow from what Christ says regarding the bread: "This is My body," and of the cup: "This is My blood." Thus from these words which are now in controversy Paul weaves his argument regarding the guilt of unworthy eating. And thus Paul clearly shows in what sense he understood these words.

Before we examine the individual words of this statement, note that he does not speak of the bread or the cup in isolation but says "this bread," or that bread of which the Son of God says: "This is My body which is given for you." In the same way he speaks of the cup of which the Lord Himself states: "This is My blood which is the blood of the new covenant," and "This is the new covenant in My blood." And the subordinate particle ὥστε, by which this entire statement is attached to the words of institution whence it is deduced and to which it refers, shows that these words must be understood and interpreted in this way.

Paul understands the eating and drinking in a literal sense, for he uses both concepts: to eat the bread and to eat of the bread; to drink the cup and to drink from the cup of the Lord. To eat unworthily means not to eat in such a way as is fitting for this Supper or as is worthy of the food which is distributed and received in this Supper. In this sense the adverb "worthily" (ἀξίως) is used in Eph. 4:1, "walk worthy of the calling"; or Phil. 1:27, "worthy of the Gospel"; or Col. 1:10, "worthy of the Lord." Likewise in 3 John 5-6, "receiving and bringing forward on their journey faithful strangers as is worthy of God and the saints"; cf. Rom. 15. From this it is possible to determine by way of antithesis what the grammatical explanation of the adverb "unworthily" is. And what is actually meant by "unworthy eating" is shown in the context. For Paul is accusing the Corinthians that among them many were eating unworthily at the Supper. He explains wherein this consisted, namely, that they were not coming to the Lord's Supper with any other spirit or in any greater reverence than in their private homes when they sat down to their ordinary meals. Likewise they were nourishing hatred in their hearts; they were despising the church, were shaming the poor, were not abstaining from idolatrous practices; they were even coming to the celebration of the Supper drunk—and yet, although this was so and they remained without true repentance and living faith, they still came to the table of the Lord. This Paul calls unworthy eating.

He adds a warning regarding the guilt which attaches to unworthy communing. This guilt consists of two things. First, it is the reason why punishment must take place. Second, it is the punishment or penalty itself. Later on Paul describes this when he says: "He eats and drinks judgment to himself." But he also describes it in a second way when he says: "He will be guilty of the body and blood of the Lord." For when in the grammatical construction something is added to the word "guilty" (ἔνοχος [1 Cor. 11:27]), it either describes the kind of punishment, as when it says: "He is guilty of death" (Matt. 26:66) or "guilty of eternal punishment" (Mark 3:29), or it describes and designates that thing for the violation of which one is condemned to be punished, as in James 2:10-11: "Whoever fails in one point has become guilty of all." And he quickly adds the explanation, that such a person "has become a transgressor of the law," that is, he is guilty of breaking the law.

Thus in Deut. 19:10, where the Hebrew reads "innocent blood will be upon you," the Septuagint uses the word ἔνοχος ["There shall not be in you one guilty of blood" LXX], and in the context it mentions "innocent blood," by the shedding of which one incurs guilt that brings the punishment of divine judgment. Therefore when Paul says: "He will be guilty of the body and blood of the Lord," he is not describing the punishment itself or the kind of penalty. For this he does afterward when he says: "He eats judgment to himself." But the cause or the crime whence he incurs the punishment of judgment he describes in the way he does in order that he may specifically mention that thing by the misuse or violation of which he brings down upon himself the penalty of judgment and may describe the manner of the violation. Therefore, because in the Lord's Supper he eats unworthily, he eats judgment to himself. This is the punishment.

But what thing has he violated to bring this penalty upon himself? That is, as Paul says, what thing has he violated to become guilty? Is he guilty only of the bread and wine? Is only the violation of some symbols the cause and the crime for which this penalty of divine judgment comes upon him? This is the contention of our adversaries. But Paul expressly mentions that thing by whose violation in the Supper the punishment of judgment is incurred; he will be guilty, he says, of the body and blood of the Lord. Therefore it is the very body of the Lord and His very blood whose misuse, violation, and despising draws down the guilt of punishment upon him who in the Lord's Supper eats unworthily. As a result those who eat unworthily in the Supper eat to their judgment because by their misuse and profanation they inflict injury and insult not only on the external symbols but upon the very body and blood of Christ. This is Paul's meaning, as we have demonstrated, when he says: "He will be guilty of the body and blood of the Lord." [1 Cor. 11:27]

These points are so clear that even Oecolampadius was critical of those who in this statement wanted, by a figure of speech, to make the word "body" mean only a symbol of the body. But just as injury was inflicted on the body of Christ through various means, so also a person can be guilty of the body and blood of Christ in various ways. Thus the soldiers inflicted injury by wounding and killing Him, Pilate by condemning Him, the Jews by accusing Him—all were guilty of the body and blood of Christ, as Christ Himself says: "He who betrayed Me to you has the greater guilt" [John 19:11]. And again: "His blood be upon us and our children" [Matt 27:25]. So it is with those who either despise the Christ hidden in the Word and sacraments or reject Him by their carnal security, their unwillingness to suffer, their godless intention, or their unbelief and thus profane the blood of the covenant. (Heb. 10:29)

But in this passage Paul is describing a particular and peculiar mode of profanation and violation of the body of Christ. He mentions it specifically when he says: "He who eats unworthily in the Supper of the Lord brings down judgment upon himself" [1 Cor. 11:27]. Therefore in the Supper judgment is incurred not by rejecting but by eating. For he says: "He eats judgment to himself." But what is it which the unworthy eat in the Supper by the misuse, profanation, and violation of which they bring down the penalty of judgment upon themselves? "He who eats this bread unworthily," he says, "and drinks the cup of the Lord unworthily."

But concerning this bread and cup, as to what it is, are we permitted to invent anything we wish? Certainly not. For this statement of Paul is not used in an absolute way but by the use of a subordinate particle is attached to the words of institution, whence it is deduced and on which it depends. And this particle (ὥστε) which draws and infers the consequences from the words of institution supplies the rationale as to how and in what way those who eat this bread of the Supper unworthily become guilty by this unworthy eating of violating the body of Christ. It is because this bread is that body of Christ which was given for us, so that those who eat in the Supper receive with their mouths not only the bread but at the same time also the body of Christ, as we have shown from the words of institution. And because those who unworthily eat this body of Christ, which together with the bread is distributed in the Supper and received by eating, violate it by profanation and misuse, therefore because of this unworthy eating and drinking they become guilty of the body and blood of Christ. Therefore the whole force of this Pauline statement lies in this subordinate particle, which brings out the meaning and causes it to depend on the words of institution, from which the meaning of this statement is clear, namely, that those who eat unworthily in the Lord's Supper become guilty of that thing which they have violated by eating unworthily.

But the Son of God affirms that in the Lord's Supper we eat, that is, receive orally, not only bread but also His own true body. Therefore by eating unworthily in the Supper they become guilty not only of the symbols but of the body of Christ itself. From this it is possible to conclude most correctly that Paul understood the words of institution in their proper and natural sense, namely, that those who eat in the Lord's Supper receive orally not only bread and wine but at the same time also the body and blood of the Lord. For those who eat unworthily become guilty of that which they violate by unworthy eating. But Paul pronounces that they are guilty of the body of the Lord. Therefore they are eating not only bread but also the body of the Lord. Moreover, they are not eating it only spiritually, because they come under judgment; therefore they are also eating sacramentally, as we have explained above.

But, someone says, Paul says that a person eats *bread* unworthily. The answer is: Paul does not refer simply to bread, but he says "this bread." But what bread is this? It is the bread which according to the word of institution is the body of the Lord given for us. For in addition to this explanation given in the account of the institution, the subordinate particle, as we have demonstrated, brings out the complete meaning.

These points are absolutely clear both from the grammatical explanation of the words as well as from the facts in the case, if only we note this one principle, namely, that this statement is so connected to the words of institution by the subordinate particle that it is inferred from them and depends on them. And it is manifest that the proper and natural meaning of the words of institution can be proved, established, and confirmed by this same statement. For the interpretations of this statement which are offered by our adversaries are forced, strange, and in conflict with the words themselves. They try to evade this meaning in three principal ways.

1. They point out that a person can be guilty of the body and blood of Christ in various ways, as we have indicated above. Therefore they say that it does not follow that if those who eat unworthily are guilty of the body of Christ they therefore actually eat the body of Christ. Answer: Paul is not speaking in a general way about guilt, but specifically about the way in which one draws guilt upon himself in the Supper, namely, by unworthily eating this bread which is the body of Christ. For they who eat unworthily inflict upon the body of Christ injury and shame no less than those who beat and killed Him.

Theodoret and Oecumenius interpret this statement in this way: Just as Judas by betraying and the Jews by afflicting the body of Christ with their reproaches brought shame upon Christ Himself, so they also dishonor Him who receive His all-holy body with unclean hands and put it into a polluted mouth. Chrysostom says that it is just as great a crime as the crime of those who butchered the body of Christ and shed His blood.

2. Some philosophize that an injury inflicted upon a symbol is inflicted upon the thing itself, as when a person treats the eagle of the emperor or the standard of a prince in a shameful manner. They consider the statement of Paul as if it were placed in so absolute and separate a position that it is not permitted or necessary for us to determine whence, why, and how those who eat unworthily become guilty of the body of Christ—although Paul through the explanatory particle weaves in both the statement and the reason for the statement, which is found in the words of institution, in such a way that he declares and shows that those who eat unworthily become guilty of the body of Christ because they unworthily eat that bread of which the Son of God Himself affirms that it is His body, given for us.

3. Calvin imagines that those who eat unworthily are indeed guilty of the offered body of Christ, but not of His received body and certainly not of His repudiated body, because to receive or eat the body of Christ is not the same as being guilty of the body of Christ. He argues this point very vigorously, but without Biblical evidence, indeed in the face of Biblical evidence. For Paul not only speaks of guilt but he describes the way in which it is incurred, namely, not by spitting out but by eating. But by eating what? That bread, he says. But what bread? The bread which Christ affirms is His body. Therefore they become guilty of the body of Christ because they eat it unworthily, and by this unworthy eating they violate it. For Christ pronounces that what is distributed in the Supper and received by our eating is His very body. Therefore this statement of Paul powerfully confirms the proper and natural meaning of the words. For he asserts that the unworthy, who do not eat spiritually, nevertheless do eat the body of Christ. For concerning that which he receives by mouth in the Supper, whether Judas or Peter, as the Greek interpreters say in their explanation of this passage, the Son of God pronounces: "This is My body which is given for you."

B. Paul's statement, 1 Cor. 11:29:
"Whoever eats unworthily eats judgment upon himself, not discerning the Lord's body."

This statement is not only related to the passage discussed above but coheres with it and with the words of institution in a continuous context. I draw attention to this because if this statement is considered separately and removed from the rest of the context, various notions can be developed regarding the discerning of the body of Christ. But to the preceding points Paul connects these which follow: "Whoever eats unworthily in the Supper eats judgment to himself, not discerning the Lord's body."

He has already explained in the preceding verses what it means to eat unworthily. But why and how can it be that men are not afraid to approach this holy table of the Lord with such security, ignorance, frivolity, temerity, and impurity as to eat this Supper unworthily? Paul answers that it happens because they do not distinguish or discern the Lord's body. This is the reason Paul gives as to why many people eat unworthily. For a worthy eating in the Supper, therefore, it is required that there be a discerning of the Lord's body. And "discern" (διακρίνειν) means to distinguish one thing from another, as when we separate, discern, and distinguish something from the common order of things. Thus in Acts 15:9 God made no distinction between Jewish and Gentile believers. And in the Epistle of Jude [22-23], where he teaches that we must preserve the difference between incorrigible sinners and those who can be cleansed, he uses the verb διακρίνειν. Therefore Paul's meaning is clear: Those who eat unworthily eat judgment to themselves in that they do not distinguish between the bread of the Lord's Supper and other, common bread, so that they fail to recognize His true presence and to attribute to Him due honor. But on the contrary He requires this kind of discrimination, so that we might discern the bread of this Supper, distinguish it from other bread, acknowledge His true honor, and in accordance with His Word attribute to Him by our discernment the preeminence which is due Him.

Up to this point the meaning is beyond controversy. For there is no one from among our adversaries who wishes to appear as saying that the bread of the Lord's Supper should be regarded simply as common bread or bread in the ordinary sense. But if this Supper is merely distinguished from ordinary food, the same question remains as to what we judge this bread to be and what kind of honor and presence we attribute to it. Here let us open our ears and listen to Paul as a most accurate interpreter. He says that this bread which is given and received in the Lord's Supper must be so distinguished that it is discerned as the Lord's body. Furthermore, Paul is not speaking at this point primarily about those people who do not rightly judge concerning Christ's human nature in itself, so that they do not attribute to Him a true and perfect human nature and do not discern it in Christ as being more excellent in glory than other creatures, but he is speaking about the distinguishing and discerning of that bread which is offered in the Lord's Supper and received orally by the communicants. He wants this bread to be so distinguished from all other bread that this bread is discerned as the Lord's body. But how can this be? Because the Son of God has declared concerning this bread: "This is My body which is given for you."

Therefore whatever a person may believe and declare concerning this bread which is distributed in the Lord's Supper and received orally by the communicants and whatever kind of preeminence he may attribute to it beyond ordinary bread, if he does not discern and judge it according to the description of the Son of God, namely, that it is the Lord's body, he is not rightly discerning but is eating judgment to himself. And we should especially note that he speaks this way concerning the bread of the Lord's Supper which even the unworthy eat. These things are manifest and certain on the basis of the unchanging context of Paul's argument, if this statement is connected both with those points which precede it and with the words of institution themselves. And it confirms by most valid proof the proper, simple, and natural meaning of the words of institution. He also gives warning, as we have now repeatedly said, as to the piety and care with which those words should be treated by which Christ affirms concerning the bread: "This is My body which is given for you." For Paul pronounces that they who do not discern the bread of the Lord's Supper in keeping with these words, namely, that it is the body of Christ, eat judgment to themselves.

Surely on the basis of this statement the frivolity, brashness, security, and impudence of the human mind, which plays and cogitates on the various interpretations of these words, ought to be struck down as by a thunderbolt. For it is horrible to fall under the guilt of divine judgment because of not discerning the Lord's body.

I am aware that this passage about the discerning of the body of Christ is interpreted by many people after taking it out of its context and then considering it, so that it can be treated in various ways. But if it is connected with the words which precede it and with the words of institution, so that it flows out of them, it will be perfectly clear that there is one simple and precise meaning for this passage. For all the words are connected by little hooks, as it were, and must be referred to the institution itself, from which they are also derived.

This is the way the ancients understood Paul's statement. Ambrose says: "We must approach this table with fear, for our mind must understand that reverence is due Him whose body we are coming to receive. For the mind ought to judge this way within itself, because it is the Lord whose blood we drink in this mystery." And Chrysostom explains it this way: "Not discerning, that is, not weighing carefully the great importance of those things which are present and set forth in the Lord's Supper and not considering the fulness of the gift. For if you have diligently learned who is present or set forth and who, being present, gives Himself to whom, no other encouragement will be necessary, but this will suffice, unless you are absolutely without hope. . . ." Thus Chrysostom. In his statement it is to be observed that he does not wish us to discern and judge things that are far removed from the Supper, removed far above the heavens. But he wants us to ponder and consider the greatness and fulness of the things that are present and distributed in the Supper, namely, that it is the body and blood of the Lord.

C. The passage of Paul, 1 Cor. 10:16:
"The cup of blessing which we bless,
is it not the communion of the blood of Christ?
The bread which we break,
is it not the communion of the body of Christ?"

This passage is extremely helpful and possesses and offers much toward the resolution of this controversy. Thus Luther writes that this passage had become a living antidote for him and a most ready remedy against all objections and cavillings, indeed against all temptations in this controversy. And he said this because his adversaries tried by means of various devices to twist even this passage to support their ideas. Indeed, it does have a certain appearance by which they can put over their ideas on the unwary, when they say that Paul in this passage most clearly wanted to show that in the words of institution the literal meaning should not be retained and that the words as they read must not be taken in their proper and natural meaning because, where the words of institution speak of the body and blood of Christ, in this passage Paul uses the term "the communion of the body and blood of Christ." And since it is certain that the communication [or communion] is not the same as what is communicated, just as the giving is something else than the gift, the sending of an ambassador is something else than the ambassador himself, so they contend that Paul in this way wanted to show that the words must not be taken in their proper and natural sense, as they read, but are figurative, their interpetation being given in 1 Cor. 10. They contend that the "body of Christ" which is distributed and received in the Lord's Supper does not mean the very substance of His body but only the communication of His body. Therefore, they say, this interpretation, which both shows that there is a figure in the words of institution of the Supper and clearly explains this figure, must be accepted without subterfuge, since the Holy Spirit has taught it through His elected instrument Paul.

But we in all earnestness ask this question, whether in those passages in which the dogma of the Lord's Supper is treated and repeated the Holy Spirit clearly and definitely shows that the words of institution are figurative and that we must depart from their proper, simple, and natural meaning, and what is the proper interpretation of this figure of speech. But up to this point, in all the passages which we have examined and weighed with some degree of care, we have been unable to ascertain this, but rather the contrary. Thus we will see whether in this passage Paul clearly, openly, and definitely demonstrates this fact. And let us adopt this axiom which in ch. VII we have shown to be beyond debate: Those things which in Scripture are spoken in a tropical way or figuratively are explained simply and literally in some other passage of Scripture where the same material is treated. Therefore if the words of the Supper are tropical or figurative when they are treated in 1 Cor. 10:16, it will be necessary that those words in 1 Cor. 10:16 which are to show and interpret the trope in the Supper ought not themselves be tropical or figurative but proper, simple, and natural.

But our adversaries, after many long dissertations, are finally saying openly that the literal meaning cannot be retained in either the words of the Supper or the words of 1 Cor. 10. But just as they put a metonymy in the words of the Supper, so also they put a metonymy in the words of 1 Cor. 10 and interpret the communication [or communion] as a symbol, a watchword, or a sign of the communication. So they themselves, both in fact and in the substance of the matter, demonstrate that what they are asserting is false. The words of the Supper are figurative, they say, and must be taken in a way different from their literal sense, because an interpretation of them is given in 1 Cor. 10. To be sure, they contend that also in the words of 1 Cor. 10 there is a figure of speech and that the words must not be taken in their literal sense but must be interpreted otherwise through a figure of speech. Likewise, they do not want us to insist on the words of institution and they try to lead us away from them under the pretext of contending that they are figurative. Moreover, they promise that they will be able to demonstrate to us the clear and certain interpretation of the figure of speech in the words of Paul in 1 Cor. 10. And we, indeed, who have determined not to contrive the explanation of the words of the Supper for ourselves or to draw it in from elsewhere, but to seek and learn it from the voice of the Holy Spirit Himself in those passages in which He teaches us this dogma, are not unwilling to follow up to this point. But when we come to this passage in 1 Cor. 10, there again among our adversaries they make a great noise that everything is figurative, metonymical, and metaphorical. And they expressly state that the literal meaning cannot be retained in the words of 1 Cor. 10 but that they must be interpreted differently from the way they sound. The result is that this passage does not disclose itself to us with a clear interpretation on the basis of figures of speech, but itself needs an interpretation different from the way the words read.

Further, I am gladly willing to hear the consequences of their argument. Paul [they say] in 1 Cor. 10 uses different words than Christ uses in the words of institution. But the words of Paul in 1 Cor. 10 are figurative, and the literal meaning or the proper and natural sense cannot be retained, as they say. Therefore [they say] the words of institution are figurative and cannot be understood as they read. Much rather this follows: If in either passage the language is figurative, the interpretation of the words of institution cannot be derived from the passage in 1 Cor. 10. For where we are dealing with the establishment of dogmas, a figure of speech is not explained by means of another figure of speech but by proper and simple language. Therefore our adversaries through their figures of speech first of all lead us away from the words of institution, so that we are not satisfied with their proper and natural meaning, and then they mix in certain figurative elements even in the other passages, in 1 Cor. 11. But on the basis of figurative statements we cannot establish a dogma or prove it. Finally, although they have made long promises, they are now contending that the interpretation of 1 Cor. 10 must also be treated as tropical and figurative. Thus in determining and proving the germane, proper, and natural meaning of the dogma of the Lord's Supper, we will not be able to take our stand on any Scripture passage in which this dogma is definitely treated and repeated. For, they contend, all these passages are tropical and figurative and their simple, proper, and natural meaning cannot be retained or followed.

How then is this dogma to be established? Where do its proper foundations lie if not on the basis of those passages and in those passages in which it is manifestly treated and repeated? Either, therefore, it will be established from irrelevant passages which do not speak of the Lord's Supper, or the dogma will be without any sure foundation, relying on the private speculations of men. But dogmas must have a passage where they are properly and clearly taught.

Further, with no reasoning can it be established that when Paul speaks of the "communion" (κοινωνία) of the body of Christ he has in mind that in the words of the Supper the word "body" should be understood not as referring to the very substance of the body but only to its communication [or communion]. For the word κοινωνία never excludes or removes the substance itself from that action in which the communion (κοινωνία) takes place. For when Paul in Rom. 8:9 and 1 Cor. 6:19 says: "The Holy Spirit dwells in you," he is saying the same thing that he says in 2 Cor. 13:14, where he speaks of the "communion of the Spirit." Are we going to say with the fanatics that the Holy Spirit does not dwell in the believers with His essence, that His essence is far removed from us, and that in His place only something drawn from the substance of the Spirit, namely, His gifts and powers, is present in us? The gifts of charity which were collected for the poor saints and sent to them are called a κοινωνία in Rom. 15:26 and 2 Cor. 8:4. Does this mean that not the substance of these gifts but only something abstract was given and sent to the poor? The word κοινωνία means a communication—sometimes actively, that is, a distribution; sometimes passively, that is, a participation; and sometimes the thing itself which is offered and received, as we can demonstrate by individual examples. But in no way does it follow that Paul by the use of the term "the communion of the body" is suggesting that therefore the words of institution are not to be understood as referring to the distribution and reception of the very substance of the body of Christ.

But for the very reason that Paul does speak of the "communion (κοινωνία) of the body and blood" of the Lord, we must now give our attention to how on the basis of clear and unequivocal principles we can determine and be certain what this "communion" in the Supper is, what its nature is, and how it takes place. For it is not permissible to establish by mere private interpretation what the nature of this communion is and how we may think it takes place. Thus Paul very clearly and definitely shows that he is speaking about that communion of the body and blood of Christ which takes place in the Lord's Supper. And when he says: "I speak as to wise or intelligent men; judge for yourselves what I am saying" (1 Cor. 10:15), he is showing that the Corinthians already knew and understood what he was going to say about the communion of the body and blood of Christ with the bread and wine. But whence were they able to know, understand, and make judgments about these matters? Beyond all doubt on the basis of the tradition he had expounded when he was present among them, as he shows in 1 Cor. 11:23 when he says: "For I received from the Lord what I also delivered to you." And we must particularly and diligently note that it is from what they had previously learned and known that Paul wants the Corinthians to judge what he says in 1 Cor. 10 concerning the communion of the body and blood of Christ. But whence had they learned this? Doubtless from the words of institution which Paul had previously taught the Corinthians as the proper foundation for this dogma. Thus in the statement in 1 Cor. 10 Paul is not trying to lead us away from the words of institution, as though the dogma of the Lord's Supper cannot be clearly set forth or understood on the basis of these words, as our adversaries do. But he is subordinating this statement in 1 Cor. 10 to the words of institution; he even subjects it to the words of institution in such a way that he wants it to be judged by them. Therefore the passage in 1 Cor. 10 must be interpreted, understood, and judged on the basis of the words of institution and not vice versa.

The very words of this statement occur in such an order that they clearly refer to and express the whole account of the institution. For when he speaks of "the cup of blessing (εὐλογία) which we bless," he is referring to and expressing the words in the institution: "He took bread and likewise the cup and blessed it or gave thanks." And we do bless God in the celebration of the Supper when we give thanks to Him for all the benefits He gives us through His Son and through the ministry of Word and sacraments. This is the way Chrysostom interprets this blessing.[1] However, it is not called "the cup of blessing" only because of this blessing by which we thank God in the celebration of the Supper. For Paul clearly says "which we bless," so that he refers the blessing to the cup itself. He does this not in the sense that by this cup we are only giving thanks to God, or because we receive this cup with the giving of thanks (for this the grammatical construction will not permit), but because we bless the very cup—not with a papistic or magical curse, but because it is not from the nature of wine that this cup has the quality of being the communion of the blood of Christ but from the Word and institution of Christ. When, therefore, this Word comes to the element, so that it becomes a sacrament, then the cup is called the cup of blessing. Thus also Oecumenius interprets it by the words "which we prepare by blessing," namely, so that it becomes the communication [or communion] of the blood of Christ and so that he might show that this blessing is valid and efficacious not only when in the first Supper it was declared by the mouth of Christ Himself. Thus he calls it "the cup of blessing which we bless," namely, with the words of Christ.

Consequently, when he says: "The bread which we break," he is referring to and expressing the words of institution relative to the distribution: "He broke and gave to His disciples." But because Christ commands that what He distributes also be received, He also says: "Take, eat, drink." Paul refers to and expresses this by the word "communion" (κοινωνία). And because Christ adds the explanation as to what it is which is distributed and received in the Supper, when He says: "This is My body, this is My blood," therefore Paul speaks of it as a communion of the body and blood of the Lord. Thus Paul by the use of this term refers to and expresses the complete institution of the Supper and includes each individual word of it.

About the rest of the words there is no controversy. But there are many meanings for the word "communion" (κοινωνία). For example, sometimes it refers to a society, a fellowship, an association, the right of participation, as in 1 John 1:3: "Our fellowship (κοινωνία) is with the Father and the Son." Or Phil. 1:5: "fellowship in the Gospel." And 1 Cor. 10:20 speaks of "fellowship with demons."

But what Paul means in this statement when he says: "It is the communion of the body and blood of the Lord," need not be learned by conjecture. For Paul adds clear explanations as to which meaning of the word "communion" he is using. For when he later [1 Cor. 10:21] says: "They partake (μετέχειν) of the table of the Lord," he does not mean only to have the right to that table but by eating and drinking to become a partaker of the food offered on that table, just as he has shortly before stated: "We all partake of one bread" [1 Cor. 10:17]. Again, when he speaks of drinking the cup of the Lord [1 Cor. 10:21] he is interpreting the word "communion." Thus Basil interprets the word κοινωνία in this passage by the word μετάληψις (a sharing), and Chrysostom by μετοχή (a participation).[2] And Calvin himself concedes that in this passage the word κοινωνία refers to a partaking [or participation]. Thus the sense is clear. In the Lord's Supper a certain distribution takes place. Likewise there is a participation or reception. For the words in the institution refer both to distribution and reception, which Paul in this passage covers with the words "breaking" and "communion."

But what is the thing whose distribution and participation or reception takes place in the Supper? The bread is broken, the fruit of the vine in the cup is distributed; but now because the Word and institution of Christ come to the bread and the cup, so that they become the bread and cup of blessing, the distribution and reception of this bread is not only the distribution and reception of physical nourishment, nor is it only the distribution and reception of the Spirit, the virtue, the efficacy, or the life-giving power of Christ, but it is a communion, that is, a participation in the body of Christ. But in what body is it a participation? It is indisputably the body of which Christ in the words of institution says: "which is given for you." But how can the distribution and participation or reception of this bread be the distribution and participation in the very body of Christ? Because concerning this bread the Son of God Himself pronounces and affirms: "This is My body which is given for you," so that not only bread but at the same time the body of Christ is present, distributed, and received in this Supper. Thus in every respect the Pauline statement most beautifully and smoothly agrees with the words of institution themselves.

Let no one say to me that this statement of Paul and this communion can be explained and understood in any other way. For I know that Scripture is not of private interpretation. And because Paul himself not obscurely but openly refers this statement to and derives it from the very institution of the Supper, every single word of which in its proper, simple, and natural sense agrees and comports beautifully with the Pauline statement in a way which is almost scientifically provable, therefore I believe and state that this is the one and only true and genuine explanation and meaning of this passage. And since for this explanation and meaning I have such foundations as I have said, I simply and safely acquiesce in it.

There still remains the question as to what this "communion" (κοινωνία) of the body and blood of the Lord in the Supper is, or how it takes place. Our adversaries state quite simply that the "communion" is only spiritual, something which is perceived only by faith. Calvin explains it this way, that when the life, vigor, and efficacy from the body of Christ which is far removed from us flood in on us, then we may be said to become participants in the body of Christ, because this life which flows in upon us is something drawn from the substance of Christ's body. These are his words. Peter Martyr defines that participation in the body of Christ thus: Faith turns itself away from the symbols of the Supper and ascends above all heavens and there lays hold on Christ in His majesty. Beza says: If a piece of ground located in Saxony is given to me while I am living here in Geneva, I would say that by this gift I have become a partaker of the field, that is, I have the right to acquire and possess something in the field or associated with that field. It is possible that even other and different kinds of "communion" can be suggested.

But Paul in his statement in 1 Cor. 10 was not trying to start a debate over the many and various kinds of "communion" that can be thought up. Rather the question is how and on what basis we can determine what sort of "communion" Paul wants understood in this passage. But since, as we have shown, Paul refers this entire statement to and derives it from the words of institution, and in them the mode of participation or reception is clearly expressed: "Take, eat and drink"—why should we labor to devise many and various other interpretations while neglecting the way the Son of God Himself has shown and expressed? It is self-evident that Paul is speaking of the communion of the body and blood of Christ which takes place in the Holy Supper. But the question is: What kind of communion comes about and how does it take place in the Supper? At this point other people are devising different modes of communion. But Paul commands the Corinthians to judge the things he says, particularly on the basis of the words of institution which had been given them. But there the Son of God Himself defines the mode of the participation or reception of His body and blood by these words: "Take, eat and drink." And Paul himself explains the word "communion" in the same way when he goes on to say [1 Cor. 10:17]: "For we are partakers of that one bread," and again when he says: "We drink the cup of the Lord" [1 Cor. 10:21]. For it is not only by the breaking or only by the blessing that the communion occurs, but by the eating and drinking. But what we eat and drink in the Supper is learned from the words: "This is My body; this is My blood," and "This is the communion of the body and blood of the Lord." Therefore will not this whole question be answered if we make up our minds to acquiesce in the teaching of Paul and the voice of the Son of God Himself?

The entire context of Paul's argument in 1 Cor. 10 is in complete agreement with what we have just said. For among the Corinthians there were certain people who at one and the same time were partakers both of the Lord's table and of the table of those who sacrificed to idols [1 Cor. 10:19 ff.], and they thought they could rightly do both, the one to their salvation and the other without harm. For because the bread which we break is the communion (κοινωνία) of the body of Christ, they thought that this communion, no matter in what manner or with what kind of conscience it took place, could always be partaken of with salutary effect. But Paul is trying to warn them away from sacrifices to idols, in order that the communion of the body of the Lord in the Supper might bring them not to judgment but to salvation. Therefore he asserts that the reasoning they are using will provoke the wrath of the Lord, that is, they are eating the Lord's Supper unworthily and thus are becoming guilty of the body of the Lord, as he also points out in 1 Cor. 11:27. And he proves this from the antithesis provided by salutary

Communion. For through such Communion the faithful are made members of that body whose Head is Christ, as Paul says: "There is one bread, and we who are many are one body, for we are all partakers of that one bread." [1 Cor. 10:17]

Yet this bread of the Eucharist is not materially one in number in all the churches which are the one body, but with the bread the one and the same body and the one and the same blood of Christ are distributed to all in the Lord's Supper and received orally by the communicants. For in the Supper I do not receive a particular body and you a different one, but we all receive the one and the same body of Christ along with the bread, in accordance with the words. And because in this way the members of the church are joined together in the one body of Christ, therefore they are also joined with one another and become one body, whose Head is Christ. Then, when in the Supper we receive the body and blood of Christ, we are most intimately joined together with Christ Himself through that nature which He has inseparably and hypostatically united to Himself, and through Christ we are united with the Father. For through the bread we are united with the body of Christ, and through the body with Christ Himself, and through Christ with the Father. Thus we are made partakers (κοινωνοί) with the Father, the Son, and the Holy Spirit. These things are the results of the salutary communion (κοινωνία) of the body and blood of the Lord in the Supper.

But now Paul says [1 Cor. 10:20 ff.]: You Corinthians, by eating things sacrificed to idols, have made fellowship with the impious and with the religion of demons and have made yourselves participants in demonic things. Therefore you have cut yourselves off so that you are no longer living members of the true church and are no longer in communion or association with Christ and God. Thus you cannot, as you have persuaded yourselves in your own imagining, salutarily partake of the Lord's Supper. But because you are at the same time drinking from the cup of demons, you are provoking the wrath of the Lord. And this is what he says [1 Cor. 10:21]: "You cannot drink the cup of the Lord and the cup of demons, nor can you be partakers of the Lord's table and the table of demons." Paul does not condemn this as though they were drinking the cup of demons in such a way that they no longer wished to drink the cup of God in the Supper, but the fact is that both were being done among the Corinthians. For if they had been eating the things sacrificed to idols in such a way that they had absolutely stayed away from the Lord's table, Paul's entire argument would have been idle, inept, and completely beside the point. But if participation in the Lord's Supper were always and only salutary, and could not be done to judgment, again his argument would be absolutely pointless.

Therefore Paul in the first place points out and explains the substance of the Lord's table and cup, namely, what this Lord's table is in which they were participating while at the same time participating in things sacrificed to idols, and what this cup of the Lord is which the Corinthians were receiving while at the same time being unworthy; that is, this bread which we break is the communion (κοινωνία) of the body and the cup is the communion of the blood of Christ. In the second place he points out the salutary use of this participation from its fruits and effects. On the other hand, he teaches that this communion of the Lord's body and blood in the Supper brings to the unworthy Corinthians not salvation but judgment. For in this whole argument he is trying to free the Corinthians from the notion that they can salutarily partake of the Lord's body and blood in the Supper while at the same time participating in the table and cup of demons.

But you do not hear that Paul makes the distinction that when the worthy eat, then it is predicated of the bread: "This is My body," and "The bread which we break is the communion of the body of Christ," but when the unworthy eat, then it is predicated: The bread is not the body of Christ but only bread, likewise: The bread which we break is not the communion of the body of Christ but only the communion of an external symbol. But just as Christ in general pronounces concerning the bread of the Supper, when He offers it both to Judas and to Peter: "This is My body which is given for you," so Paul in this passage, where he speaks both of himself (for he says *"we* break" and *"we* bless") and of those who were drinking the cup of the Lord unworthily because they were provoking His wrath, says in general: "The bread which we break is the communion of the body of Christ," and "The cup which we bless is a participation in the blood of Christ." Thus it is not merely some spiritual communion (κοινωνία) which becomes salutary only by faith and is always so, but it is that communion of which the words of institution of the Supper speak: "Take, eat, drink; this is My body, this is My blood." This communion gives salvation to those who eat it worthily but judgment to those who do so unworthily.

Therefore just as in the words of institution, so also in this passage Paul deals expressly and first of all with the substance of the Supper, namely, that the bread is the communion (κοινωνία) of the body of Christ and the cup of the blood of Christ. In the second place he describes its saving use and benefit, namely, that it joins us both to

Christ Himself and to His church. And from the antithesis he shows that those who do not add salutary use to their participation in the body and blood of Christ in the Supper (which is the substance of this Supper) provoke the wrath of God, that is, eat judgment to themselves. Thus in this passage Paul simply and completely agrees with the proper and natural sense of the words of institution.

I know from the context of the Pauline argumentation that, if the various points are not properly distinguished, it has become customary to bring in various sophistries in order to escape the proper and natural meaning. For example, because Paul makes mention of the fellowship in the body of the church, Bullinger explains the words thus: Those who partake of the bread and cup of the Lord become the communion (κοινωνία) of the body and blood of Christ, that is, the congregation and the church of those redeemed by the body of Christ and washed by His blood, and so the body or the members of Christ. Or again, because Paul says that they who partake of the table of demons are partakers (κοινωνοί) of demons, and yet they do not eat them with their mouth or receive them bodily, many contend that there is only a spiritual communion of the body of Christ in the Supper.

Paul does treat and explain these three matters together, to be sure, but separately: 1. The external distribution, participation, or reception which takes place in the Lord's Supper, which Paul defines as the communion of the body and blood of the Lord; 2. The fellowship, which derives from this, with the members of the body of Christ, which is the church; and 3. The communion or joining with Christ Himself and through Him with God the Father. That is, to speak even more clearly, there is a threefold communion (κοινωνία): 1. The communion of the body and blood of Christ; 2. The fellowship of the body of the church; and 3. The communion with the whole Christ and all His benefits. But the two latter Paul classifies as effects or fruits of the first kind of communion, that is, of the communion of the body and blood of Christ in the Supper, through which the communion both with God and with the members of the church takes place.

He demonstrates this by examples taken both from the sacrifices under the Law and from those offered to idols. For in the Old Testament through the practice of certain rituals a communion into the one body of the Israelite religion took place, and those who added true faith were made partakers (κοινωνοί) with God. This was a spiritual communion (κοινωνία). Moreover, it was a kind of medium through which this fellowship both with God and with the church took place, because those who were offering the sacrifice partook of the same victims which they offered to God on the altar. And this was a communion (κοινωνία) which came about by an external action. In a similar manner idolaters came together in a certain structure of their religion, as they thought it to be, and became partakers (κοινωνοί) of demons, in order that they might enjoy their protection. To be sure, this participation (κοινωνία) did not consist of any kind of physical eating of demons; but yet this sacrifice through which the Gentiles unified their religion and through which they became partakers of demons, this I say, took place by an external participation. For they afterwards ate of the things which were sacrificed to idols or demons, and they drank of the libations which were made to idols. And so this was the medium through which they became partakers (κοινωνοί) of demons, in order that they might make certain that they would receive and become partakers of the things which they imagined could be obtained from the demons through those sacrifices. And thus in this text Paul refers distinctly and with express words to a participation with demons and the table of demons.

Thus Paul in speaking of the Lord's Supper posits the association of the members in one body, the church, whose Head is Christ, and the union with Christ Himself and with God as its fruit or effect. Then he goes on to show that the participation (μετοχή) in the Lord's table, or the communion (κοινωνία) in the Lord's cup, in the external celebration of the Supper is the medium or means through which this spiritual association both with Christ and with the members of the church is brought about. For he says: "We being many are one body, for we are all partakers of that one bread" [1 Cor. 10:17]. But is it only bread and wine by whose participation such great benefits are bestowed and sealed, namely, not only fellowship with the members of the church but also communion with Christ Himself and with all His merits and benefits? Surely the Son of God Himself affirms concerning this bread of the Supper: "This is My body which is given for you," and of the cup: "This is My blood of the new covenant." And Paul says: "The bread which we break is the communion of the body of Christ, and the cup is the communion of His blood."

Surely this is a worthy and appropriate sign and guarantee that Christ with all His merits and benefits is ours, so that as in those examples which Paul cites, so likewise in the Supper of the new covenant the same victim which was sacrificed to God for our sins is also given to us in the Lord's Supper and shared in by the communicants, so that through this participation in this same victim we are joined to Christ and made partakers of all His merits. And what more certain seal and what more sure guarantee can there be by which it is confirmed and sealed to us that as individuals we possess and are made partakers of those things which the Son of God by the giving of His body and the shedding of His blood merited and acquired, than the distribution of and participation in that very body which was given for us and that very blood which was shed for us for the remission of sins? Moreover, this distribution and partaking take place, as Christ says, in this way: "Take, eat, drink; this is My body, this is My blood." Or as Paul says: "The bread which we break is the communion of the body of Christ, and the cup is the communion of His blood."

The ancients also (whose interpretations Oecumenius gathered) divided and explained this passage of Paul in this way, namely, that the participation in the body and blood of the Lord in the Supper is a means through which we are both joined to Christ Himself and brought into fellowship with the true members of the church. They write thus: The blood of Christ joins us to Christ as members to the head through that participation or reception which takes place in the Supper. Again: If we are not joined by the body and blood of Christ into the fellowship (κοινωνία) of the church, which is His body, through what other thing shall we be one body? Again: Because the things which are sacrificed to idols are sacrificed to demons, therefore it is an abomination to take part in the sacrifice of demons, for through this we enter into fellowship with the demons themselves. For just as those who partake of the bread of the Lord's table become partakers of Christ Himself, so likewise those who partake at the table of demons come into fellowship with the demons themselves. But what is that bread of the Lord's Supper through which we become partakers of Christ Himself? Theodoret answers: We partake of the Lord through His precious body and blood; but of demons through food sacrificed to idols.

Chrysostom likewise says that through the bread of the Lord's Supper and through the cup of the Lord we are joined to Christ Himself and to the members of the true church, because this bread is the body of the Lord and the cup is His blood. However, he does not understand the body and blood to be removed and separated a great distance from the bread and cup of the Lord's Supper; but the words "The cup of blessing is the communion of the blood of Christ" he interprets this way: "Paul is trying to say that what is in the cup is what flowed from the side of the Lord, and of this we partake." And he goes on to say: "When we hold in our hands the cup of blessing, we are celebrating the marvelous fact that He poured this very thing out for us, and not only did He pour it out, but He gave or imparted it to us all."[3]

Up to this point, then, we have faithfully and diligently considered and commented on the individual words in those Scripture passages in which the dogma of the Lord's Supper is clearly and expressly treated and repeated. Our purpose has been to inquire as to whether the Holy Spirit in any of those passages shows by a manifest and sure testimony that the words of the Supper should be taken and interpreted in any other way than in the proper and natural sense. If so, we could safely depart from the simple and natural meaning. But before God I affirm that on the basis of a diligent comparison of all those passages I cannot find clear, sure, and firm testimony that the simple and natural meaning is to be abandoned. Rather, all those passages with marvelous consensus demonstrate, prove, and confirm this proper and natural meaning, that the Lord's Supper consists not only of the external symbols of bread and wine but also of the very body and blood of the Lord, and that in the celebration of this Supper there is distributed and received by the mouth of the partakers not only bread and wine but at the same time also the true and substantial body and blood of Christ. But how this takes place or can happen is not mine to ask. For I know and believe that He who has thus instituted this His Supper is truthful, wise, and powerful; yea, He is truth, wisdom, and power personified. Therefore, although I would not deny that I am moved and often even disturbed by the numerous specious and plausible objections of the adversaries, nevertheless my conscience is held bound and convinced by those testimonies of the Holy Spirit in those Scripture passages where He treats and repeats the dogma of the Lord's Supper. Thus I do not dare depart from that proper, simple, and natural meaning which is treated, repeated, proved, and confirmed in so many passages and with so great consensus. For this statement of Paul is always sounding in my ears, not so much the ears of my body as of my mind: "He who does not rightly discern the bread of the Lord's Supper eats judgment to himself and becomes guilty of the body and blood of the Lord." [1 Cor. 11:27]

Chapter X

Arguments from the testimonies of the true, learned, and purer ancient church.

They make a great mistake who first bring those Scripture passages in which the dogma of the Lord's Supper is established, treated, and repeated, either implicitly or explicitly, under the suspicion of ambiguity or unclarity, thus leaving the whole settlement of this controversy in doubt, and then refer the matter to the fathers as honorable arbiters. As if this doctrine were dealt with more clearly and certainly in the writings of the fathers than in those Scripture passages in which this dogma has its proper setting, and as if faith could find a clearer, surer, and firmer assurance in the statements of the fathers than in the voice of the Son of God Himself! For by this line of argumentation the matter is brought to the point where no matter how clear and convincing the words of institution and related passages are, yet we may freely depart from them when some statement from the fathers which seems to speak and hold differently can be set in opposition. But what else destroyed the church's entire doctrine under the reign of the pope but that people persuaded themselves and others that the words of Scripture are difficult, obscure, and ambiguous and therefore their true meaning must be sought in the writings of the fathers? And hence it finally came about that Scripture was not taken seriously, no matter how clearly, surely, and firmly it dealt with something, as long as some statements of the fathers which seemed to speak and mean something different could be put into opposition. Thus the very treatment of Scripture itself was finally reduced to the point where there was no attempt to discuss how the true and genuine meaning was to be drawn from the words of Scripture, but only how the very words of Scripture could in some way be accommodated to certain statements of the fathers, and very often violently twisted, so that Scripture was now forced to speak not its own natural meaning but the opinions of the fathers. Thus judgment was committed not to Scripture over the fathers but to the fathers over Scripture. The universal church deplores the consequences of this, and yet exactly the same thing is happening in this controversy regarding the Lord's Supper.

Therefore this warning is necessary in order that the correct faith regarding the Lord's Supper may not rely on the statements of any of the fathers, however ancient or learned or numerous they may be, but only on "canonical authority," as Augustine says. We must not first establish what is to be believed about the Lord's Supper on the basis of the fathers, so that we may then twist the words of the Supper to fit that presumed opinion. But this dogma must first be studied and established on the basis of those Scripture passages in which it is treated and founded in its own proper setting, not through guesswork but on the basis of the clear, certain, proper, and natural meaning of those passages. Afterwards, when faith has been built in this way on this firm rock and this solid foundation, testimonies and opinions from the ancient church can usefully be added. For because we believe that the universal church, in which the Son of God works at all times, has by His Spirit raised up certain learned writers to the kingdom of heaven, who follow the natural and genuine meaning of the words, therefore by their confession, which is in agreement with the natural meaning of the divine Word, the weak may be aided and greatly strengthened.

Moreover, what we do in the case of other articles of faith or dogmas must of necessity also be done in this controversy, namely, when the statements of the ancients are not sufficiently clear or in agreement with one another, we select and espouse those which agree with the proper, simple, and natural meaning of the divine Word. For we must not judge concerning the Word of God in accordance with the opinions of the ancients, but as Augustine says, *Contra Cresconium,* Bk. 2, ch. 31: "Therefore the canon of canonical books has been established, that according to them we may freely judge other books, whether of believers or of unbelievers."[1]

Moreover, in the case of this controversy it is easy to pile up varied and different opinions of the ancient fathers. 1. Sometimes they are speaking about the external symbols of the bread and wine as to what kind of benefit they give and what function they serve in the Supper, namely, that they are visible signs or symbols by which the invisible presence of the Lord's body and blood is represented and through these external media distributed and received. 2. Sometimes they are explaining the spiritual or salutary use of the bread which is distributed in the Lord's Supper, that is, they are discussing spiritual eating, which is not characteristic of unworthy communicants but only of believers. 3. Sometimes they are arguing about the words of Christ in John 6, namely, that it is beyond controversy that these words are figurative and speak only of spiritual eating. 4. Sometimes they are refuting the idea of a Capernaitic eating of the body of Christ. 5. Sometimes they are not dealing with this dogma in the sense of a full explanation but are only making passing mention of it.

But when these statements are piled up without any order or distinction, as our adversaries are accustomed to do, the result can easily be that consciences are more disturbed than instructed. Therefore, when these different opinions of the ancients have been categorized, it is asked what the ancient and purer church thought, believed, and taught according to the Word of God regarding this question in which the point at issue in this whole discussion is set forth, namely, what it is which, according to the word of Christ, is present, offered by external distribution, and received in the mouth of the participants along with the bread and wine in the celebration of the Lord's Supper.

Now there are extant certain particularly important statements regarding this controversy, gathered from all of antiquity according to the chronological order in which the fathers lived, which have been collected by most outstanding men of great judgment. And recently Marbach has prepared an outstanding work dealing with the statements of the ancients. But in my simplicity I believe and have learned that even more light can be shed on this controversy if we do not merely gather these testimonies from antiquity according to chronological order but rather according to the order of the concepts, under certain headings, by which the whole point at issue in this controversy can be grasped and divided and observations noted under particular categories. From these we can oppose all hair-splitting and can clearly and surely determine what was the true and genuine opinion and confession of the ancient church in regard to this dogma. I have followed this method in an earlier study and have noticed that it was not disapproved by educated people. Therefore I will now try to explain this method more clearly and distinctly.

[A. The Eucharist consists of two things, the bread and the body of Christ.]

In the first place we learn from the significant words of Justin, *Apologia 2,* that the bread of the Lord's table and the drink of the Lord's cup, which are present, distributed, and received in the celebration of the Supper, were called the Eucharist by the ancients.[2] But Irenaeus affirms in *Adversus haereses,* Bk. 4, ch. 18, that this Eucharist did not consist of only one thing or substance, but of two.[3] Augustine in his statements to Prosper treats the Sacrament in a similar manner, namely, that it does not consist of or comprise only one element but two; and what these two are, of which the Eucharist is comprised and consists, this Irenaeus explains when he says: "One thing is earthly, the other heavenly."[4] And regarding the earthly element we agree that it is bread and wine; but what is that second, heavenly thing of which the Eucharist consists?

Some say that it is a giving of thanks or a sanctification; others, a word of promise in regard to the bestowal of the merits of Christ; others contend that this heavenly element, of which, together with the earthly, Irenaeus affirms the Eucharist consists, has a symbolic significance. But there is no need for conjecture or books of divination, for Irenaeus himself clearly and specifically calls the bread also the body of Christ, the cup also the blood of Christ.[5] Indeed the statement of Augustine at this point speaks still more clearly, when he says: "What we are saying and what we are contending for in every way is to establish that this sacrament is made up and consists of two elements: the form of the visible elements and the invisible flesh and blood of our Lord Jesus Christ." Nor are the words "body and blood" ambiguous. For Irenaeus in *Adversus haereses,* Bk. 5, ch. 2, adds a completely clear explanation. He says that the blood is nothing less than what flows from the veins, the flesh, and the rest of human substance, which was truly made the Word of God who redeemed us by His blood.[6] Hesychius, *In Leviticum,* Bk. 2, ch. 8, says that [Moses] prescribed that flesh be eaten with bread in order that we might understand that this was spoken about the mystery which is bread and flesh at the same time.[7] And it is noteworthy that immediately after the time of the apostles those were proscribed as heretics and put out of the church who were not willing to confess that the Eucharist, that is, the bread of the Lord's table, consists of these two things. For Theodoret in *Dialogus 3* cites this statement from Ignatius, who described the heretics of his time thus: "They do not confess that the Eucharist is the flesh of our Savior Jesus Christ, with which He suffered for our sins and which the Father raised from the dead by His mercy."[8] And lest because of the heavenly element, of which the Eucharist is said to consist at the same time with the earthly element, someone might argue that the heavenly element should be understood as only the fruit or the power or the strength or the efficacy which comes to those who worthily participate in this sacrament, Bernard in his *Sermo de coena Domini* distinctly speaks thus: You must note three things in the Sacrament of the Altar, the outward appearance of bread, the true flesh, and the strength of spiritual grace. For what we see is the outward appearance of bread and wine; what we believe is under that outward appearance is the true body of Christ which hung on the cross and the true blood of Christ which flowed from His side.[9]

[B. The simile of the two natures in the person of Christ.]

In the second place, there are some in our time who, when they cannot deny that the Eucharist consists of two things, contend that these things are completely separate from one another, namely, the bread is on earth but the body of Christ is only in heaven and therefore is called a heavenly thing. They maintain that these two things are conjoined and united in the Eucharist not according to their substance but either by signification or relationship or by the power and efficacy of the body which is far distant. These philosophical notions are beyond and beside the statements of the ancients. But the ancients have expressed themselves so clearly regarding the manner in which they held that the Eucharist consists of two parts, that this fabrication cannot be maintained. For the heretics who did not acknowledge that in the one person of Christ there were two complete, distinct, and unmixed natures, but rather denied either His divine or His human nature or at least separated them, these people were refuted by nearly all the ancient fathers on the basis of the dogma of the Lord's Supper; cf. Justin in his *Apologia 2*,[10] Cyprian in his *Sermo de coena Domini*,[11] Augustine in his statements to Prosper, Chrysostom in *Ad Caesarium monachum*, [12] Gelasius in *Contra Nestorium et Eutychem*,[13] and Theodoret in *Dialogus 2*.[14] For they asserted that the person of Christ consists of two natures which are neither disunited nor confused but joined together and united, just as the Eucharist consists of two things, namely, the external appearance of the elements and the invisible body and blood of Christ. But if the ancient church had held and taught that the Eucharist consists of these two things in such a way that according to the substance they were not at all simultaneously joined together but were entirely disunited from one another and separated by a very great distance, and only could be called united by signification or relationship or power or efficacy, in no way could they from the similarity of the Eucharist have refuted the fabrications of the heretics who recognized in the person of Christ either only one nature or substance or else separated His two natures and set them apart from one another, or else imagined that the divine nature was not in Christ substantially but only through some peculiar power or efficacy. Rather they would greatly have supported and proved that fabrication of the heretics by using this comparison that it is similar to the Eucharist consisting of two things. But the ancients also turned this point of comparison around and taught that the Eucharist consists of two things, namely, the bread and the body of Christ, the wine and the blood of Christ, just as the person of Christ consists of two natures which are distinct, to be sure, but not separated or divided, but united.

They also stated that the mode of the union is not the same in both cases. For in the person of Christ the union of the two natures is inseparable and hypostatic or personal, which is not the case in the Eucharist. But in this there is a similarity between the union of the two natures or substances in the person of Christ and in the Eucharist, that as in the person of Christ so also in the Eucharist there is not only one nature or substance but there are two distinct natures; moreover, they are not separated or divided but according to their substance are truly and incomprehensibly joined together or united, even though the mode of their union is not the same. And Augustine adds: "This is so because everything contains in itself the nature and genuineness of the things of which it is composed." This point sheds so much light on the thinking of the ancient church, as to how they understood that the Eucharist consists of the bread and the body, the wine and the blood of Christ, that there is no escaping the fact, unless one is trying to make darkness out of light and to confess that he practices the sophist's art, "He lies there and he does not lie there" (κεῖται οὐ κεῖται).

[C. The substance of Christ's body is present wherever the Lord's Supper is celebrated on earth.]

In the third place, the ancients carefully explained these two things of which the Eucharist consists. But because the earthly parts, namely, the bread and wine, are substantially present in the celebration of the Supper, and because the senses affirm this, the ancients did not undertake much discussion of this matter. But in regard to the other part which pertains equally to the completeness of the Eucharist, they spoke in such a way as to indicate that it was not far removed and very remote from the bread and cup of the Lord, but that in the Lord's Supper when the bread and wine are present and are being used in the outward celebration in accord with the institution, then, they teach, along with the bread and in the cup there is also present the very substance of the body and blood of the Lord. Bede cites Augustine, *Ad neophytos:* "Receive in this bread that which was hanged on the cross; receive in this cup that which was poured from Christ's side. For he will gain death, not life, who thinks Christ a liar."[15] Chrysostom in explaining the passage in 1 Cor. 10:16, "The cup of blessing is the communion of the blood of Christ," says: "That which is in the cup is that which flowed from His side, and that is what we participate in." Thus he calls the cup a fearful and awesome thing.[16] And in the same place he soon adds: "When we hold that cup in our hands we glorify God and stand amazed at that ineffable gift, namely, that He shed this very thing (αὐτὸ τοῦτο), and not only shed it but also distributes it to us all."[17]

Likewise in his *Sermo de encoeniis* Chrysostom says: "The blood in the cup was drawn from His immaculate side for your purification."[18] He also often uses the expression "set forth" (προκείμενα) when he is speaking of the things which are distributed, present, and handled in the external celebration of the Lord's Supper. He says in *Homilia 24 in 1 ad Corinthios:* "When you see the body of Christ set forth (προκείμενον), tell yourself, 'I hope to receive heaven and the blessings which are there because of this body,' that is, the body which was nailed to the cross, scourged, but not overcome by death; when the sun saw this body crucified, it averted its rays; because of this body the veil of the temple was rent and the stones and all the earth shook."[19] Thus in the *Oratio de philogonio* Chrysostom says: "The table of the Lord takes the place of the manger, for in it lies the body of the Lord, not indeed wrapped in swaddling clothes but clothed with the Holy Spirit."[20]

Likewise the word προκείμενον is used in the Nicene canon which Oecolampadius cites: "On this divine table let us not humbly fix our gaze on the bread and the cup which are placed there, but raising our minds or our thoughts in faith, let us meditate on or think of the fact that there is also placed on that sacred table the Lamb of God who takes away the sin of the world, who is sacrificed by the priests but not in the ordinary manner of a sacrifice. And when we truly receive His precious body and blood, we must believe that this is the symbol of our resurrection. And because we do not receive a large amount, but very little, we should understand that these are received not to fill us physically but for our sanctification." And this canon expressly states: "On the holy table of the Lord there lie (προκείμενα) two things which are present and set before us, namely, the bread and the cup and then also the Lamb of God Himself with His precious body and blood. And on that sacred table not only those things which are perceptible to the outward senses must be noted and observed, but the mind must also be elevated, so that faith may think also of those things which are not apparent to the senses, namely, the presence of the very body and blood of Christ." But to what place is the mind to be elevated? Is it to be turned away from the present external celebration of the Supper and spread its wings above the heaven of heavens? Or where ought faith to seek the presence of Christ? Do I lay hold on Him only in heaven? The canon surely does not say this, but expressly and distinctly affirms that the mind should be so elevated and faith should so meditate that it recognizes that on this sacred table has been placed the Lamb of God with His body and blood. On this table we see the bread and the cup placed and dealt with by the external action of the priests. And when we receive a little from the external bread and the cup in the Supper, then at the same time faith, on the basis of the Word, recognizes that we also truly receive the body and blood of Christ which are present on the table. How these are symbols of our resurrection we shall explain later.

Thus the other fathers hold that before the consecration there is only one substance there, namely, the bread and wine. But when the Word and institution of Christ comes to these elements, then not only one substance is present as before, but at the same time also the very body and blood of Christ, as Ambrose says, *De sacramentis,* Bk. 4, chs. 4 and 5: "This bread is bread before the words of the Sacrament. But when the words of Christ come to it, it is the body of Christ."[21] Again: "Before the words of Christ it is a cup full of wine and water. When the words of Christ become operative, the blood which has redeemed the people is caused to be there."[22] And Augustine in many places repeats that in the Eucharist there are two things, one of which is visible and external, namely, the elements of bread and wine; but the other is invisible, that is, the body and blood of the Lord, not because the body of Christ is by nature invisible or because it is invisible in heaven, but because it is present in the Lord's Supper in an invisible, heavenly, and incomprehensible way. Thus he says in his statements to Prosper: "The Eucharist consists of the visible appearance of the elements and the invisible flesh and blood of our Lord Jesus Christ."

In the same place he says: "In the outward appearance of bread and wine which we can see we honor something which we cannot see, that is, the flesh and blood of Christ." But he explains this statement thus: In the Eucharist there is the sign and the reality. The sign is that which is perceived outwardly, namely, the bread and the wine, but the reality is the body and blood of Christ, which is truly believed inwardly. Bessarion cites a statement of Hilary which says the same thing.

Gregory of Nyssa in a certain homily says: "'This is My blood which is shed . . .' It is not a case of this being one thing and that being another, but this and that are one and the same. For tomorrow there will pour from My side that which you are now drinking and which you see in the cup."

[D. The body of Christ is in heaven and at the same time present in the Lord's Supper.]

In the fourth place, because the adversaries contend that the body of Christ is now only in heaven and nowhere else and that thus all the statements of the fathers are to be interpreted in the sense that the substantial presence of the body and blood of Christ is believed to be nowhere else than in heaven only, because it was the custom in the liturgies of the ancients to admonish the people to lift up their hearts to the Lord, therefore it is useful to observe that the ancients recognized and confessed that it is a stupendous miracle that the one and the same body of Christ which is in heaven is at the same time, although in a different mode, present also on earth in all those places where the Lord's Supper is celebrated according to His institution, because Christ says: "This is My body; this is My blood."

Chrysostom, *De sacerdotio,* Bk. 3, exclaims: "O the miracle, O the blessing of God, who with the Father sits above and in that very point of time is handled by the hands of all and gives Himself to those who wish to receive and embrace Him! And this does not take place by any sleight of hand but before the very eyes of those who are standing there and looking around, namely, along with these earthly things which are visible there is at the same time believed to be present the body and blood of Christ."[23]

Again in his *Homilia 24 in 1 ad Corinthios* he says: "Christ ascended, not only to the visible heaven above but to the very highest throne; there He conveyed His body, this very body which He gives to us to take and to eat, because of His great love."[24] But hear how Chrysostom explains this. He says: "This mystery makes for you a heaven on earth. Fly to the gates of heaven, yes, to the heaven of heavens, and look around. You will then see the things which have been said (that is, about the Eucharist), for what there ἐκεῖ in the heaven of heavens is the most precious thing of all, this I will show you has been placed on the earth. For as in palaces the most important thing of all is not the walls, nor the golden roof, but the body of the king sitting on his throne, so also in the heavens the body of the King Himself is the most important of all; but this you are permitted to see here on earth. For I show you not angels or archangels or the heaven of heavens, but Him who is their Lord. Now you will understand how you are able to see on earth that which is the most precious of all things in heaven. You will not only see but touch, you will not only touch but also eat, and having received it you will return home."[25]

Similarly in *Ad populum Antiochenum homilia 2,* speaking of Elijah, who was carried into heaven leaving his mantle to Elisha, he adds these words: "Now what if I shall demonstrate to you that there is something else which is much greater than this and yet all of us who are baptized into these sacred mysteries will receive it? Elijah, to be sure, left his mantle to his disciple; but the Son of God when He ascended gave us His very flesh, while Elijah left only his cloak. Moreover, Christ both left His flesh for us and yet ascended into heaven with it."[26] Likewise, *Homilia 17 ad Hebraeos:* "We always offer the same thing, not one lamb now and another tomorrow, but always the same; nor does it follow because it is offered in many places that there are many Christs, but only one."[27]

These words have been cited in a comment of Ambrose on Heb. 10, but translated thus: "Because this sacrifice is offered in many places, does this mean there are many Christs? By no means, but the one Christ is everywhere, and He exists fully here and fully there, one body. For just as that which is offered everywhere is one body and not many, so also there is one sacrifice, which is the copy and the remembrance of His sacrifice offered on the cross."

Gratian also cites this statement of Chrysostom and Ambrose in his *De consecratione,* dist. 2.[28] And Cyril, *Ad reginas,* says that the Logos, because it is incorporeal, is not edible, and therefore the mystery of the Supper consists in the flesh of Christ, of which there can be a proper eating because it is a corporeal substance.[29] But because there arose out of this a concern as to how the flesh of Christ could be present in all the celebrations of the Supper without being divided, Cyril explains this, *In Johannem,* Bk. 12, ch. 32: "His clothes were divided into four parts, and His tunic alone was not divided, which I might say is a symbol of this mystery. For the four corners of the earth have been led back to His salvation and have divided among themselves the clothing of the Word, that is, His flesh, but without dividing it. For the Only-begotten comes to individuals who are divided and sanctifies both their soul and body through His flesh, yet He is undivided and complete in all, since He is everywhere one and in no way divided."[30]

Gratian several times cites this statement of Augustine regarding the eating of Christ in the Sacrament: "We do not divide Him into parts, but He remains whole and complete in heaven, and He remains whole and complete in your heart."[31]

Among the sermons of Bernard there is a certain statement concerning the Lord's Supper where he says: "Whence does it come to us, most blessed Lord, that we worms who are crawling over the face of the earth, we who are dust and ashes, should be rewarded with Your presence in our very hands and before our very eyes, You who sit whole and complete at the right hand of the Father, You who in a moment are present and one and the same in all places, in many places, in different places from the rising to the setting of the sun, from north to south? Whence does this come, I say? Certainly not from anything You owe us or that we deserve, but out of Your own will and the blessing of Your kindness." And again he says: "Give thanks, O bride, rejoice greatly. You have your Groom as protector and guide in the battles of your present exile. You have a guarantee, you have a seal by which you will be blissfully united with your Bridegroom in your fatherland. Here on earth you have your Bridegroom in the Sacrament, and you will possess Him in heaven without concealment; both here and there the Truth, but here in a pale form, there in all His glory."

Likewise, in the liturgies of the ancients we read this prayer in almost the same words: "Give ear, Lord Jesus Christ our God, from Your holy tabernacle, from the throne of Your glorious reign, and come, that we may be made holy, You who sit on high with the Father and who walk among us invisibly and deign by Your powerful hand to impart to us Your uncorrupted body and precious blood and through us to all the people." And lest anyone take exception and has doubt regarding the authority of these liturgies, in an earlier part virtually the same words occur which Chrysostom had used in another place, as we have already pointed out. Moreover, Chrysostom often repeats the sense of the earlier portion, namely, that Christ Himself who was crucified is here present in this His Supper which is placed before the communicants in order to consecrate them and to offer them His body and blood. In his *Homilia de proditione Judae*[32] and his *Encoeniis*[33] and his *Homilia 57 in Matthaeum*[34] Chrysostom says: "When you see the hand of the priest holding out to us the body of the Lord, we must remember that it is not the hand of the priest stretching to us but the hand of Christ who says, 'Take and eat; this is My body.'" Leo in his *Epistola ad Anastasium* says: "Although He is seated at the right hand of the Father, yet in the same flesh He received from the Virgin He comes with His sacrament of propitiation."[35]

The little book *De duplici martyrio,* which is ascribed to Cyprian, interprets the passage in 1 John 5 concerning the three witnesses who testify on earth as applying to the Spirit, to the water of Baptism, and to the blood of the Lord's Supper. Thus it very clearly affirms that the blood of Christ is not only in heaven but also on earth in the Lord's Supper.[36]

Here those statements of the ancient church are also pertinent which teach that the ancients venerated and worshiped Christ the God-man, indeed the very flesh of Christ, not only in the Supper but also on the altar where the mystery took place, Gregory of Nazianzus, *De Gorgonia sorore;* Ambrose, *De Spiritu Sancto,* Bk. 5, ch. 12;[37] Augustine, *In Psalmum 98;*[38] and Chrysostom, *Homilia 24 in 1 ad Corinthios.*[39] They did not adore the external elements of bread and wine on the altar; therefore they held that Christ is present with His very body and blood not only in heaven but also there where the Lord's Supper is celebrated according to His institution. For this reason they call it a fearful and awesome mystery.

Nor is it true that the ancients by this form of exhortation (we lift up our hearts unto the Lord) wanted to indicate that Christ was not present with His body and blood in the celebration of the Lord's Supper, or that faith ought to turn itself away from the outward celebration of the Supper and ascend into heaven and seek Christ there. For the Nicene canon, when it teaches us to raise our minds, says that faith must recognize that on the holy table has been placed the Lamb of God which takes away the sin of the world. And Chrysostom in his *Homilia de encoeniis* says that those who respond to the exhortation to lift up their hearts say, "We lift them up unto the Lord."[40] And after they leave the congregation and the Communion and at the hour of the mystic table they are occupied in idle talk; he says that lies come in. Therefore the *Sursum corda* does not lead minds away from the table which has been spread; but this is to lift the heart high, when in the celebration of the Supper we consider not only those things which are apparent to the senses but in accordance with the Word hold that Christ Himself with His body and blood is present at the table. For this is the way both the Nicene canon and Chrysostom explain it. Likewise, Chrysostom in *Homilia 24 in 1 ad Corinthios* says: "In a long speech it is interpreted to mean that we should approach our participation in the mysteries by laying aside all earthly thoughts, cares, and preoccupations, set aside our vices, and with a pure mind consider the greatness both of the Giver and the gift."[41] And in the same place he not only says to lift up our hearts, but also that we ought, "as though we had been made eagles, to soar to heaven itself, 'for where the carcass is, there the eagles are gathered.'[41] He calls the body of Christ a carcass, because of His death; for if He had not fallen we could never rise. And he uses the term 'eagles' to show that he who approaches this body ought to be high or lifted up (ὑψιλὸν εἶναι) and must have no communion with earthly things, nor cling to the earth or seek it, but always fly to the heights and seek the sun of righteousness. For this is the table of eagles, not of jackdaws."[42]

But the question will be asked of Chrysostom: Does he want to say that we are not at all to seek Christ with His body and blood in the celebration of the Supper here on earth? However, he is the clearest interpreter of his own words. For in the same discourse he says those words we have cited above, that we celebrate the mysteries in order that the earth may be heaven for us because that which is most precious in heaven has now been placed on earth. But why, then, does Chrysostom say that we must not cling to earth but rather soar into heaven? He explains this point in the last part of the homily: "Let us not cling with the mind to the world or the earth or the things that are in them, but rather let us seek and be concerned with the things that pertain to the kingdom of God and the future life."[43] So also Gregory in *Dialogus 4*, ch. 58, says: "The hour of the mysteries opens heaven, the choir of angels is present, the lowest things are joined with the highest, earthly things are joined with heavenly, and the visible and the invisible are made one."[44]

[E. The body of Christ in the Lord's Supper is not only received in the heart or the spirit but also in a person's physical mouth, orally.]

In the fifth place, the thinking of the ancient church and the clearest confession from that period can be demonstrated to show that the fathers affirm expressly and by common consent that the body and blood of Christ are in the Supper, and not only in the heart or spiritually through faith but also received orally. And thus the confession of the ancients diametrically contradicts the opinion of our adversaries who contend that our physical mouth receives only bread and wine in the Lord's Supper, as external symbols, but that the body of Christ is received only by the soul and by faith but not orally.

But let us give ear to the confession of the ancient church. Irenaeus, who teaches that the Eucharist consists of two things, namely, the external symbols and the very body and blood of Christ, affirms that our bodies receive this Eucharist which consists of those two elements.[45]

Tertullian, *De resurrectione carnis,* says that in eating the body of Christ in the Supper, His works, the body and soul of man, are joined together. And in this sense he goes on to say: "Our flesh eats the body and blood of Christ so that the soul is filled with God. Therefore what He joins together in His work cannot be separated in His reward.[46]

Augustine in his *Contra adversarium legis et prophetarum,* Bk. 2, ch. 9, says that it is indeed more horrible Capernaitically (that is, with our imagination) to eat human flesh than to destroy it or to drink human blood than to shed it. "We, however," he says, "take into our believing hearts and mouths the Mediator between God and man, the man Jesus Christ with His flesh given us to eat and His blood given us to drink."[47]

But in regard to this passage from Augustine our adversaries shout that in the same place and context he also includes some items which are figurative. Therefore I have carefully scrutinized this passage and have discovered that Augustine calls something figurative when a certain act which in itself is true and literal at the same time signifies something spiritual. For example, the marriage of Abraham with the slave and with the free woman [Gal. 4:22 ff.] is a matter of fact. But because it signifies the two testaments, Augustine calls the fact figurative. Two people in one flesh [Eph. 5:22 ff.] signify Christ and the church. Thus, that we receive orally the body and blood of Christ is the mystery of the spiritual union by which we through the Spirit are united with Christ. And yet nevertheless this receiving of the body of Christ which takes place orally is real, just as the marriage of Abraham was real and the union of marriage is real, even though it signifies something else.

Leo in *Sermo 6 de ieiunio* in disputing against the Eutychians, who denied the reality of the human nature in Christ, says: "You ought to commune at the holy table in such a way that you cast absolutely no doubt on the reality of the body and blood of the Lord; for that is received orally which is believed by faith. The Amen is spoken in vain by those who argue against that which is received."[48]

Gregory in his *Homilia paschali,* 22, says: "You will learn what the blood of the Lamb is not by hearing but by drinking. This blood is placed above each doorpost when it is drunk not only with our bodily mouth but also with the mouth of our heart."[49]

Cyprian, *Sermo de lapsis:* "When their mouths have been purified by the heavenly food, after the body and blood of the Lord, they spew out all worldly contagion and the relics of idolatry."[50]

Again, in *De coena Domini* he says that the body of Christ is eaten by means of a bodily ministry. "We eat the bread of angels in the Sacrament here on earth, and we will eat the same without the Sacrament in heaven, but not by means of a bodily ministry, repeatedly returning to it, but the completed sacrificial work of Christ will remain permanent and be established, with His sufficiency filling and refreshing us because of the fact that He offered Himself openly and without any covering, in the sight of all performing the highest sacrifice."[51]

Chrysostom, *Homilia 27 in 1 ad Corinthios,* in speaking against drunkenness and its results, such as laughter, frivolity, filthy talk, riotousness, etc., says: "And you do this when you come to the table of Christ, on that very day when you are considered worthy to touch His flesh with your tongue. Therefore, lest these things happen, purify your right hand, your tongue, your lips, those things which are the entryway through which Christ comes to us. We are the temple of Christ, and therefore we kiss the entrance of this temple."[52]

Again, *Homilia 29 in 2 ad Corinthios,* in speaking of the holy kiss he says: "For through these doors and portals Christ has entered and still enters in to us when we commune. You who are participants in the mysteries know what is being said. For our mouth in receiving the body of the Lord is not pursuing an ordinary honor. Those who speak filthiness and foul talk, let them listen and cringe in horror that such things should pollute their mouth."[53] For here in the liturgy of Chrysostom the priest prays that the Lord Jesus Christ might deign to enter into his soul and his body, even though they are corrupted.

Bede in commenting on John 1 on the basis of Augustine says: "The body and blood of Christ were not given and shed at the hands of unbelievers for their destruction but rather are received in the mouth of believers for their salvation."

Many other examples can be brought from the writings of the ancients, but these are sufficiently illustrative. For it is not our intention to pile up all the statements of the ancients. Moreover, the ancients do not feel that the body of Christ is destroyed or torn to shreds or dishonored when they say that it is received orally. Therefore when Augustine calls that body invisible, spiritual, heavenly, and divine which acording to Christ's words is received orally, he is not saying this for some physical reason or because of some mode of this world, as certain statements of Augustine cited by Gratian teach. For if it were common flesh or even that of some specially holy man and not the true flesh of the only-begotten Son of God in which the whole fulness of the Godhead dwells bodily, then its eating in the Supper with the mouth would truly be cannibalism, as Cyril says.

[F. Christ joins Himself to us not only in spirit but also with His body.]

In the sixth place, beside these points we have thus far noted, there are testimonies among the ancients concerning the substantial presence, distribution, and reception of the body and blood of the Lord in the Supper which are so clear, so manifest that our adversaries by no trick are able to escape them without doing obvious violence both to the words and to the very clear arguments of the ancients. For the ancients teach that Christ is united with us not only by the Spirit or by His divinity through faith, but also through that participation which takes place in the Supper in a bodily and natural way and by natural participation. For these are their very words, which speak not only of the mode but of the very nature or substance of the body of Christ.

Some, of course, try to get around these statements of the ancients by saying that Christ is united with us only by some unique spiritual connection which nevertheless is called bodily, that is, true. Others restrict the bodily union only to the incarnation, namely, that Christ assumed, with the exception of sin, the same nature which we possess. Others interpret the bodily or natural participation thus, that the advantages or benefits of the spiritual union consequently apply also to our bodies. Finally, those are most of all pleased with themselves who think they can escape the statements of the ancients by means of the following sophistry. Christ is said to be in us by nature, bodily, and by natural participation because His life, which in the flesh remains very far removed from us, is poured out upon us through the channel of the Spirit. Thus the spiritual properties of which our nature has been deprived because of sin are now by means of the most holy humanity of Christ, although it is very far away, bestowed upon us.

These notions seem plausible and can be embellished by specious arguments. But the fathers stated their position in such ways that they expressly, as it were, rejected such sophistries. For Cyril, *In Joannem*, Bk. 11, ch. 26, distinctly deals with three modes of our union with Christ: 1. The union by participation through faith with the one Holy Spirit, who by His grace renews our spirit; 2. The union which takes place by reason of our disposition, emotion, or pious attitude or conformity.[54] The word σχέσις means an affectionate relationship (*affectio*) of things which are compared with one another, which indicates what agreement one has with another. Thus σχέσις which comes about through love, as Chrysostom and Cyril speak, includes the efficacy and communication of properties. But Cyril has still a third kind of union, distinct from the two previous, namely, that Christ is in us not only with His Spirit and His divinity, not only with the power and efficacy of His flesh, but also with the bodily or natural participation of His flesh. And lest this be restricted only to the incarnation, Cyril says that this participation takes place in the Lord's Supper. Hilary in *De Trinitate*, Bk. 8 [ch. 13 ff.], speaks still more clearly. He distinctly makes these two points: 1. "We are in Christ through the incarnation because He, being born a man, has inseparably taken to Himself the nature of our flesh, except for sin" (these are his words); 2. Christ is in us by nature, because by that nature which He has assumed from us He has again joined Himself to us by the participation of His flesh in the Supper. Here are his words: "He has added to us the nature of His flesh in addition to the nature of eternity under the Sacrament by the communication of His flesh, and we under the mystery receive the flesh of His body. And thus Christ is in the Father through the nature of the deity, and we are in Him through His physical birth, and He again is in us through the mystery of the sacraments."[55] This line of argumentation which Hilary uses demonstrates most clearly that these words of his cannot be understood only of symbols or only of efficacy or only of transfusion of properties or conformity of will or consensus or similarity of qualities, on the grounds that Scripture teaches us that the Father is in Christ and Christ is in us. On this basis the Arians used to formulate the following argument. Just as Christ is in us, so the Father is in Christ. But [they said] Christ is not in us with the nature or substance of His flesh but only with His power and efficacy, that is, only with the acquiscence or consensus of His will; therefore the Father is also in Christ not with the very substance or nature of His divinity but only with His power and efficacy.

Now Hilary, in order that he might prove that the Father is in the Son not only with His efficacy but with His substance or the nature of His divinity, showed that Christ is in us according to the flesh not only with His power or efficacy but also through the very nature or substance of His flesh. And he proved this from the communication and participation of the flesh of Christ which takes place in the Lord's Supper. For he affirmed that Christ in the mysteries again communicates to us the flesh which He assumed from us, and that we by eating and drinking that flesh truly do receive it, and thus we not only by nature are in Christ through His incarnation but Christ is also by nature in us through the communication and participation of His flesh in the Supper. But if we imagine that by this communication Christ is not in us with the very substance or nature of His flesh but only with His power or efficacy, not only are the Arians not refuted but their opinion is quite simply proved and confirmed. Hilary himself openly points this out, for he says: "Even as Christ lives through the Father, in the same way we also live through His flesh." He adds: "If we therefore live through Him by nature according to the flesh, that is, having acquired the nature of His flesh, how does He not by nature, according to the spirit, have the Father in Him, since He lives through the Father?" He also says: "We have Christ remaining through the flesh in us bodily beings, that is, He remains not only in the soul through the spirit but also in our body through His flesh."[56]

These matters are clearer than the midday sun, and yet there are people who hope that they can persuade the world that the sun is not shining at midday.

Cyril, *In Johannem,* Bk. 10, ch. 13, says that our spiritual union with Christ takes place in two ways: 1. By faith through the Spirit or the divine nature; 2. by love, that is, by His efficacy.[57] But with a strong affirmation he goes on to say that there is still another way whereby we are united with Christ, namely, according to the flesh. For he undertook the refutation of these words of the Arians: Not the flesh of Christ but the deity is called the vine, because our bodies do not derive from the flesh of Christ the way shoots grow out from a vine; therefore the deity of the Son is the vine to which we are attached through faith. But Cyril responds that when someone suggest that we are joined to Christ only by faith and love and not by the flesh, we will demonstrate that he has perverted the meaning of the sacred writings. Certainly we do not deny that we are spiritually joined with Christ through faith and love, but we categorically deny that there is no way whereby we are joined to Him according to the flesh. Cyril explains this mode of union with Christ by saying: "The mystical blessing comes to us when we all participate in that one bread by which Christ is caused to dwell in us bodily by the communication of His flesh." And finally he concludes by saying: "Therefore we must consider that not only in the manifest way which is understood through love does Christ dwell in us, but also by participation in His nature."[58] But if you ask whether Cyril in using these words has in mind only the spiritual indwelling of the Deity or that this indwelling consists only of His efficacy, he himself is the best interpreter of his own words. For in the same place he says: "Just as if one were to mix some melted wax with some more melted wax so that one entity is made of the two, so by the communication of the body and blood of Christ He Himself is in us and we are in Him."[59] And in Bk. 11, ch. 27, he says: "Christ is spiritually united with us as God, by the communication of the divine nature and the grace of the Spirit, that is, He is united with us by His efficacy; but He is bodily united with us as man through the mystical blessing."[60]

And in ch. 26 he says that having been joined with Christ through His body we receive His Spirit. "And this is the bodily union with Christ which is acquired by participation in His flesh. . . . The bond of this union is Christ, who is at the same time both God and man. There is, to be sure, a spiritual union, by which the Holy Spirit is received and in a certain way a union is created between God and us.[61]

Likewise, Chrysostom in his *Homilia 82 in Matthaeum,*[62] *45 in Johannem*[63] and *60—61 ad Antiochenos*[64] says the same thing, namely, that there is a threefold kind of union between us and Christ: 1. By faith through the Spirit; 2. by love, which along with other gifts is the work of divine efficacy and renewal. But he also contends that there is still another, more intimate kind of union between us and Christ, namely, not only by the Spirit and by efficacy, but we are truly united with His very flesh or body, so that we together with Him are joined as though into one lump (*massa*), through eating that which is bestowed upon us in the Lord's Supper when He says: "This is My body." This does not take place in such a way, however, that the flesh of Christ is far distant in heaven and unconnected with us, but in such a way that when we eat His body we have Him in us in totality. In *Homilia 51 in Matthaeum*[65] and *Homilia 82 [in Matthaeum]*[66] he says: "He does not give you His clothes or shoes, but He gives you Himself, so that when you touch the food and eat it you have Him within you."

These testimonies are crystal clear, and the comparisons with wax and a lump, although not precisely analogous with this union, yet show a most intimate union of the substances themselves, which therefore is called a bodily or natural union, even though it is not *only* bodily or natural. For this union is supernatural and heavenly and it does not take place either by a continuum or by contiguity or by mixing, but rather it is an incomprehensible union which we yet believe in because the words of the last will and testament of Christ teach it: "Take, eat; this is My body."

But the ancients were not debating about idle matters, nor were they disturbed about inconsequential things, but rather they drew the sweetest consolations from these teachings. For because of sin our nature was separated and alienated from the Deity, which is the fountain of life (Is. 59:1 ff.; Eph. 4:17 ff.), so that the divine majesty, if He had acted without a mediator between Himself and our human nature, could have fallen upon us like a consuming fire on a pile of straw (Deut. 4:24; Joel 2:3 ff.). Therefore the Son of God assumed our nature, without sin, and first so sanctified it in His own person that He made it not only alive but also life-giving. Then, through this nature by which He is our brother and of the same substance with us, He brought us into the most intimate union with Himself, so that we are brought back into union with God the Father, the fountain of life. The connecting link of our union with God is Christ, with us as a man through the blessed mystery, and as God He is united with God the Father by nature, as Cyril says, *In Johannem,* Bk. 11, ch. 27.[67]

Chrysostom, *Homilia 24 in 1 ad Corinthios,* says that because the old nature of the flesh has been corrupted by sin, we have lost our life and are subject to death. Therefore Christ, in a sense, introduced a second lump *(massa)*, namely, His own flesh, which is indeed the same in nature as ours but free from sin and full of life. This He communicates to all, so that nourished by it we may set aside the old death and be restored to immortal life through this feast.[68] So far Chrysostom. But we have noted down many more comforting statements of this kind from the ancients in another book, concerning the hypostatic union. Let no one tell me that all these things could have taken place even if the very substance of the body of Christ were not joined to us substantially. For no one has commissioned us to argue as to how this union could take place in the most explainable way or to determine whether it could or ought to take place, but God Himself has revealed to us in His own Word how He willed to accomplish it. Nor let us argue that only a spiritual union would be more than satisfactory. The fact is that in addition to a spiritual union the Son of God in His holy Supper in that nature which He has assumed from us, namely, in the very substance of His body and blood, wishes to join Himself to us in a most intimate way, as a head is joined to its members. Therefore let us not argue against it, but with grateful mind believe, confess, uphold, and proclaim this highest philanthropy (φιλανθρωπία) of our Savior.

[G. The resurrection and salvation of the flesh are demonstrated by our participation in the Lord's Supper.]

In the seventh place, Valentinus, Marcion, and others argued that only the soul is capable of eternal life, but human flesh either by nature or by substance is evil and comes from an evil god or certainly is so vile and abject that it is not capable of regeneration, incorruptibility, salvation, or eternal life, but will return to nothingness. Irenaeus and Tertullian judged that they could not more clearly or powerfully refute this error than on the basis of the doctrine of the incarnation. Thus Irenaeus says: "They are absolutely wrong who deny the salvation of the flesh or reject its regeneration. For this would mean that the Lord did not redeem us with His blood, for it would not be blood if it had not come from His veins and from the rest of that substance which made up His human nature which was truly made the flesh of the Word of God, who has redeemed us by His blood, as the apostle says: In whom we have redemption through His blood [Eph. 1:7][69] This is the argument based on the incarnation.

Besides this, he draws another argument from the doctrine

concerning the participation in the body and blood of the Lord in the Supper, and he often repeats this.

Further, the reader should note that Irenaeus does not base his argument, as the adversaries do, on our bodies receiving only the external symbols of the body of Christ and that only the soul really receives the body of Christ and that from the soul a power afterwards redounds to our body. But Irenaeus argues in this way: "Just as that which is bread from the earth, when it receives the call of God is no longer common bread but the Eucharist, consisting of two parts, the earthly and the heavenly, so also our bodies when they share in the Eucharist which consists of these two things are no longer subject to corruption but possess the hope of the resurrection."[70]

And in [*Adversus haereses*] Bk. 5 [ch. 2] he says: "Christ has testified that the cup which is a created thing is His blood, and He has confirmed that the bread which is a created thing is His body, from which our bodies draw strength. Therefore when the mixed chalice and the bread receive the Word of God, there is a Eucharist of the blood and body of Christ, from which the substance of our flesh draws strength and whereby it exists. How can they deny that the flesh is capable of receiving this gift of God, which is life eternal, since it is nourished by the blood and body of Christ and made His member, as the apostle says, 'Since we are members of His body, of His flesh and of His bone' [Eph. 5:30 KJV]? It is not of some spiritual or invisible man that he says these things, for 'a spirit does not have flesh and bones' [Luke 24:39], but he is speaking of that quality which is characteristic of a human being, who is made up of flesh and nerves and is nourished by the cup which is His blood and the bread which is His body."[71] Moreover, he affirms that this takes place because the Eucharist consists of two things, the external symbols and the actual body and blood of Christ, and because our bodies receive not only one part of the Eucharist but that Eucharist which consists of two parts.[72]

However, Irenaeus [*Adversus haereses,* Bk. 5, ch. 2] is not speaking of the natural and bodily nourishment and strengthening for this life through the digestion of the bread and its change into the substance of our body; but he is speaking of the existence, the nourishment, and the strengthening of regeneration, incorruption, salvation, and eternal life not only of the soul but also of our flesh itself, which through this participation in the body and blood of the Lord is called back from its weakness to the place where it belongs, that is, it is re-formed for life eternal, it is brought back to incorruption, and it ascends to life and immortality,[73] as Cyril says, *In Johannem,* Bk. 3, ch.

36—37;[74] Bk. 4, ch. 14.[75] Indeed this mystic benediction (as he calls the Eucharist) draws the whole man to itself and by its grace fills him completely, just as a small amount of yeast leavens a whole lump and as when a person pours some melted wax into more melted wax, as Cyril says, *In Johannem,* Bk. 4, ch. 17.[76] Also Augustine in *Confess.,* Bk. 7, ch. 10, is saying much the same thing: "I am sublime bread; you will not change me into you, as the bread of your flesh, but you will be changed into me."[77] And this is what Justin is saying: "Our blood and flesh are nourished by the bread of the Eucharist by a process of change (κατὰ μεταβολήν)." Leo in *Sermo 14, De passione,* says: "Participation in the body and blood of the Lord does nothing else than transform us into that which we have received."[78]

Therefore the opinion of antiquity is that "the essential quality (*proprietas*) of the Only-begotten, that is, His life, itself enters into us and remains in us"[79] through that nature by which He is made our Brother and of the same substance with us, namely, through the most holy body and blood of the Lord.

Cyril, *In Johannem,* Bk. 3, ch. 36, says that as we receive the body and blood of the Lord, in this way He Himself is found in us and we in Him. Bk. 4, ch. 17:[80] "We have this blessing of immortality in our midst." Bk. 3, ch. 36:[81] "And thus we have life in us, since we are joined to this flesh which has been made life-giving"; cf. Bk. 4, ch. 14. But the adversaries take exception and say that only the soul receives the body and blood of the Lord by faith and only later does power redound from the soul to our body. But the ancients, as we have just demonstrated, clearly teach that the body and blood of Christ in the Supper are received not only with the mouth of the heart or the soul but also with our physical mouth. And Cyril, *In Johannem,* Bk. 4, ch. 14, says: "It is absolutely necessary that not only the soul through the Holy Spirit must ascend into a blessed life, but also that this body, rude and earthly as it is, be brought back to immortality when it has received, touched, and tasted this bread."[82] But these qualities cannot be attributed to the bread and wine, but belong only to the flesh of Christ.

Most clearly of all Tertullian explains the position of the ancient church over against those who deny the salvation of the flesh, in a book on the resurrection of the flesh.[83] His point is that the flesh is the servant or handmaid of the soul, that is, a kind of medium through which or by whose ministry, as Cyprian says, the soul itself is brought into communion with God and made a sharer of salvation. These are his words: "Now let us look at the proper form of the name 'Christian,' how much privilege before God belongs to the vain and filthy flesh;

and if it suffices for it that the soul in no way can acquire salvation unless it believed while in the flesh, therefore it follows that the flesh is the heart of our salvation, through which the soul is bound to God. It is the very thing which makes it possible for the soul to be bound to God. The flesh is also cleansed, just as the soul is purified; the flesh eats the body and blood of Christ, just as also the soul is nourished by God." And then he very carefully adds that this participation in the body and blood of the Lord in the Supper takes place not only by works of the soul, but by joint works both of the body and the soul, for he says: "Therefore the flesh and the soul cannot be separated as to the benefit, for He has joined their works together."[84]

Therefore the ancient church proved the salvation of the believers' flesh from this, that not only our soul but also our flesh or body receives the body and blood of Christ in eating the Supper. But our adversaries publicly write against this position of the ancient church, saying that it is not proper to receive heavenly and supernatural things with our physical mouth but that for the reception of the body and blood of the Lord in the Supper we need a nobler instrument, that is, only the soul and faith. For these are their words.

[H. The unworthy partake of the body of Christ but not to their salvation.]

In the eighth place, when the ancients disputed concerning the participation of unworthy communicants in the Supper, they very clearly showed what the ancient church thought regarding the substance of the Lord's Supper, that is, what is present and distributed in the celebration of the Lord's Supper together with the bread and the wine, and that this is not received only spiritually by faith but also in the mouth of the participants. For those who eat unworthily eat judgment to themselves, and it is certain that their soul is not spiritually through faith eating the body and drinking the blood of Christ. For to eat and drink spiritually is to embrace Christ by faith, so that we draw life from Him and thereby became participants in Christ and in all His benefits unto righteousness and salvation. The question therefore is what is distributed to the unworthy in the Lord's Supper, and what they receive when they eat, since it is certain that they are not spiritually eating the body and blood of Christ. Many of the adversaries feel that only the external signs are distributed to the unworthy and only the elements of bread and wine are taken into their mouth. But Calvin and his followers see that the words of institution very strongly oppose this notion. For Christ did not make a twofold institution of His Supper, one for the worthy and another for the unworthy, so that to Peter the words do indeed mean: "Take, eat; this is My body," but to Judas the words are different, namely: "Take, eat; this is only plain bread." But He says in general to all who come to the Supper: "Take, eat; this is My body."

Thus when Paul writes to the Corinthians, among whom there were many who were eating and drinking judgment to themselves, he does not vary the words of institution, so that he says to the unworthy: "Take, eat and drink; these are only bare symbols of bread and wine." And Calvin concedes that in the use of the Lord's Supper not only are the external symbols of bread and wine offered to all who eat, both worthy and unworthy, but at the same time also the body and blood of Christ. But he holds that the body and blood of Christ are not received by all, but only by the believers. Now if this is understood to refer to the spiritual reception through faith unto salvation, then it is true. But Calvin extends this also to the sacramental reception, so that what those who eat unworthily in the Lord's Supper receive in their mouth is not the body and blood of Christ but only bread and wine.

But the words of institution in no way sustain this meaning. For if because of the words of distribution Calvin is forced to concede that in the sacramental distribution the body and blood of Christ are offered to all the participants in the Supper together with the symbols, then it is most manifest that in the institution there are, so to speak, not only words of distribution but also words of reception or participation: "Take, eat, drink." And these words: "This is My body, this is My blood," do not refer only to the words of distribution ("He gave it to them") but more properly pertain to the words of reception: "Take, eat, drink; this is My body, this is My blood." Therefore the Son of God says in general to all who partake of this Supper, whether they eat worthily or unworthily: "What you are receiving, eating, and drinking, this is My body and My blood." For the genuineness and integrity of the sacraments does not depend on the worthiness or unworthiness of either those who distribute or those who receive, but it rests solely on the divine institution. Therefore in 1 Cor. 10, where Paul is disputing about those who provoke the wrath of God because they participate at the same time at the table of the Lord and the table of demons, he is saying in a comprehensive way that the cup of blessing which we bless is the communion (κοινωνία) of the blood of Christ and that the bread which we break is the communion of the body of Christ. Moreover, in this passage Paul speaks very clearly not only of the distribution but also of the reception or participation. Therefore the substance of the Lord's Supper, which does not consist only of the external symbols but also of the very body and blood of Christ, as it is offered and distributed to all who partake at the Supper, whether worthy or unworthy, is thus also received by all. For the distribution and reception are joined together: "He gave it to them saying, 'Take, eat, drink; this is My body, this is My blood.'" But the salutary use or benefit accrues only to the believers. The unworthy eat judgment to themselves, as Mark says, namely, that they all drank from the cup concerning which Christ pronounced: "This is My blood," but not all of them did this in memory of Christ. For Judas drank judgment to himself.

Thus Augustine in his *Contra Donatistas* distinguishes the completeness, the genuineness, the sanctity, that is, the substance, of the sacraments from their benefit, efficacy, or saving features. He attributes the benefit or salvation associated with the sacraments only to believers but applies the genuineness and completeness, that is, the substance, of the sacraments in common to all who use them. Thus he says in *Contra Donatistas,* Bk. 3, ch. 14: "When we are dealing with the completeness and sanctity of the sacrament, there is no difference as to what a person believes or with what faith he who receives the sacrament is imbued; there is a very great difference as to the matter of his salvation, but as to the question of the sacrament there is no difference at all. For it can happen that a man possesses the complete sacrament and yet has a perverse faith."[85] And in Bk. 7 [ch. 33] he says: "Salvation belongs alone to those who are good, but the sacraments are given to the good and bad alike."[86]

But what Augustine understands by the sacrament or the completeness of the sacrament of the Eucharist he explicitly explains when he says: "This sacrament is made up of these two elements and consists of two things, namely, the visible appearance of the elements and the invisible flesh and blood of our Lord Jesus Christ." Moreover, Augustine argues clearly that the substance of the Lord's Supper is one thing and its salutary use and benefit are quite something else.

And because there were at that time those who imagined that all who in the Lord's Supper partook of the body and blood of the Lord were saved, regardless of how they lived or in what heresy or impiety they might be, because it is written: "He who eats My flesh shall live forever" [John 6:54], therefore Augustine in *De civitate Dei,* Bk. 21, ch. 19, distinguishes between the spiritual eating of John 6, which is always unto salvation, and the eating of the body of Christ which takes place in the Supper, which is given to believers unto salvation but in the case of the impenitent gives place to judgment. And with solemn warning he contends against the position that those who without repentance and faith partake of the Lord's Supper eat the flesh of Christ as described in John 6. For he expressly says in ch. 25 that the question is how we are to understand what Christ says in John 6:51: "If anyone eats of this bread, he shall live forever." And because those fanatics said that those who partook of the Lord's Supper without repentance and faith, if only they were members of the church by external profession, actually and truly ate Christ's body and drank His blood with that eating which is described in John 6 (for the question centered here), Augustine denies the words of these fanatics in the following way. He says that those who cannot be considered members of Christ cannot be said to eat the body of Christ. And then he says that He who speaks the words: "He who eats My flesh and drinks My blood abides in Me and I in him" [John 6:56] demonstrates what it means truly to eat the body of Christ and drink His blood apart from the sacrament.[87] For He said this as if to say: He who does not remain in Me and I in him should neither say nor think that he is eating My body or drinking My blood. And this is correctly and accurately said concerning the spiritual eating which is described in John 6. Further, Augustine expressly shows that he is talking about this, *In Evangelium Johannis tractatus 26,* where he says: "Therefore this is what it means to eat that food and drink that cup, namely, to remain in Christ and have Him remain in you. And thus he who does not remain in Christ and in whom Christ does not remain certainly does not eat the flesh of Christ *spiritually* or drink His blood."[88] And he there calls this spiritual union between Christ and us a sacramental thing, which he correctly points out is received by no one to his destruction but rather yields life for all who partake of it.

He repeats the same thing in *Sermo* [71, ch. 11,] *de verbis Domini:* "If what is received visibly in the sacrament is in very truth eaten spiritually, and is drunk spiritually, then the holy eating is judged to be beneficial."[89] And that the mouth of this spiritual eating is spiritual Augustine correctly states, *In Evangelium Johannis tractatus 26:* "Brethren, you see the heavenly bread; eat it with your spiritual mouth."[90] These things are correctly said with reference to the spiritual eating.

But the question is: What do the unworthy receive and eat in the Lord's Supper, since it is certain that they do not eat the body of Christ spiritually?

Our adversaries indeed are frank to say that the unworthy certainly do not receive or eat the body of Christ, but only the external symbols. For they feel that the body of Christ is only spiritually received and eaten, by faith alone. But now let us investigate the thinking of the ancient church. For Augustine, who is correct in denying that the unworthy eat the body of Christ spiritually, expressly teaches that there is more than one mode of eating the flesh of Christ, namely, the spiritual by which they who eat His body and drink His blood remain in Christ and He in them, but that those also eat the flesh of Christ and drink His blood of whom the apostle says that they eat and drink judgment to themselves, *Sermo* [71, ch.] 11, *de verbis Domini.*[91] But in this citation the adversaries find this way of escape, namely, that Augustine speaks of the sacrament of the body and blood of Christ. Therefore they say that the unworthy do eat the flesh of Christ, that is, the sacrament of His flesh, that is to say, only the element of the bread. But Augustine in his *Sententiae Prosperi* expressly explains his meaning, namely, that by the term "sacrament" he includes both ideas, the external elements and the body and blood of Christ.

But we shall note from time to time other statements of the ancients by which they make clear that they are speaking not only of the external symbols but also of the very body of Christ when they describe what is distributed to the unworthy in the Supper and what those who eat unworthily receive by mouth.

Augustine, disputing with the Donatists, *Contra Donatistas,* Bk. 5, ch. 8, says that even evil people if they are rightly baptized, although they lack the saving benefit of baptism, still receive and possess a complete, true, and holy baptism. He proves this by the example of the eating of the unworthy in the Supper. He says: "If someone receives the sacrament of the Lord's Supper unworthily, the fact that he is evil does not make the sacrament evil, nor does it mean that he receives nothing because he does not receive it to his salvation. For it is nevertheless the body of the Lord and the blood of the Lord, even for those of whom the apostle says: 'He who eats unworthily eats and drinks judgment to himself.'" You are hearing Augustine affirm that the difference between those who eat worthily and those who eat unworthily is not that those receive the body of Christ but these only the bread. And lest anyone interpret the body as only a symbol, he says that what is distributed and received in the Supper is the body of Christ not only for those who eat worthily, but, he says, it is no less the body of the Lord even for those who eat unworthily.[92] Nor does Calvin have a way of escape with his idea about only the distribution. For Augustine clearly speaks of reception and taking by the unworthy.

This statement of Augustine rests firmly on the foundation of the words of institution. For Christ says in the same way to both Judas and Peter: "Take, eat, and drink; this is My body, this is My blood." And the meaning of these words is the same, namely, it applies to the substance of the Eucharist, whether the words are spoken with reference to reception by the worthy or the unworthy. Therefore Augustine proves from the context of Luke that Judas was present at the first Lord's Supper, that together with the rest of the apostles he received what was distributed by Christ Himself, even though he not only did not receive the saving benefit of the Supper but rather ate to his own judgment, *Sermo* [71, ch.] 11, *de verbis Domini;*[93] *Contra Fulgentium,* ch. 6.[94] In *Ennaratio in Psalm. 10* he teaches that He gave the first Eucharist to Judas as well as to the other apostles.[95] *Epist. 163:* He gave the first sacrament to all in common, before Judas had been excluded.[96] *Contra Petilianum,* Bk. 2, ch. 47: "The table of the Lord was the same for both Judas and Peter, but each did not give it the same value."[97] *Collat. contra Donatistas,* ch. 6: "From the same bread and from the same dominical hand Judas received a portion and Peter received a portion."[98] Theodoret on 1 Cor. 11 says that Christ gave His precious body and blood not only to the eleven apostles but also to Judas the betrayer.[99] Likewise Chrysostom confirms the same idea in *Homilia 82 in Matthaeum*[100] and in his comments on 1 Cor. 11.[101] Oecumenius on 1 Cor. 11 [*Homilia 27 in 1 ad Corinthios*] likewise affirms the same thought on the basis of the ancient interpreters.[102]

With one voice all confess that the unworthy in the observance of the Lord's Supper take in their hands and into their mouth not only the external elements of bread and wine but at the same time also the very body and blood of Christ. Origen in discussing Ps. 37 [*Homilia 2*] says: "You value the judgment of God lightly and you despise the church which admonishes you. You have no fear of partaking of the body of Christ as if you were pure and clean, and in all these things you think that you shall escape the punishment of God. You do not recall what is written: 'Therefore many of you are weak' (1 Cor. 11:30). And why are many of them weak? Because they do not evaluate themselves and do not examine themselves. They do not understand what it means to take Communion in the church and what it means to approach such great and extraordinary sacraments. They suffer this, which those who have a fever are accustomed to suffer, that although they eat good food, they bring destruction upon themselves."[103] Again in *Homilia 2* [on Ps. 37] in a different context he says: "When you receive that sacred bread, you are eating and drinking the body and blood of the Lord; then the Lord enters under your roof and you therefore humble yourself to imitate that centurion and say: 'Lord, I am not worthy that You should enter under my roof' [Matt. 8:8]. For where He enters an unworthy person, there He enters to the judgment of the one who receives Him."[104]

Cyprian, *De lapsis:* "Though lying fallen he threatens those who are standing and though wounded he threatens those who are whole; and the sacrilegious man becomes angry at the priest because he does not immediately receive the body of the Lord in his polluted hands or drink the blood of the Lord with his befouled mouth."[105] Again in the same writing he says: "They return from the altars of the devil and come to the sanctuary of the Lord with hands stinking of roasted meat; exhaling their wickedness from their throat . . . they rush upon the body of the Lord."[106] Again: "The apostle . . . denounces people who are stubborn and obstinate, saying: 'Whoever eats the bread or drinks the cup of the Lord unworthily will be guilty of the body and blood of the Lord.' They despise and hold in contempt all these warnings and do violence to His body and His blood; yet they offend more against the Lord with their hands and their mouth than when they denied Him."[107]

Basil, *De baptismo,* last chapter, says: "We ought to be concerned as to what this judgment is which befalls the person who eats and drinks unworthily. For if a man who saddens his brother because of bread is lacking in love, what must we judge about him who dares to eat the body of the Lord and drink His blood in an idle and meaningless way?"[108]

Likewise in the *Regulae* under question 172: "With how much fear and with what kind of assurance ought we partake of the body and blood of Christ? Answer: Concerning fear we have the words of the apostle, who says: 'He who eats and drinks unworthily eats and drinks judgment to himself'; but faith is aroused by the words of the Lord, who said: 'This is My body which is given for you; this do in remembrance of Me.'"[109]

The same thought is also present in the *Liturgiae* of Basil: "Act in such a way that none of you partakes of the body and blood of your Christ to your judgment or condemnation."

Ambrose in discussing 1 Cor. 11 says: "Therefore he says: 'Many of you are sick,' in order that he may prove that there will be an examination of those who receive the body of the Lord. Here he shows a picture of the judgment coming upon those who in an unthinking way receive the body of the Lord, so that others may learn from them and know that to receive the body of the Lord in a thoughtless manner will not go unpunished."

Chrysostom, *Homilia 3 ad Ephesios:* "How will you, who with unclean lips and hands have dared to touch His body, stand before the tribunal of Christ? You would not dare to kiss your king with an unclean mouth. But the King of heaven you kiss with an ill-smelling soul."[110]

Jerome in discussing Mal. 1 says: "We pollute the bread, that is, the body of Christ, when we approach the altar unworthily and drink His pure blood in a wicked way."[111]

Augustine, *In Evangelium Johannis tractatus 62:* "When the apostle says: 'He will be guilty of the body of the Lord,' his remarks pertain to those who eat the body of the Lord in an indiscriminating and negligent way, like any other bread. If this bread is seized, it is done by him who does not judge it, that is, does not distinguish the dominical body from other bread. Why should he not be condemned as one who approaches this table feigning friendship but is really an enemy?"[112]

Oecumenius in discussing 1 Cor. 11 says: "Just as Judas betrayed Him and the Jews treated Him shamefully, so they bring shame upon Him who lay hold on His all-holy (πανάγιον) body with impure hands—just as in those days the Jews seized Him—and bring it to their detestable mouth."[113]

Leo, *Sermo quadrages. IV, De Manichaeis:* "In the participation in the sacraments they water things down in such a way that they receive the body of Christ with unworthy mouth, and they absolutely refuse to drink the blood of our redemption."[114]

Theophylact on Heb. 10: "When we by Communion have become participants in His immaculate body and blood, do we not, if we by an impure Supper befoul this very body which has received this body and blood, trample down the Son of God?"[115]

But the adversaries evade all of these and many more statements like them with one argument, namely, that the word "body" does not refer to the true body of Christ itself but only to its external symbol, that is, we must understand only the bread. And although this comment is in conflict with absolutely clear statements of the fathers and can be rejected with the same ease with which it is asserted, yet in keeping with overpowering evidence we shall show that the fathers were describing the body which they believed was received by the unworthy in the celebration of the Supper, so that it cannot be understood in any other sense than as the actual, true, and substantial body of Christ.

Hesychius, *In Leviticum,* Bk. 7, ch. 26: "To the body of Christ in which there is all holiness, for in Him dwells the whole fulness of the Godhead, we come without any subtle judgment of our own, remembering Him who said: 'Whoever eats this bread and drinks this cup of the Lord unworthily will be guilty of the body and blood of the Lord.'"[116]

Chrysostom, *Homilia 45 in Johannem,* says: "The unworthy receive the same body which the Jews pierced with nails, and therefore both come into the same judgment."[117]

Again, *Homilia 24 in 1 ad Corinthios:* "But if no one can touch the garment of a man with impunity, by what agreement do we so shamefully receive the body of the Lord of all, pure and immaculate, a participant in the divine nature, through which we exist and live, through which the gates of hell are broken down and the gates of heaven opened?"[118]

Augustine, *Epist. 162:* "The Lord Himself tolerated Judas and permitted him along with the innocent disciples to receive what the faithful knew was the price of our salvation."[119] Again, *Contra Cresconium,* Bk. 1, ch. 25: "What shall we say of the very body and blood of the Lord as a true sacrifice for our salvation, of which the Lord Himself says: 'Unless you eat the flesh of the Son of Man you will not have life in yourselves'? Does not the same apostle also teach that this can be received to great damage by those who use it in an evil way? For he says: 'Whoever eats unworthily will be guilty of the body of the Lord.'"[120]

Leo, *Sermo quadrages., IV:* "They receive the body of Christ with an unworthy mouth, and they absolutely refuse to drink the blood of our redemption."[121]

Oecumenius on 1 Cor. 11, on the basis of the interpretation of the ancients, says: "That body which the Jews laid hold on and killed is seized with impure hands and brought to an unworthy mouth."[122]

Eucherius on 2 Kings 6 says: "If that priest who touched that ark (which was a type of the Lord's body) with less than the proper reverence was struck dead, we ought to consider how great a wrong he does who approaches the body of the Lord while guilty."

So also Basil, *De baptismo,* Bk. 2, sets up an antithesis between those who treat the figures of the body of Christ in an unworthy manner and those who eat the Lord's Supper unworthily. For to the question as to whether one who does not cleanse himself from the filth of body and soul can without peril eat the body of the Lord and drink His blood, Basil replies: "When God in His law establishes the supreme penalty for one who dares to touch, without being purified, those things which have been sanctified by men, what must we say of the person who dares to pollute so great a mystery? Since much more, therefore, than the temple is here, according to the voice of the Lord, so it is much more serious and horrible for a person who lives in uncleanness of soul to dare to touch the body of Christ than to touch a sacrifice of rams and bulls."[123]

The chief argument by which the adversaries impugn this

statement regarding the eating of the unworthy is drawn from Augustine in his controversy with the Donatists. This argument, which has been long since refuted, goes this way: The flesh of Christ is life-giving. But the unworthy are not given life, for they eat judgment to themselves. Therefore they do not receive the true body and blood of Christ but only the external symbols.

Augustine himself, however, gives the answer in his *Contra Donatistas,* Bk. 5, ch. 8: "He who receives the sacrament unworthily does not make the sacrament evil because he is evil, or receive nothing because he does not receive it to salvation. For the body of the Lord was nevertheless there even for those who partook unworthily (1 Cor. 11)."[124]

Contra Fulgentium, Bk. 9: "Judas the betrayer received the good body of Christ and Simon Magus received the good baptism of Christ, but because they did not use these benefits for a good purpose, they as evil men were destroyed in their evil use of them."[125]

Contra Cresconium, Bk. 1, ch. 25: "What shall we say about the very body and blood of the Lord as a unique sacrifice for our salvation, when the Lord Himself said: 'Unless one eats My flesh he shall not have life'? Did not the same apostle also teach that a danger would befall those who use the sacrament in an evil way? For he says: 'He who eats unworthily will be guilty of the body and blood of the Lord.' Behold how hard it goes for those who use divine and sacred things in an evil way."[126]

In Evangelium Johannis tractatus 6: "Holy things can inflict injury; for in good people they work to salvation, but in evil people to judgment. For surely we brothers know what we receive and that what we receive is certainly holy. And what does the apostle say? 'He who eats unworthily, etc.' He does not say that this sacrament is evil, but that he who receives it in an evil way receives a good thing unto his own judgment."[127]

Contra Donatistas, Bk. 3, ch. 14: "It must be understood that a good thing can work not only life for those who use it rightly, but also death for those who use it for evil. It makes no difference, when the question concerns the integrity and sacredness of the sacrament, what kind of belief one has who receives it. The difference indeed is very great in regard to the way of salvation. But this does not affect the sacrament."[128]

Thus also the other fathers do not agree that it follows that the unworthy who eat judgment to themselves do not receive the true body of Christ which gives life.

For example, Origen on Ps. 37 [*Homilia 2*] says: "They suffer this, which those who have a fever are accustomed to suffer, that although they eat good food they bring destruction upon themselves."[129]

Chrysostom, *Homilia de proditione Judae:* "Just as physical food when it comes into a stomach filled with sickness does more damage and brings no help, so this spiritual food, if it comes to a person who is polluted with a spiritual illness, ruins him even more, not because of any evil of its own but because of the evil of the one who receives it."[130]

Again in *Homilia 61 ad Antiochenos:* "Just as food, although it is nutritious, if it is eaten by a person who has indigestion brings everything to naught and becomes a cause of illness, so also with these tremendous mysteries." Jerome, on Mal. 1, gives the following as the reason for the judgment which befalls those who eat unworthily: "They pollute the Lord's body and in so doing declare that they despise the Lord's table."[131] Chrysostom says that it is because they defile it. Oecumenius says that it is because they dishonor the body of Christ when they receive Him with impure hands and a cursing mouth. Theodoret says that it is because wanton men work injury to the body of Christ.

These statement surely demonstrate most clearly the thinking of the ancient church regarding the eating of the unworthy, namely, that they do not only receive the external elements but the very body and blood of Christ Himself, although to their judgment. And on the basis of this we can establish most firmly that the body of Christ is eaten in the Lord's Supper not only with the soul, spiritually through faith, but is also received and eaten with the physical mouth in a manner which is supernatural and above our understanding.

From these observations we may clearly and with certainty conclude that the ancient church taught and defended this belief, which is also ours, concerning the true and substantial presence, distribution, and reception of the body and blood of Christ with the bread and wine in the Lord's Supper. And in this faith the ancient church concurred with all simplicity, so that they consulted neither the senses, nor the rational mind, nor the order of nature, but simply clung to those words of Christ which He pronounced regarding the bread of His Supper: "This is My body," and regarding the wine: "This is My blood."

Cyprian, *De coena Domini:* "At the celebration of the Lord's table a carnal man is not received; whatever flesh and blood dictates is excluded from this feast; whatever human subtlety undertakes has no wisdom, contributes nothing; all seems to be at variance with his rational thinking; the wise men of this world consign to madness everything that deviates from their reason, and consider it alien to the truth, but the truth cannot be comprehended by erring men."[132]

Epiphanius in *Ancoratus* argues that we must believe the words of Scripture that man is made in the image of God, even though we do not see this image either in the body or the mind. All people have this image according to likeness (τὸ κατ' εἰκόνα) but not according to nature. But the Lord, who is truthful, has given us the image by grace. He uses a similar line of reasoning regarding the bread in the Lord's Supper. We see, he says, that the Savior took the bread in His hand, and when He had given thanks He said: 'This is My body. . . .' And we see that it is not equal or similar to either a corporeal image, or the invisible Deity, or the arrangement of the members of the body. For it is of rounded shape and without feeling as far as its power is concerned. But He wanted to say by grace: 'This is My body . . .' and no one should refuse to believe this statement. For he who does not believe that He is truthful, as He Himself has said, cuts himself off from grace and salvation. But what we have heard, that we believe, namely, that it is His body and blood."[133]

Chrysostom, *Homilia 82 in Matthaeum:* "We must everywhere believe God and not contradict Him. Even if what He says seems absurd to our senses and our ideas, let His Word supersede both our senses and our reason. Let us do this in all things and particularly in the mysteries, not looking only at those things which are placed before our eyes but also clinging to His words. For we cannot be deceived by His words, but our senses are very prone to deception. Since therefore He has said: 'This is My body,' let us not be hung up on some ambiguity, but let us believe it and grasp it with the eyes of our understanding."[134]

Cyril, *In Johannem,* Bk. 4, ch. 13, in dealing with the doctrine of the Lord's Supper in regard to John 6 says: "The mind is arrogant and wicked, and whatever things defy its comprehension it soon rejects as foolish or false; for it surely behooved those who saw the divine power of the Savior established by so many miracles to believe His word and, if some things seemed difficult, humbly to inquire and seek His explanation of these matters. But instead these people, not without great impiety, cry out to God: 'How can He give us His flesh?' For it did not enter their mind that with God nothing is impossible. But, I beseech you, let us make progress beyond the sins of others and, showing a firm faith in the mysteries, let us never in these sublime matters either consider or utter the word 'how.' For this is a Jewish word and the cause of ultimate punishment. Therefore as those who have learned something from the guilt of others let us never ask how, but let us leave to Him alone the way and the understanding of His work. For just as no one knows what God is by nature, and yet we are justified by faith, so even though a person does not understand the reason for His works, yet if he does not doubt but with sure faith believes that He can do all things, the rewards of his trust that follow are not to be despised. For He who so excels in wisdom and power will work in so miraculous a way that the reason for His works will far exceed our understanding. Do you not see that even things made by human genius and industry often quickly exceed our understanding? How, therefore, can those escape the supreme punishment who despise the Architect of all things, God, so that they dare to ask how He performs His works, when they know Him to be the Giver of all wisdom and the One who can do all things, as the Scriptures themselves teach us?"[135] Thus far Cyril.

Ambrose says in regard to those people who are entering the mysteries. "In this discussion that and how the bread of the Supper is the body of Christ should not be inquired after, nor the order of nature in this, since this same body is not according to the order of nature but was conceived by the Holy Spirit and born of the Virgin."[136]

Chapter XI

How useful and comforting for consciences this doctrine is which is based on the proper and natural meaning of the last will and testament of Christ.

It is our task not only to consider what is present, distributed, and received in the celebration of the Lord's Supper as to its substance, but the useful and necessary teaching regarding the importance, the benefit, the efficacy, and the salutary value of this Communion should also be added. Concerning this aspect of the doctrine there is no particular controversy at this time. For our churches correctly and diligently teach the kind of penitence and faith which are needed for approaching the Lord's table, lest anyone eat judgment to himself and that he might gain the fullest consolations. We are also adding comments regarding the strong and sweet strengthening and sealing of our faith which follows from the salutary use of the Lord's Supper.

Thus I do not wish at this point to inaugurate a full discussion of this doctrine but only briefly to call attention to the main points regarding the benefit, usefulness, and saving efficacy of the Communion of the body and blood of Christ in the Supper, which bring great weight and strength in shedding light on and confirming the proper and natural meaning of the words of the Supper. The result is that after considering these things the mind is moved and excited, so that we may all the more love and diligently retain and defend the proper and natural meaning of the last will and testament of Christ and not lightly allow it to be snatched away or removed from us, as many are doing who think it is unimportant to our faith even if the substantial presence of the body and blood of Christ is entirely removed from the Supper. For this study shows how many pious meditations, what sweet and useful consolations, what firm and necessary confirmation this interpetation regarding the substantial presence, distribution, and reception of the body and blood of the Lord in the Supper, which the proper and natural meaning of the words gives, brings to good and fearful minds. All of these are either rendered absolutely null and void or certainly weakened and shaken if the substantial presence, distribution, and reception of the body and blood of the Lord are removed from the Supper farther than heaven is from the earth.

Furthermore, there is no argument as to what kind of consolation and confirmation in our judgment brings surer, more beneficial, and more effectual results. For we certainly ought not arrogate this judgment to ourselves, we who ought to depend on the word of Him of whom the Father has said from heaven: "Hear Him" [Luke 9:35]. But because the proper, simple, and natural meaning of the words of the last will and testament of Christ teaches the substantial presence of His very body and blood in the Supper, and because from this so many sweet and useful comforts come to our conscience, which through the opposing opinion are entirely taken away or torn down, we therefore rightly come to the point that we must fight to retain the proper and natural meaning of the testament of Christ lest such comforts be taken from the church. For what kind of comfort and strengthening is best suited and most necessary for us in our infirmity no one knows better than our true Good Samaritan, who heals all our infirmities. In addition to all the other remedies for our infirmity He has instituted in His last Supper, in the form of His last will and testament, this ever-present antidote, when He says: "Take, eat and drink; this is My body, this is My blood." And we must give pious and reverent attention to its benefit, use, and efficacy.

Luther is correct in saying that even if only the bare mandate had been handed down in the institution by Christ, without any express mention of the benefit or usefulness of the Sacrament, still the words of Christ could not be set aside, and it would have to be certainly and firmly maintained that Christ in His will would not have instituted anything either useless or dangerous to salvation. But now Scripture clearly shows the usefulness of the Sacrament; for if one who eats it unworthily becomes guilty of the body of Christ and eats judgment to himself, then one who eats worthily surely becomes a participant in Christ and of all His merits unto salvation. And the words of institution themselves are so stated that each of them gives admonition regarding both the benefit and the efficacy of the Sacrament. For when Christ says: "This do," He is including the entire act of institution, namely, that while I am distributing you are with the bread receiving and eating My body which is given for you, and while I am distributing you are with the wine drinking My blood, which is the blood of the new covenant which is shed for many for the remission of sins.

"This do in remembrance of Me." But what kind of remembrance is it? It is the kind in which for the restoration of your fallen and lost nature I (1) have assumed "body and blood," that is, human nature, (2) have given My assumed body into death and shed My blood as a ransom (ἀντίλυτρον) for you, and (3) offer for you to receive in the Supper this body which has been given and this blood which has been shed, in order that this memory of Me, which is faith, may by this eating be more and more aroused, preserved, and confirmed in you. In this way the new covenant is applied, confirmed, and sealed to each person who eats in faith. Thus in the words of institution there is included in a summary way the entire doctrine of the benefit, usefulness, and efficacy of this sacrament. But in order that the antithesis between our adversaries and ourselves may be clearer, we shall review the principal points part by part.

In the first place, our faith ought to lay hold on Christ as God and man in that nature by which He has been made our neighbor, kinsman, and brother. For the life which belongs to the deity resides in and has in a sense been placed in the assumed humanity. The adversaries teach that faith ought to turn itself away from the present celebration of the Supper and in its thoughts ascend above all heavens and there seek and embrace Christ in His majesty, although they themselves admit that they do not know in what place in heaven He is dwelling according to the mode of His true body. But the proper, simple, and natural meaning of the words of institution teaches that Christ Himself is present with us in the celebration of the Supper with both His deity and His flesh, and that He comes to us in order to lay hold on us (Phil. 3:12) and join us to Himself as intimately as possible. This brings sweetest comfort. For Christ, both God and man, must lay hold on us in order that there may be a union between Him and us. But we, weighed down by the burden of sin and pressed under the weight of our infirmity, are not yet able to enter the secret places of heaven (Col. 2:18) and penetrate to Him in glory. He Himself therefore comes to us in order to lay hold upon us with that nature by which He is our Brother. And because our weakness in this life cannot bear the glory of His majesty (Matt. 17:2 ff.; Acts 9:3 ff.), therefore His body and blood are present, distributed, and received under the bread and wine. Nor does He will that we wander around the gates of heaven uncertain in which area of heaven we ought to look for Christ in His human nature or whether we can find Him; but in the Supper He Himself is present in the external celebration and shows by visible signs where He wills to be present with His body and blood, and there we may safely seek Him and surely find Him, for there He Himself through the ministry distributes His body and blood to the communicants. These most sweet and necessary comforts will be completely snatched away from us if the substantial presence, distribution, and reception of Christ's body and blood are removed from the Supper.

In the second place, our adversaries teach that the deity of Christ is the medium through which we are joined to His flesh, which is separated from us by a very long distance. But [we teach that] because we have been so alienated through sin from the life of the Deity that our weakness cannot bear Him to be dealing with us except through a medium, therefore He assumed our nature in order that through that which is related to us and consubstantial with us the Deity might deal with us.

And thus the humanity of Christ is the point of connection between us and God Himself, as Cyril says[1] and as we shall demonstrate more fully later on in the book concerning the hypostatic union.[2] Therefore, in order that we might be able to lay hold on Christ more intimately and retain Him more firmly, not only did He Himself assume our nature but He also restored it again for us by distributing His body and blood to us in the Supper, so that by this connection with His humanity, which has been assumed from us and is again communicated back to us, He might draw us into communion and union with the deity itself. And from this it is possible to understand what is involved when by disputations the substance of Christ's flesh is carried from the Lord's Supper out of the world.

In the third place, there is a salutary change of which the fathers often reminded us with a special joy of the Spirit. Our nature, at the beginning created in God's image, had been adorned with all heavenly and divine gifts, blessings which had been bestowed upon Adam as the founder of our race. But through his fall not only were these blessings lost, but our nature became corrupted by sin and doomed to death. The Son of God, therefore, in order that He might become the second Adam, assumed our nature, but without sin, and in that nature condemned sin, destroyed death, and restored that nature to life. Thus first of all in His own person He sanctified, restored, and blessed human nature. And now, in order that we might be made certain that these blessings apply also to us and our wretched nature, and have truly been communicated to us, Christ in His Supper again offers us that very nature which He has assumed from us and in Himself first restored, so that when we receive it with our poor flesh we are no longer in doubt concerning the salvation also of our nature through Christ. For in this way He, as it were, grafts our miserable and corrupt nature into the holy and life-giving mass of His human nature, as Cyril says,[3] so that our depravity and misery are cured and renewed through the remedy of this most intimate union. These concepts, which are filled with the most abundant comfort, diminish and disappear if we remove from us by an immense distance the assumed human nature of Christ in the Lord's Supper.

Briefly and only for the sake of warning I am calling attention just to the main points of these tremendously important matters, which can be understood better by pious meditation than explained by human language.

In the fourth place, the price of our redemption is the body of Christ which is given for us and His blood which is shed for us. Among Christians no one doubts that by this giving of Christ's body and shedding of His blood the wrath of the Father has been satisfied and eternal redemption gained. But the question is, to whom does this promise pertain and who are the receivers of this benefit of Christ? To be sure, the teaching of the Gospel in general pronounces that everyone who believes in Him shall not perish but have eternal life [John 3:16]. But anxious and fearful minds, when they consider their sins, their unworthiness, their weaknesses, and their many temptations, become so terrified and disturbed that dangerous doubts arise concerning the individual application, that is, whether I myself have with sufficient certainty grasped the benefits of Christ and so faithfully cling to them that my conscience can stand before the judgment of God. For this reason Christ in His Supper willed to confirm and seal to His disciples the demonstration and application of the promise of the Gospel with a certain and firm guarantee, so that in the face of all temptations faith can stand strongly and firmly in the assurance that it is a participant in Christ and all His benefits unto salvation.

But how? For this purpose He uses bread and wine, to be sure, but because these elements are diminished by use, as Augustine says, or are partly expelled from our system, as Origen puts it, it is manifest what kind of confirmation and sealing this is if in addition to these external elements nothing else is present and distributed in the Lord's Supper. Therefore Christ in the Lord's Supper distributes to us His very body which has been given for us and His very blood which has been shed for us, and He offers them to us to take and eat.

Surely there can be no more faithful, firm, or efficacious sign and seal of the promise and grace which have been shown and applied to us than that Christ Himself in the Supper shows to us His very body which has been given for us and His very blood which has been shed for us, not at some enormous distance, but He offers and gives it to us in so present a manner that we receive it to our very selves. For even in the Old Testament there was evidence of this uniting, because from the same victim which had been sacrificed to God they later ate and from the blood which had been shed before God a part was sprinkled on the people, as we have shown in the preceding pages.

Nor is this demonstration in the Supper made only in a general way, but to the individual communicants the Son of God Himself bears witness that He is offering and giving His body and blood, and without doubt at the same time also all those things which by the giving of His body and the shedding of His blood have been gained for our salvation. Therefore there is a most beautiful formula which the ancients used in their distribution of the Lord's Supper. Ambrose is the author. In this formula, as is the case also in Baptism and absolution, the words of institution are adapted to the individual recipient: "Take [singular], eat; this is the body of Christ which is given for you [sing.]; take, drink; this is the blood of Christ which is shed for you [sing.], for the remission of sins." And the person who received the elements would respond: "Amen."

But lest the infirmity, unworthiness, and uncleanness of our flesh disturb or overturn our faith, the Son of God affirms that in His Supper He is offering His body and blood to us in such a way that with the bread and wine we receive them in our mouth, that we may be even more certain that the unworthiness and uncleanness of our flesh can be covered and hidden before the tribunal of God through the most holy body and most precious blood of our Lord Jesus Christ. Now let everyone consider how much of these most beautiful and sweet comforts would be lost and destroyed if we move the very substance of the body and blood of the Lord immeasurably far away from the Supper, so that we would conclude that with our mouth we receive only bread and wine. Nor let us give credence to those profane arguments that the same things can take place no less truly or efficaciously through a spiritual communion, even if the substance of the body of Christ is actually far distant from us. For the Son of God Himself in the words of His own will and testament has revealed how He wishes this sealing to take place, and He of all people knows best what method of reassurance is useful and necessary for us. Some prayers of the ancient Greek fathers are extant in which with the sweetest words they say that the body and blood of Christ, when they are eaten by us in the Supper, become for us the "acceptable offering" (εὐπρόσδεκτος ἀπολογία) which we can bring before the tribunal of God [Rom. 15:16, 31]. Likewise they speak of it as our guarantee (ἀρραβῶν) of eternal life and salvation.

In the fifth place, the human nature of Christ, its limitations having been set aside, has been removed from all the miseries and injuries of this world and now resides in the glory of the Father. But our nature, although according to the promise we have the hope of glorification, is still befouled with uncleanness, oppressed with miseries, and exposed to all the darts of Satan, the world, and the flesh. As a result our faith is under the cross and still terribly tossed about by temptations. Therefore in the Supper Christ offers us His own body and blood which have been exalted above all miseries into the glory of the Father. He does this in such a way that through them He joins Himself to this miserable nature of ours, so that with this most present and sure guarantee and seal He may give us the certainty that He does not wish us to remain in these miseries forever but that we shall someday be conformed to His glorious body which He offers to us in the Supper as a seal of our own coming glorification.

In the same way the early church most sweetly confirmed the resurrection, salvation, and glorification of our flesh on the basis of this doctrine, as we have said earlier. The Canon of Nicaea calls the body and blood of Christ we receive in the Supper symbols (σύμβολα) of our resurrection—a most appropriate name, for the ancients spoke of identifying tokens (σύμβολα) which were given to guests so that they might possess them, carry them around with them, and show them so that they might be recognized as a guest and thus be received and treated in a friendly and hospitable way under the legal right of need and hospitality. Thus the Son of God willed that in His Supper there might be certain symbols to identify our flesh, by which we might be recognized and possess the right of need and hospitality in the heavenly fatherland so that we might be received there and treated in a friendly and hospitable manner. Further, this identifying symbol is not only the bread and wine which the ancients knew were consumed and then cast out into the drain, but the very body and blood of Christ, by which we are admitted to the heavenly fatherland, which the Lord now holds and governs, and they are the surest symbols of our own resurrection and glorificaton. For He offers these to us in the Supper in such a way that we receive them unto ourselves and possess them in ourselves, as Chrysostom says. But where will this most beautiful comfort be if we imagine that in the Lord's Supper our bodies receive only the elements of bread and wine, while the actual body and blood of Christ are distant from us as far as all heaven?

In the sixth place, the New Testament is that covenant of grace which is described in Jer. 31:33, 34: "I will be merciful toward their iniquities, and their sins will I remember no more. . . . I will be for them a God, and they shall be for Me a people." This covenant toward God the Father is established and confirmed by the shedding of Christ's blood on the cross. But it is necessary for the salvation of individuals that they be brought into this covenant and remain in it. To be sure, we are received into this covenant by the Spirit through Baptism and preserved in it through the Word. But fearful minds are concerned as to whether they actually are firmly and surely in this covenant. They desire, they long for this, that they may be certain they are going to remain forever and persevere in this covenant of grace. Therefore the Son of God willed that in His Supper our faith should be strengthened by a definite pledge and guarantee, so that we might be assured that we are under this covenant and included in it; and to this end He bears witness that He strongly wills to preserve us in this covenant. For He says: "Drink, this is My blood which is the blood of the new covenant." Therefore by this very blood, by the shedding of which this covenant with God the Father has been established, He also ratifies, confirms, and seals the covenant with us, so that He offers this very blood for us to receive, as we have explained more fully in our discussion of the words of institution.

But we poor souls often violate this covenant of grace into which we were received through Baptism. We often transgress it and break it. And through faith and in true repentance we return to that covenant and are received back into it. However, in order that faith may have a fuller assurance that we are truly, surely, and constantly received and restored into this covenant of the New Testament, even after we have fallen, the Son of God Himself offers us His very blood to drink from the cup of blessing. It is the blood of the new covenant, and by thus offering us this blood He is ratifying and confirming the new covenant to us. This pledge, this sign, this guarantee of the blood of the new covenant is substantially offered to us in the Lord's Supper by Christ Himself so that we receive Him to ourselves and with true faith oppose all temptations and doubts. Furthermore, it conflicts with the nature of a pledge, a sign, or a guarantee if we are separated by an immense distance and cut off from those things which ought to strengthen us and instead receive and possess only bread and wine.

In the seventh place, Christ says: "This do in remembrance of Me." And the word "remembrance" (ἀνάμνησις) means that when things begin to slip from our mind because of forgetfulness or neglect they are brought back to memory (Mark 14:9; 2 Tim. 1:3). And just as the loss of faith is called forgetfulness (2 Peter 1:9), so a true remembrance is an arousing, a preserving, and an augmenting of living and growing faith. Moreover, each of us experiences how manifold is the infirmity of faith, how weak its exertions, how often it is almost buried in false security, indifference, and forgetfulness, how easily it is overgrown with the thorns of this life and wallows in the billows of temptation. Therefore Christ, our true Samaritan, in addition to the ministration of and meditation on the Word, has also instituted against this dangerous forgetfulness this most efficacious antidote, namely, the Communion of His very body and blood in the Supper.

For because Christ lays hold on us more strongly than our faith lays hold on Him (Phil. 3:12), therefore by our taking hold of His life-giving flesh He has willed to train us, to nourish, preserve, increase, and confirm us in a true and living recollecton of the fact that for our salvation He has assumed our nature, has given this assumed nature into death for us, and again distributes and offers it to us to eat in the Supper, in such a way that it may be joined and attached to our poor nature as intimately as possible.

Finally, the Eucharist is not only a figurative admonition regarding our mutual, fraternal fellowship and love for one another, in the way that bread is produced from many grains and wine from many grapes, as Augustine says, *In Evangelium Johannis tractatus 26.*[4] But because Christ in the Supper joins Himself most intimately to us by that very nature with which He is our Head, namely, by His body and blood, at the same time through this assumed nature of His, which is akin to ours, He will work powerfully and efficaciously in the believers, so that, because our Head Himself is among us, we also may be members of one another. For we being many are one body because we all partake of that one bread which is the body of Christ (1 Cor. 10:17), and we all drink into the one Spirit. (1 Cor. 12:13)

I wanted to review these points thus briefly and in order, so that we can see more clearly and consider more diligently how many comforts can come to our consciences on the basis of the proper and natural meaning of the words of institution concerning the true and substantial presence, distribution, and reception of the body and blood of the Lord in the Supper, and that these most beneficial comforts will be taken from us and snatched away if we imagine that the substance of the body and blood of Christ has been removed and separated from the Supper and from us by an immense interval of space, farther than the heaven is from the earth, and that our bodies receive only bread and wine in the Eucharist. As a result there is much less frequent use of the Lord's Supper among those who have embraced the position of Zwingli and

Calvin. Indeed, they publicly teach that for those who are ill or dying, who cannot come to the public gathering of the church, the use of the Lord's Supper, even when they can have it, is not necessary.

But in our case, the more we love it, the more diligently we will defend it and the more tenaciously we will retain the proper, simple, and natural meaning of the words of Christ's last will and testament, so that these sweet consolations are not snatched away from us.

Chapter XII

Concerning the arguments of the adversaries.

Up to this point we have, with a certain amount of diligence and in good faith, spent our time on those passages of Scripture in which the dogma of the Lord's Supper is clearly taught and repeated. We have also pointed out the certain and unchanging analogy which the Spirit Himself has preserved and has commanded us to preserve in the interpretation of such passages. Nor have we been able to discover any compelling arguments which force us to depart from the proper and natural meaning of the words of the testament of the Son of God. Moreover, we have noted that all these passages—not with ambiguous or obscure indications but with manifest, certain, and firm testimonies and with marvelous consensus—demonstrate, express, prove, and confirm that meaning which the proper and natural sense of the words conveys. Therefore the pious mind can rightly and safely rely upon this certain and firm foundation, and faith can securely acquiesce in this assurance, even if it cannot extricate itself from all these notions which are put up in opposition by sharp argumentation and learned response, as Augustine says in regard to heresies: "The believing heart is a great help in knowing what not to believe, even if one cannot refute it with one's own ability in argumentation."

And Fulgentius, *Ad Donatum,* makes this statement: "I praise first of all this quality in you, that you did not possess so great an ability to respond, and yet there remained in your heart a firm belief in the truth. For not all who are members of Christ can defend what they believe by the art of rebuttal. But it is part of our victory that when a person cannot make a speech to defend the truth, nevertheless he wards off error by his believing heart."[1] Thus Fulgentius.

And Justin in his *Expositio fidei* says: "In controversies we confess that we are ignorant of the clear knowledge (τὴν ἐναργῆ γνῶσιν) of the truth, and this is the most important part of our victory."[2] In the same place: "When I search out these things and cannot answer, then I call upon the amazing mysteries of the Christians, which are above our understanding, above argumentation, above the comprehension of the nature of creation." He goes on to say that faith is the surest solution to all the objections that are raised, faith which leans on the clear divine voice. He gives us this rule: Let faith alone solve the difficulties of controversies and tremble at the divine Word, in accord with what is written. And in questions which were addressed to Justin, where it was asked how the body of Christ, being of solid substance, could enter in when the doors were closed,[3] he answers with this rule: "Those supernatural things which occur in nature by divine power cannot be demonstrated according to the laws of nature."[4]

Therefore faith, which relies on the express and consentient testimonies of Scripture in those places where the dogmas have their proper setting, must not at once lose its assurance when it is unable to give a learned and convincing refutation of all the points which are raised against it. For it is not our task either to inquire into or explain the ways of the divine mysteries, but it is our responsibility in a simple, humble, and obedient way to believe the expressions of the divine voice. For as Theodoret cites Ambrose, it is ours to believe but His to know.

However, because many people have been upset by these clamors, when they hear that many articles of faith are shaken, destroyed, and overturned if the proper and natural meaning of the words of the testament of Christ is received and retained, this teaching [of the adversaries] ought not simply be neglected or rejected out of hand, but we ought to look into the chief objections of the adversaries to see whether their arguments have the validity they claim for them. For it is certain that we are to receive nothing which is in conflict with the articles of faith. For Scripture does not teach contradictions, but the harmony of the entire faith is everywhere in agreement and consentient with itself.

In fact, by this very treatment of the objections the sincere mind is greatly strengthened, when it learns that the proper and natural meaning of the testament of Christ is actually not in conflict with any article of faith but rather is confirmed by those very passages which are raised in opposition.

Moreover, we ought to repeat the Pauline warning of which we made mention above in ch. VII: When we have the sure, clear, and consentient testimony of Scripture concerning a certain dogma, in those passages where the proper setting of the doctrine actually resides, we should not at once be upset and turn to some other meaning when some appearance of a contradiction is raised. For it is neither new nor strange that people can devise and oppose various ingenious antitheses (ἀντιθέσεις). But Paul in 1 Tim. 6:20 says: "If you wish to keep the sound doctrine which has been committed to your trust and not depart from the true faith, avoid the oppositions (*antitheses*) of knowledge falsely so called."

It must also be observed whence or from what passages of Scripture the adversaries seek their main arguments. For it is manifest that these arguments are not based or constructed upon the passages of Scripture in which the dogma of the Lord's Supper is expressly taught and repeated, but on other passages which do not speak of this dogma. We have already demonstrated with two clear examples from Abraham (Gen. 15 and 22) that when God Himself in those places where He treats and repeats the same dogma does not expressly show a different explanation than the words convey, that then no objections whatever, brought in from elsewhere, ought to have so much weight that on their account we depart from the clearly expressed divine Word which He teaches in those passages where the dogma has its setting, and thus permit ourselves to be won over to another position.

So in the arguments of the adversaries we will consider only this one point—since all the passages in which the dogma of the Lord's Supper is treated and repeated in its own setting, as it were, if they are accepted on their own terms, produce a consensus and demonstrate and confirm the proper and natural meaning—whether there is sufficient force, strength, and evidence in these arguments, which the adversaries bring up in opposition, to compel us to conclude that it is right, safe, and necessary because of them to depart from the natural meaning which by such a great consensus is the clear teaching of the pertinent passages dealing with this dogma. If the explanations of the objections are directed to this point, the entire discussion will be simpler, plainer, and easier.

We shall now divide the chief arguments of our adversaries into certain categories and general headings, so that matters which are similar and of the same classification may be dealt with and refuted on the basis of the same fundamental principles. For our adversaries have learned in the school of the rhetoricians to fight not so much with the weight of their arguments as with their number, so that if they cannot prevail by the force of their arguments they can at least be victorious because of their number, according to a dictum of Quintilian. Hence it develops that their books with great literary flourish present not only whole battalions of arguments but entire legions of them. And they insult us by saying that our faith is merely a five-word faith, for to such a degree do they hold in contempt those sacred words: "This is My body; this is the blood of the new covenant." But the question before us is not the matter of the gymnastics of the sophists in piling up a huge number of arguments, but it concerns the divine word expressly stated in those Scripture passages where the dogma of the Lord's Supper is treated in its own setting. For there is found the one point of primary weight and force rather than in the innumerable myriads of other arguments.

A. The arguments from the physical properties, that is, the measurements, circumscription, and localization of a true and finite human body.

This is the fountain from which flow all these billows of arguments and objections of every kind in this controversy set up in opposition to the proper and natural meaning of the words of Christ's last will and testament. For human reason understands and our senses themselves grasp that a true human body by reason of its proportion and size cannot be extended and diffused into infinity, but rather has a certain symmetry of its proportions and a certain position of its parts and members, and is circumscribed to one particular place in such a way that by its own natural power it cannot at one and the same time be truly and substantially present in many different places. Now Scripture certainly affirms that the Son of God according to His human nature has been made like unto His brethren in all respects except for sin.

Therefore, although the proper and natural meaning of the words of institution asserts the true and substantial presence of the body and blood of the Lord in all those places in which the Lord's Supper is celebrated, yet because the human mind cannot comprehend how this can take place while the true integrity of the human nature remains intact, it seeks various pretexts on the basis of other Scripture passages in order that it can under some appearance of being Biblical depart from the proper and natural meaning of the testament of the Son of God.

Further, the explanation of this argument will be easier and plainer if the individual points of this argument are considered in their bare and dialectical brevity minus the ornamental flowers of the rhetoricians.

If the major proposition of this argument is stated thus: The human body according to the common and usual condition of its nature is circumscribed to one certain place in such a way that by its own physical nature and power it cannot be in many idfferent places at the same time, then the proposition is true, but it draws no conclusions which are in opposition to the substantial presence of the body of Christ in the Supper. For this does not come about by the common and usual mode of nature, nor by natural power and human reason, but by divine power and heavenly reason.

In order to give this argument binding force it will therefore be necessary to state the major proposition in such a way that not even with divine power can a true human body, while retaining the integrity of human nature and while not destroying the substance of the body, be in many different places at one and the same time. But if the premise is put in this way, then it will have to be established by certain, manifest, and firm testimonies from Scripture that divine wisdom does not know any way and divine omnipotence does not have the power to discover a means whereby, if it so desires, it knows how and is able to cause a human body, with the integrity of its substance intact, to be at the same time in many places. Moreover, I am certain that such impotence attributed to God cannot be demonstrated or established from any passage of Scripture. And who in the church would ever bring up such an argument without any proof from the Word of God, indeed contrary to the express testimony of Scripture and to the absolute, infinite, immeasurable, and incomprehensible omnipotence of God, a notion which someone has created and strung together with a physical chain and geometric shackles? In what Scripture passage and where is such an idea taught, that the divine omnipotence, if it so willed, could not cause a true human body to be in many places while still preserving intact the integrity of its substance? If someone should say that it cannot be imagined or comprehended by human reason how this could take place with the actuality of the body preserved, this is certainly not a sufficient reason to say that therefore the divine omnipotence could not do a certain thing when we know it can do things superabundantly (ὑπερεκπερισσοῦ) above all that we can imagine (Eph. 3:20). And yet unless the major premise is posed in this manner, this argument opposing the presence of the body of Christ in the Supper is inconclusive.

Certain of our adversaries have noticed this point and therefore do not use the entire argument but only propose the conclusion; or at least they do not propose the major premise in its proper form or in the place or order where it ought to be, but conceal it among their rhetorical declamations.

On the other hand, some of them are not afraid to write publicly that God with all His universal omnipotence cannot cause a true human body to be at one and the same time in more than one place, with the substance of the body remaining intact. For they scream that this would cause a contradiction whereby it would both be a body and not be a body—as if there were no difference between substance and accidents. Localization and circumscription are certinly not the very substance of human nature, but rather they are properties which are consequent upon the fact that the substance is physical.

But such properties in created beings are included even by the philosophers and dialectitians among the accidents. Even though by virtue of their creatureliness these cannot be separated from the substance, and even though we cannot imagine or comprehend how they can be separated from the substance while the substance retains its integrity, yet who is to say that these things cannot take place under divine omnipotence?

These points are plain, clear, certain, and firm; and when the major premise is stated in this way, no true conclusion can be drawn from it which is contrary to the natural meaning of the words of institution. Thus I am often amazed that the substantial presence of the body and blood of the Lord in the Supper, which the natural meaning of the words of institution clearly teaches, can be opposed with such strong force, with such propositions (αἰτήματα) as, "It is impossible; it cannot happen while still preserving the integrity of the human nature." Or again, "If this were admitted, then the destruction and abolition of the substance of the human nature in Christ would follow; Christ would be stripped of His true body," etc. But to what is this impossibility attributed in this line of argumentation? Surely not to created nature, but rather to the divine omnipotence. But where is it written that God does not will this, that He cannot do this? Nowhere. Rather, there are the clearest testimonies in Scripture to the immeasurable, incomprehensible, and free divine omnipotence.

But they take exception and argue that nothing can be settled on the basis of the absolute omnipotence of God or because it is written: "He has done whatever He has willed" [Ps. 115:3]. Nor do we ourselves argue from the absolute omnipotence of God, but we begin with the clear Word of God, which in the very testament of the Son of God, according to the proper and natural meaning, asserts the substantial presence of the body and blood of the Lord in the Supper. But because our adversaries say that this can in no way take place while keeping the substance of the body of Christ intact, we raise in opposition the article of faith regarding the immeasurable omnipotence of God and we assert that there is no passage of Scripture which can be used to prove that God either does not will this or cannot do it. And so to the will of Christ which has been revealed in the very words of His last will and testament we join His immeasurable wisdom and omnipotence. And we cannot depart from the proper and natural meaning of Christ's testament on the grounds that this is in fact impossible for any created thing. "For with God nothing is impossible" (Luke 1:37); "He who has spoken is also able to perform it" (Rom. 4:21); ". . . beyond what we are able to imagine" (Eph. 3:20). Let the careful reader note this point regarding the major premise in all the arguments of this kind, in all of which the nerve is cut with this absolutely true and trustworthy statement, so that they cannot really come to any conclusion which is in opposition to the proper and natural meaning of the words of institution of the Supper.

In the same way we should examine the minor assumption or premise. For we believe and confess that the Son of God assumed the true and complete substance of human nature, along with those essential properties which naturally belong to the substance of human nature and derive from it. (The argument regarding the assumed weaknesses properly does not pertain here.) He has retained this substance with its essential properties even after the resurrection, when He had laid aside the weaknesses, and we believe that He retains it true and unimpaired also in glory. Now according to these natural and essential properties, and because of the natural mode of a true body, these things are described in Scripture in these ways: "I rejoice not because I am there but because we are going there" [Phil. 1:23, etc.]; likewise: "If You had been here, my brother would not have died" [John 11:21]; "He has risen, He is not here; behold the place where the body of the Lord was laid" [Mark 16:6]. According to these properties and according to the nature of a true body, Luther together with Augustine and along with the scholastics felt that the body of Christ even now in glory is seen in heaven by the angels and the saints in that circumscribed form in which He showed Himself to Paul and Stephen, in which He also will return to judgment.

But, you say, if these things are so, then we cannot retain the proper and natural meaning of the testament of Christ, namely, that with His true body and blood He is substantially present at the same time both in heaven and in all those places where the Lord's Supper is celebrated on earth. I know that our adversaries rely most strongly on this argument and its consequences and judge that we are unable to respond to it without completely doing away with those essential properties in Christ which naturally make up the true integrity of the substance of His human nature. [They rely on this argument] because they know that they are in conflict with the meaning of Scripture and the opinion of the ancient and accepted councils. So on the basis of this argument they proclaim an undoubted victory for themselves.

But the simple, plain, true, and convincing answer is that Christ does retain the true integrity of the substance of the human nature and its essential properties, through which and according to which He functions in His human nature when and how He wills, as we have already said in regard to the matter of localization. But I ask: Does the human nature in

Christ possess its natural or essential properties only in such a way that it received absolutely nothing as a result of the hypostatic union with the divine nature? Likewise I ask: Does Christ in His human nature and through His human nature act only according to its natural or essential properties and do nothing beyond it? For Scripture clearly asserts that Christ according to His human nature has been anointed above and beyond all His fellows (Ps. 45:7). And Peter explains this anointing in Acts 10:38, where he says that Christ has been "anointed with the Holy Spirit and with power." In John 3:34-35 the Baptist says: "God gives not the Spirit by measure . . . and has given all things into the hand of His Son." John 13:3: "Knowing that the Father had given all things into His hands." In John 5:26-27: "God has given to the Son to have life in Himself, and has given to Him authority to execute judgment, because He is the Son of Man." Matt. 28:18: "All power is given unto Me in heaven and on earth." This giving to the Son of Man took place in time, as Dan. 7:13-14 clearly describes. Heb. 1:6: "When God brought Him who is His first-begotten among many brethren into the world, He said: 'Let all the angels of God worship Him.'" Eph. 1:20-22: "He set Him at His own right hand in heavenly places, far above every power . . . and every name which is named, not only in this world but in that which is to come; and He put all things under His feet." Heb. 2:8: "For in that He put all things in subjection under Him, He omitted nothing that is not put under Him."

Furthermore, I have gathered many statements of this kind together in a little monograph[5] in which I have explained this entire doctrine more fully and where I have also shown both from pertinent Scripture passages and from the explanations of the entire ancient church that these statements must be understood of the human nature in Christ. We have also added the rule of the ancients: Those things which Scripture teaches that Christ received in time, must be understood according to His human nature, yet in such a way that the essence of the human nature in Christ is not understood to have been absorbed or changed into the deity, nor made equal with the properties of the divine nature, as we have explained more fully in this little monograph. This truth is so evident among the adversaries that many of them neither dare to nor can deny it. Therefore the human nature in Christ not only has its own natural or essential properties but beside and beyond them, as a result of the hypostatic union with the divine nature, it has received innumerable prerogatives which exceed and surpass every name and every condition and all the essential or natural characteristics of our nature in infinite ways, as Paul says.

And Christ acts with and through His human nature not only

according to its natural or essential properties but also, when and how He wills, according to those supernatural (ὑπερφυσικά) prerogatives which have been added to His humanity as a result of the hypostatic union with His divine nature. For example: "God has redeemed the church with His own blood" (Acts 20:28); "In His blood we have redemption" (Eph. 1:7); "In His blood we are justified" (Rom. 5:9); "The blood of Christ . . . cleanses our conscience" (Heb. 9:14); "By His stripes we are healed" (1 Peter 2:24). By His flesh He gives life (John 6:54); when His body was touched, power went out from Him (Luke 6:19; 8:46); He walked on the waves of the sea (Matt. 14:25); He came through locked doors and stood among them (John 20:19); He became invisible (Luke 24:31); by His physical breath He gave the Holy Spirit (John 20:22).

But our adversaries, even when they concede these points, immediately take exception that we must not develop arguments on the basis of these passages, either the argument from analogy (a paribus) or from greater to lesser, without an express word of Scripture. It does not follow, they argue, that if the flesh of Christ can do what is greater, namely, to make alive, therefore it can also do what is lesser, namely, to be in several places at the same time. Human beings can understand and use their reason, which is greater; but yet they cannot fly, which is lesser, something even the most contemptible birds can do.

But our argumentation by no means relies on bare dialectics without an express word of God. For although it is true beyond all doubt what Paul affirms, namely, that the exaltation of the human nature in Christ is above every name which is named not only in this world but in the world to come, yet Luther with great restraint says only that in this controversy regarding the Lord's Supper we must not debate about the ubiquity of the body of Christ nor make this matter the point of controversy. But because we have the express word of Christ: "This is My body; this is My blood," this axiom suffices for us, and it cannot be denied, that Christ with His body can do what He wills and can be wherever He wills (Jena Ed., 8, 375; Wittenberg Ed., 2, 187). Therefore the safest way is that, because this exaltation is above every name (Eph. 1:20 ff.), we should not by our private conjectures and arguments, without an express word of God, attribute whatever seems good in our own eyes to the human nature in Christ. Nor, on the other hand, should we decide by our own judgment, without an express word of God, what seems to us to agree with Christ's human nature, its integrity remaining intact. Let the Word of God be the judge. For to Him this mystery is known best of all, and He has revealed to us in His Word as much of it as He wants us to know in this life.

Therefore, whatever Scripture has in express word predicated and asserted regarding the human nature of Christ, these things we should rightly, safely, and necessarily believe, even though they may far exceed the essential properties of our bodies, even be entirely alien to our bodies. For we do not believe that Christ according to His assumed nature is "like unto His brothers in all respects . . . except for sin" [Heb. 2:17; 4:15] in such a way that when Scripture predicates and affirms something regarding the humanity of Christ which is alien to the essential or natural properties of our bodies it must be rejected and explained in some other way than as the words sound, under the pretext that otherwise He would not be "like unto His brothers in all respects . . . except for sin." But we believe it when Scripture teaches that Christ has assumed, possesses, and retains the true and complete substance of the human nature and the essential properties of that substance. We also believe it when the same Scripture affirms that the human nature in Christ has received and possesses something as a result of the hypostatic union with the divine nature, even if this may far exceed the essential properties of our nature—even, indeed, if it is something above every name. For Scripture predicates many such things of the human nature in Christ, and not only do we believe them but we are commanded under peril of our salvation to believe them—things which can be attributed to no man or angel without idolatry and blasphemy, such as that also the humanity of Christ pertains to the work of redemption, justification, and vivification, even to the point of being an object of adoration. These things are certain and firm, and they can in no way be denied unless a person is willing to deny all of Scripture and completely overturn the doctrine of the hypostatic union.

Having therefore thus established these points on the basis of the true, clear, and solid foundations of Scripture, we shall now proceed on a smooth and easy road to the very heart of the argument which is raised in opposition. For we have not out of our own conjectures dreamed up the substantial presence of the body and blood of Christ in the Supper, or put it together without the Word of God as a result of our own disputings. But Christ Himself in His last will and testament with express word has predicated and affirmed concerning that which is present, distributed, and received orally in the Lord's Supper, wherever it is celebrated here on earth in accord with His institution: "This is My body; this is My blood." And what the proper and natural meaning of these words is, if the literal sense (τὸ ῥητόν) is retained, is perfectly clear, as we have demonstrated above.

But they object that the essential or natural properties of a body are finite and circumscribed, which we freely grant; but Christ in His Supper is not acting according to the natural properties of a body. For because Scripture predicates them, we accept and believe many other things concerning the flesh of Christ because of the hypostatic union with the divine nature, things which far exceed the natural or essential properties of our bodies, far above every name, as has been indicated. Similarly, because we have an express word regarding the substantial presence of the body and blood of the Lord in the Supper, just why should we depart from the natural meaning of the words of Christ's testament? It is not a sufficiently great or compelling reason, on which conscience could rightly or safely rely, that it does not coincide or agree with our notions of the essential or natural properties of a true body. For it is absolutely certain that the human nature in Christ has received from the hypostatic union with the divine nature countless other gifts which are not only far above the essential properties of a true body but above every name. Therefore under what guise and with what kind of conscience are we to say that it is impossible for Christ to have this one unique prerogative concerning which we have no less an express word than about the other prerogatives, and that in the last will and testament of the Son of God Himself?

They repeatedly assert that the other prerogatives do not destroy the substance of the human nature, but if one should concede that Christ with His body is substantially present in all those places on earth where the Lord's Supper is celebrated, then they say Christ is absolutely stripped of His true body, His substance is absolutely destroyed, and in no way can this take place while maintaining the integrity of the substance of the human nature in Christ and not destroying it. I hear, to be sure, that they affirm this with great strenuousness; but I question how they can prove this. To be sure, I am aware of the physical principles, but faith, whose object and foundation is the Word of God, neither can nor ought to rely on these.

Therefore what is the testimony of the Word of God, what is the Scripture, and where is it revealed and taught that the Son of God can indeed do the other supernatural things (ὑπερφυσικά) which have the express testimony of Scripture, with His true body and with the integrity of its substance left intact, but that this one unique thing, whereby according to the literal meaning of the words of institution He is present with His body in the Supper wherever it is celebrated here on earth in accord with His institution, can in no way take place while preserving intact and not destroying the substance of Christ's body? I am certain that this cannot be demonstrated by a single express testimony of Scripture.

Indeed, it seems to be entirely a matter of human judgment, and the approval of all philosophy is brought in to prove the case. But this rule still stands firm and established: We must judge concerning the prerogatives of the human nature in Christ only on the basis of the Word of God. For who knows better what supernatural gifts the body of Christ can receive and possess, while retaining its substance and avoiding its own destruction, than the Son of God Himself? But just as He has brought us His own word concerning the other prerogatives, so with His express voice and in His own will and testament He teaches us what is present, distributed, and received orally in the Lord's Supper, wherever it is celebrated here on earth: "This is My body; this is My blood." A pious mind therefore justly recoils when reading these words in the writings of our adversaries: that God with all His omnipotence cannot cause the true body, not of some ordinary man but even the body of His own Son, while its substance remains intact and undestroyed, to be substantially at one and the same time in many places rather than in only one. Scripture certainly nowhere teaches this, but rather affirms that with God nothing is impossible.

Let us now repeat the status of this whole controversy. Do the words of the last will and testament of the Son of God in their proper and natural sense teach and affirm the substantial presence of His body in the Supper? But why do you not simply believe and accept this? Because, they say, it does not agree with the essential or natural properties of a true human body. But from Scripture it is absolutely certain that by reason of the hypostatic union with the divine nature innumerable things have been added to the human nature in Christ which far exceed the essential properties of human nature, because He has been exalted above every name.

But they take exception and say that those things which would destroy the integrity of the human nature in Christ or abolish its substance neither can nor ought to be attributed to Him; for it is an article of faith that the reality of the human nature remains intact and complete in Christ. I agree with this. But I do not agree with or receive what they weave in from physical principles without an express word of God, namely, that Christ is stripped of His true body, that its substance is destroyed, and that the integrity of His human nature cannot remain, if we believe according to the literal meaning that His body and blood are substantially present in a supernatural and heavenly manner in the Lord's Supper wherever it is celebrated here on earth. For what Scripture passage teaches that the divine omnipotence, which is infinite, cannot possess this ability and that God's wisdom, which is beyond calculation, cannot find any way in which this can take place while still retaining the integrity of His body?

What testimony can be brought from the Word of God to teach that the integrity of the human nature in Christ cannot, without being destroyed, endure being present by divine power in all those places where the Lord's Supper is celebrated according to its institution? I would be the first to agree that this cannot take place in keeping with the laws of nature. But what can take place through divine power in regard to the body of the Son of God, while still retaining its integrity intact, can and ought to be certainly and safely determined not from the principles of the physical universe or from our human arguments but only from God's Word, which in its proper and natural meaning teaches the substantial presence of the body and blood of the Lord in the Supper.

Therefore who am I to say that this cannot happen in any way while preserving the integrity of the body of Christ? I have the words of the last will and testament of the Son of God, and I understand what these words mean in their proper and natural sense. My adversaries command me to depart from this express word of God. If I ask their reason for this, they reply in this way: It is impossible that the body of Christ can be present at the same time both in heaven and on earth and in all those places where the Lord's Supper is celebrated; further, the reality of Christ's body cannot admit or bear such variation (πολυτροπία) in form without the destruction of its substance. Yet no Scripture passage teaches this. Can I then without Scripture rightly and safely depart from Scripture?

This is a matter of the utmost importance. It involves the last will and testament of the Son of God, the infinite omnipotence of God, and the high exaltation of Christ's human nature. Such matters certainly should be considered in the fear of God, with reverence and concern, lest we dream up something which is contrary to these very basic articles and as a result draw down upon ourselves the just wrath of our eternal Judge. But if I say that the divine will does not wish that we understand the words of the Supper in their proper and natural sense, then I fear that I might be accusing the Son of God in His last will and testament of lying. If I say that the omnipotence of God cannot accomplish this while preserving the substance of the human nature, and that the integrity of Christ's body does not permit this, I am saying this without a passage of Scripture and an express word of God. And I fear that I may be found careless and impudent toward the infinite omnipotence of God and the incomprehensible exaltation of the human nature in Christ, if for this kind of reason I should depart from the proper and natural meaning of the testament of the Son of God. For if I believe that Christ according to His humanity has all things in subjection to Himself, so that nothing is excepted except He alone who subjected all things to Him (Heb. 2:8), how can I determine with certainty that Christ according to His humanity does not have places in subjection to Himself, but rather that He is subject to places in such a way that because of His circumscription and localization we must set aside the proper and natural meaning of His testament?

Since these things are so, I find no more certain and safe way in this controversy than simply, humbly, and reverently to embrace and retain the words of the last will and testament of Christ just as the proper and natural meaning of the words declares it.

Very compelling for me are those examples from Scripture which admonish us as to what we should attribute to arguments of this kind when Scripture predicates something about the body of Christ which is alien to the condition of our bodies and when arguments are then lined up in opposition which are based on the similarity with our bodies, namely, that our bodies could not undergo this process without being reduced to phantoms.

In the Gospel story in Matt. 14:25 ff. the apostles saw and recognized Christ when He was walking on the waves of the sea and did not drown. But because they realized that this was not in keeping with the essential properties of a true body, they thought it was not His true body which they saw but a phantom. But Christ assured them: "It is I." And in order that He might prove to them that this action did not destroy the actuality of His body, by His divine power He caused Peter to walk with his body on the waves.

Likewise in John 20:19 ff., 26 ff., when the doors had been closed, Jesus came with His own true body and stood in the midst of them, and the apostles saw and recognized the true body of Christ. But because they made the judgment that the actual substance of a body could not do this and undergo this, namely, that while the doors remained shut a body could enter in such a way that two bodies at the same time could occupy one space through the penetration of dimensions, therefore they concluded that it was a spirit and not a body. But Christ in a long discussion confirmed the fact that although it was in conflict with the essential or natural properties of a true body, yet by divine power this had taken place, and the true substance of His body remained intact and was not destroyed. Thus He offered His flesh and bones to be touched and seen, and He ate in their presence. [Luke 24:36 ff.]

But if these arguments concerning the actuality of the human nature and the essential properties of a body could so disturb the apostles, when they at that very time saw the body of Christ before them and could touch it, it is not strange that these same arguments arouse so much disturbance today in regard to this mystery in which faith is asked to believe not only in that which the senses reject but particularly in that which is not seen but only affirmed by the words of Christ.

I am also much impressed by the consideration that the fathers disputed a great deal with the Eutychians about the circumscription and localization of the body of Christ; for they rightly attributed these qualities to Him, because of the nature of a true body and the essential or natural properties of a body, according to which He acted and still acts when and how He wills. But I found no one in the entire purer antiquity who used this argument about circumscription or localization in such a way that he would contend that in order to preserve the integrity of the body of Christ it is impossible that His body be truly and substantially present in all those places where the Lord's Supper is celebrated. But in regard to circumscription and localization they argued in such a way that they detracted nothing from the substantial presence, distribution, and reception of the body and blood of the Lord in the Supper; they both believed and taught the things we have noted above in ch. X.

Thus Augustine indeed says that because of the nature of a true body and by the law of nature the body of Christ is somewhere in one place. However, he does not press the matter of the mode of a body and the law of nature to say that Christ neither wills nor can do anything different and beyond them with His body. These are his words: "If He walked on the waters, where is the weight of the body? If He entered through closed doors, where is the mode of the body? Let the weight and the mode recede a little; He for whom nothing is impossible has done these things." Again: "The law of nature will yield a little and the human body will leave fixed tracks in the waves of the sea."

But we have explained this entire doctrine of the essential properties of the human nature in Christ and the prerogatives which have come to it as a result of the hypostatic union with the divine nature, while preserving the actuality of the human nature, in a special monograph[6] which we are anxious to add to this discussion because of this concern. At this point we only want to indicate that the arguments from localization and circumscription neither cause nor compel us to believe that we either can or ought rightly, safely, and necessarily depart from the proper and natural meaning of the words of the testament of the Son of God. In fact, the natural meaning is more strongly confirmed by the article of the infinite omnipotence of God and the sublime excellence with which the human nature in Christ, far beyond its natural properties, has been adorned and exalted above every name.

B. The arguments from the article of Christ's ascension to heaven, His session at the right hand of God, and His return to judgment.

The rule is sure and certain: When the absurdity of the literal sense clearly touches on the articles of faith, then the literal sense (τὸ ῥητόν) must not be retained, but with the aid of figures of speech another interpretation must be sought which is in keeping with the articles of faith. With long treatises the adversaries contend that the proper and natural meaning of Christ's testament regarding the substantial presence of the body and blood of the Lord in the Supper is in conflict not only with one article of the Creed but with three which follow in order: "He ascended into heaven, sits at the right hand of God the Father almighty, and from thence He shall come to judge the quick and the dead."

They prove their point in this way: Christ with His body has ascended into heaven and there sits at the right hand of the Father, but the Lord's Supper is celebrated in the meeting of the church among us here on earth. Therefore the statement about the substantial presence of the body of Christ in the Supper conflicts with these articles of faith. For Scripture when it wishes to describe a very great distance speaks of something being exalted from earth to heaven, for example, Is. 55:9: "As the heavens are higher than the earth, so My ways are higher than your ways . . ." And there is a further point made, which the Creed adds, namely, that Christ has so ascended into heaven that He shall also return from there to judgment; but if on the day of judgment He shall come from heaven to earth, then it follows that He is not now prior to the judgment present with His body here on earth where the Lord's Supper is celebrated. Therefore the words of Christ's testament must be interpreted differently than is indicated in the proper and natural meaning, lest they conflict with these articles of faith.

This is the summary of the argument, and it must not be rejected out of hand. For no dogma in the church can stand which expressly and diametrically conflicts with the articles of faith. But we have shown several times in the preceding pages that various and specious contradictions (ἀντιλογίαι [Heb. 7:7]), contraventions of the Law (ἀντινομίαι [not in NT]), and antitheses (ἀντιθέσεις [1 Tim. 6:20]), as Paul says, can be dreamed up right out of Scripture itself and set in opposition even to the surest and truest dogmas. Therefore we should not immediately depart from the proper and natural meaning of those passages in which dogmas have their setting, just because some specious argument is made that there is conflict with certain articles of faith.

We must, therefore, consider more closely and examine more diligently whether the meaning of these articles of faith really is such that what is conveyed by the proper and natural meaning of the words of Christ's testament cannot in any way stand, even through the power of God, and still let these articles remain in force. For it is necessary to formulate the argument in this way if we really intend to come to a consistent and necessary conclusion opposing the substantial presence of the body and blood of the Lord in the Supper. Furthermore, we shall state these points individually and in order and as briefly as possible.

Now the account of the ascension must be taken in its simple sense, as the words describe it. For He was taken up on high in a visible way which was perceivable to the senses. Acts 1:10 and 1 Peter 3:22 use the word "to go" (πορεύεσθαι), Luke 24:51 uses "He was carried" (ἀνεφέρετο [Textus Receptus]), and Acts 1:9 uses "He was taken up" (ἐπήρθη). And the account expressly points out that this act of ascension did not take place through a sudden disappearing of the body but in the circumscribed form and the localization of Christ's body. For the clouds received (ὑπέλαβεν) Him out of the sight of the apostles (Acts 1:9) in such a way that He continually ascended farther and farther away from their sight by a visible interval of space; for "while they were watching" (Acts 1:10) "He was parted from them" (διέστη ἀπ' αὐτῶν, Luke 24:51), "He was taken up into heaven" (Mark 16:19)—on high where the angels ascend, where Elijah was taken, where the elect will be received. The entire account of the ascension shows this with almost every single word. Therefore the words in the account of Christ's ascension remain in their proper, simple, and natural meaning.

But then, they say, it follows that Christ with the substance of His true body is not present in the Lord's Supper when it is celebrated here on earth. But I do not see how this is a sure and necessary consequence. In its visible, physical, and circumscribed form the body of Christ has been taken into heaven; and in that form in which He was seen to ascend He will also descend from heaven unto judgment (Acts 1:11; 1 Thess. 4:16). In that form He now appears to His saints who are in heaven, as Augustine says, for they follow the Lamb wherever He goes (Rev. 14:4). He does not live among us here on earth now in such visible and physical form as this, in the ordinary and familiar way He did before His resurrection and again after the resurrection and before the ascension. But it in no way follows from this that the wisdom and power of Him who in the proper and natural sense of His testament affirms the presence of His body in the Supper neither knows nor has another mode of presence, although unknown and incomprehensible to us. In such a mode He could, just as the words sound, be truly present with His true body, not only in heaven but also in His Supper which is celebrated on earth. And unless this point of theirs can be surely, clearly, and firmly proved, the entire argument taken from the article of the ascension can bring us to no definite or compelling conclusion against the substantial presence of the body of Christ in the Supper, which relies on the words of the last will and testament of Christ.

But how would their point follow, since it does not even follow that also before the judgment Christ cannot be present and show Himself when and where He wills here on earth in the physical, circumscribed, and visible form of His body while preserving the article of the ascension? For we already possess the clearest example of this, which cannot be evaded, in Acts 23:11, where the Lord stands before Paul and appears to him in the prison. But some people figure that this was not the true body of Christ but a specter or a phantom which stood beside Paul and appeared to him. But this is an impertinent and impious idea, for then the resurrection of the flesh of Christ, which Paul in 1 Cor. 15 proves on the basis of such appearances, would not be a true resurrection but a game of fantasies.

Nowadays there are many who, like the scholastics of a bygone age, in a free and easy manner philosophize about where the place or seat of God's habitation and that of the saints is. Is it above the crystal heavens, in a spacious realm of definite boundaries and circumscription where in a physical location there are expanses, stations, meeting places, promenades, etc.? But such assertions are made without a basis in Scripture, which indeed teaches that there is a heaven above, the dwelling place of God and the saints; but where it is and what its nature is Scripture not only does not explain but it expressly states: "Eye has not seen, ear has not heard, and into the heart of man has not entered what God has prepared for His saints" [1 Cor. 2:9]. and Paul was carried in a rapture beyond the airy heaven and the starry heaven into the third heaven [2 Cor. 12:2], but he says so little about the physical aspects of the place that he confesses he does not even know whether he was carried there in the body or outside the body. He says that the things he saw and heard in the celestial light of heaven are ἄρρητα, things that cannot be explained in words. [2 Cor. 12:4]

But we, if it pleases the gods, feel free to philosophize and make assertions regarding the place, nature, and conditions of the third heaven as if we had been there ourselves, and we do so in such a way that because of our own imaginings we do not hesitate to depart from the proper and natural meaning of the last will and testament of the Son of God Himself.

Indeed, because of these fantastic notions of ours we pronounce that the words of Christ's testament cannot be understood the way they sound. But we really ought to consider before Immortal God how much certainty and firmness this argument possesses. In the testament of the Son of God we have the express word which in the proper and natural sense affirms the presence of His body and blood in the Supper. The adversaries try to lead us away from this natural meaning. But listen to what line of reasoning and what kind of argumentation they use in trying to do this: The location of that heaven, they say, into which Christ ascended is such and its nature and condition are such that it is impossible for Christ to be present with His true body at one and the same time both in the highest heaven and in His Supper which is celebrated here on earth, while still maintaining the integrity of His body and the article of His ascension.

But what Scripture passage teaches that the nature and condition of that heaven is the way they philosophize? There is absolutely no Scriptural basis, but Scripture on the contrary asserts that the nature of the third heaven cannot be comprehended by our thought or explained with our words. Therefore the things they philosophize about the nature of the third heaven are not established propositions (ἀξιώματα) but merely guesswork (αἰτήματα), unknown to Scripture and without any Scriptural warrant. Indeed, they are brash assertions promising to explain things which Scripture affirms are incomprehensible and ineffable.

With what kind of conscience, therefore, will a person on account of these uncertain and ill-considered assertions dare or be able to depart from the proper, natural, and clear meaning of the testament of the Son of God Himself? And unless an argument establishes for certain that the nature and conditions of the third heaven cannot bear or admit the substantial presence of the body of Christ in the Supper, we can draw no conclusion in opposition to that presence.

It is assumed, almost in the form of a confession, that the body of Christ is now in heaven in such a mode and with such a nature that, preserving the article of the ascension, it cannot be present in the Supper which is celebrated on earth. But Augustine in a plenary meeting of a council of all Africa in explaining the faith and confession of the church spoke most earnestly concerning the faith and the Creed, ch. 6: "It is very odd and most unnecessary to inquire where and in what condition the body of the Lord is in heaven; it is our duty only to believe that it is in heaven. For it is not the task of our fragile mind to discover the secrets of the heavens, but it is the duty of our faith to know the sublime honor and dignity of the body of the Lord."

Even Bucer says properly and correctly: "Since the heavens to which Christ has ascended are above all the heavens, I would certainly not dare to define them, except in keeping with the words of Scripture, and certainly not with the proclamations of our own reason. Scripture does not define them except in terms of blessedness, majesty, sublimity, and divine power, not in terms of expanses of space; and it clearly testifies that they have not entered the heart of man." Thus far Bucer.

Therefore a person ought to give careful thought as to what it means to depart from the natural meaning of the testament of Christ on the basis of these brash assertions. For they [the adversaries] do concede that the exaltation and glory of the human nature in Christ is as high as it can possible be and therefore incomprehensible, but they take exception to this one point, namely, that it can be at the same time in heaven and also in all those places where the Lord's Supper is celebrated according to Christ's institution. And surely if there were no definite word of God regarding this presence in the Supper, I would not want to dispute at length about this possibility. But because the Son of God in His own last will and testament has spoken with strong assertion concerning that which is present, distributed, and received in the Lord's Supper: "This is My body; this is My blood," and since the exaltation of the human nature in Christ into glory, majesty, and power is incomprehensible, I do not find any testimony in Scripture which can give us the certainty [we would need in order to grant] that exception.

Augustine says in regard to the glorification of the saints, *De civitate Dei*, Bk. 22, ch. 21: "What the grace of the spiritual body is and how great it is I am hesitant to describe because it has not yet come into the realm of my experience, lest there be only rash guessing and rhetoric."[7] And in ch. 30: "What powers of movement such bodies will possess yonder I do not dare to describe rashly because I am not able to conceive of it."[8] Therefore what temerity, to say nothing of impiety, to circumscribe the exaltation of Christ's body in heaven in such a way that, although we have clear Scripture regarding its presence in the Supper, we make pronouncements without any Scriptural basis that this cannot take place while preserving the actuality of His body and the doctrine of the ascension of the body of Christ.

Augustine has written clearly in the same place regarding the glorified bodies of the saints: "Where the spirit shall will, there shall the body immediately be; nor shall the spirit will[9] anything that cannot be suitable[10] for the spirit or the body."[11] Again in Bk. 5, ch. [9]: "Bodies are subject to wills, certain of them to our wills, certain to the wills of angels, but all of them are particularly subject to the will of God."[12] And in the monograph regarding the knowledge of true life which is found among the works of Augustine we can read the discussion, ch. 45, concerning the spiritual bodies of those who are glorified: "It will not be necessary for the spiritual body then to be maintained in some special place but as a spirit it will subsist illocally in the Highest Spirit, who is God, lest by chance we understand 'place' to mean that which is substantially and personally circumscribed." Again: "Since the spiritual bodies are in the Highest Spirit, they will not remain spiritually localized."[13] Furthermore, the glory of these bodies is not to be contemplated by our reason but only by faith. And Augustine on Psalm 30, *Sermo 5,* says: "Let everyone but God be silent, who cares for us in the place of this life so that after this life He may be our place."[14] Why therefore do we humans oppose as an impossibility what the words of His testament state concerning the body of Christ and its presence in the Supper, as if He cannot be where He wills with His body, or as if the will of Christ revealed in the Word wills something which is not proper for His body unless we help ourselves with the aid of a figure of speech?

Therefore these arguments on the basis of the ascension of Christ into heaven contribute nothing which compels us of necessity or gives sufficiently weighty, certain, and firm reasons to cause us to depart with good conscience from the proper and natural meaning of Christ's last will and testament. And this argument is of great weight, that Christ after His ascension, when He had already brought His body to heaven, yet so teaches the dogma of the Supper to Paul that He affirms that what is present, distributed, and received by eating and drinking in the Lord's Supper which is celebrated on earth is His own body and His own blood. If He had judged that the article of the ascension would not bear or permit that presence in the Supper, then He surely would have indicated this by some kind of clear declaration. For who knows better than Christ Himself what can take place while still preserving intact the integrity of His own body and the article of the ascension? And how can we pretend with certainty, seriously, and consistently that for the sake of the article of the ascension we cannot retain the proper and natural meaning of Christ's testament, when at the time of the first Supper Christ had not yet ascended into heaven? Nor can we say that at the first Supper these words had retained the proper and natural meaning, but that now this can no longer be the case because of the article of the ascension. Add to this the fact that among the ancients this line of argumentation is not found in such form or meaning, namely, that Christ ascended into heaven and therefore cannot be present with His body in the Supper which is celebrated on earth.

To be sure, Capernaitic notions regarding the mangling, chewing, and digesting of the body of Christ, as is the case in the natural order of physical food, were raised in opposition to the article of the ascension. But as to the presence of His body in the Supper, they clearly affirmed that the same body which is in heaven is at the same time also present in the Supper, as the testimonies of the ancients which we have cited above point out. For example, Chrysostom in *Ad Antiochenos homilia 61* says: "As often as we taste the blood in the Supper, let us remember that we are tasting Him who sits on high and is adored by angels." *Homilia 5 ad Ephesios:* "Remember that this is His body and blood who sits above the heavens—His, I say, who stands close to the immortal power of God, whose blood we taste and who gives us His own body to partake of." *Homilia 24 in 1 ad Corinthios:* "He has taken this body to the highest throne, the body which He also distributes to us that we may touch it, eat it, and having received it return to our homes."[15] And in the same place he says that we have the body of Christ on the altar. *Ad Antiochenos homilia 55:* "Feed upon Me both here and in heaven; and in heaven I will possess you as the firstfruits, and on earth I will be joined to you; I do not want any interval between us." Moreover, in other places he expressly says that this takes place through the flesh of Christ, by which He is united with us in the Supper.

Up to this point we have demonstrated that the article of the ascension does not present sufficiently certain, serious, firm, urgent, and necessary causes and reasons so that with a tranquil conscience we can rightly and safely depart from the proper and natural meaning of Christ's testament. For it is a matter of very great importance to undertake to make the testament of the Son of God say something different than the words expressly state. Moreover, we shall now show that the article of the ascension neither takes away nor overturns but rather confirms and strengthens that natural meaning of Christ's testament for whose retention we are fighting. And this will not be obscure if we learn and consider on the basis of Scripture what the article of Christ's ascension into heaven really entails and for what purpose He ascended into heaven.

Elijah was carried into heaven in a whirlwind. And of his ascension Elisha said: He is not here, that you should seek him on earth, whether in the mountains or in the valleys; for he has been taken into heaven [2 Kings 2]. But if the ascension of Christ consisted of nothing more, nothing greater, nothing more sublime than the ascension of Elijah, and if we did not have the word regarding the presence of His body in the Supper, then we might justly come to the same conclusion. And our adversaries (indeed, in order that they might reach their end of having Christ ascend into heaven with His body in such a way that He either wants to or can be present only there and in no way among us on earth, not even in His Supper, although it has His express word concerning the presence of His body and blood) do not hesitate to change the statement of Peter in Acts 3:21: "It is necessary that Christ be received into heaven" (ὃν δεῖ οὐρανὸν δέξασθαι) by a manifest corruption in translation to mean that He had to be kept in heaven, contained, laid hold of, closed in until the day of judgment. The grammar, however, shows that it is not the meaning that heaven captured Christ or incarcerated Him, but that Christ took possession of heaven or occupied it, which Luther very meaningfully translated into German with *den Himmel einnemen.* Calvin himself has written regarding this statement of Peter: "It is an ambiguous passage, because we can understand both that Christ was taken by heaven and that He took heaven. Therefore let us not urge a word of dubious meaning." Thus far Calvin. The reader ought to note diligently how sure these foundations are on the basis of which they want us to desert the proper and natural meaning of Christ's testament.

The sequence and context of the entire speech demonstrate what the meaning of this passage in Acts 3:21 actually is. Peter is here making the point of his entire oration, namely, that the heavenly Father has adorned that Jesus who was crucified out of weakness [2 Cor. 13:4] with the highest and most incomprehensible glory and power, which He has demonstrated to some degree in the miracle of the restoration of the lame man. And by this argument he is encouraging those who denied and killed Christ that they should repent of that sin, lest they experience His vengeance. But at the same time he is showing by this very argument what those who believe can expect from that glory and power of Christ. However, because the objection can be raised that Christ did not exercise that glory and power of His in person, either in the face of His enemies or for the sake of those who believed in Him, Peter replies that Christ has received heaven itself. Moreover, there is a common Scriptural expression that God Himself is described as inhabiting the heavens, not in the sense that He is locked up there so that He cannot be on earth also, but in the sense that in the heavens He manifests Himself and His majesty and power more clearly and gloriously. For He shows that in heaven He is not to be known through means, but He reveals the quality of His majesty, glory, and power face to face for us to look at, and there He communicates His benefits without means, but He Himself fills all things with His blessing, so that there is no misery, no weakness, no confusion, no cause for sin there. On earth God also presents Himself to be known, but only through means, only in part, through a glass, in riddles; He also communicates His benefits on earth, but He shows His glory and His power only through means, under a veil, as it were. In the meantime His blessings are mixed with misery, weakness, sadness, confusion, and various temptations to sin. It is absolutely certain that this is what Scripture wants to say when it attributes to God that He dwells and has His habitation in heaven. And Peter is using this language when he describes the reign of Christ.

But because the impious are offended and the pious are disturbed by this kind of reign for Christ here on earth, Peter says that the time is coming when there will be a restitution (ἀποκατάστασις [Acts 3:21]) of all things. The riddles, the dark glass, the veil, and everything which is partial will vanish away; the enemies, the miseries, the weaknesses, the scandals, and the confusion will pass away. God will be all in all, and Christ will demonstrate and exercise the majesty and power of His reign publicly and gloriously, everywhere, as now in heaven so also on earth, both against His enemies and for the benefit of those who believe. It is perfectly clear that this is the sense of Peter's speech, on the basis of the context.

Therefore what Peter said, that it is necessary for Christ to receive heaven until the time of the restitution, is exactly the same as what David says: "Sit at My right hand until I make Your enemies Your footstool" [Ps. 110:1], and what Paul says in 1 Cor. 15:25-26: "He must reign until . . . the last enemy, namely death, is destroyed."

· Now let the argument be stated and considered as to its consequence: Christ [they say] according to His human nature received heaven in the way that has now been shown from Peter's speech; therefore He neither wills nor can according to that nature be present in the Supper which is celebrated here on earth, even though the words of His last will and testament in their proper and natural sense say this.

By the same line of reasoning it would follow that God Himself cannot be present here on earth because Scripture calls heaven "God's habitation" (Deut. 26:15), "the place of God's habitation" (1 Kings 8:30), "the Father's house" (John 14:2), "the throne (sedes) of God" (Ps. 103:19). But they say that we have the express word of God which teaches that God is in heaven in such a way that He can fill both heaven and earth at the same time. But we in the same way also have the word, and indeed in the testament of the Son of God, which instructs us that Christ is in the heavens in such a way that Christ Himself both before He ascended into heaven and after He received heaven pronounces concerning that which is present, distributed, and received in the Lord's Supper which is celebrated on earth: "This is My body; this is My blood." Further, I do not believe or want to say that the humanity of Christ either has been turned into the deity or made equal with the deity so that thereby whatever we believe regarding the deity we must also immediately believe regarding the humanity without an express word. But because I see what the words of Christ's testament say in their proper and natural sense, I have demonstrated on the basis of the article of Christ's ascension into heaven that we cannot certainly, firmly, and necessarily conclude that we have to repudiate and reject the proper and natural meaning of Christ's last will and testament.

For what the article of the ascension includes and to what purpose Christ ascended into heaven must not be judged and determined on the basis of our imaginings but from the testimony of the divine Word. The adversaries contend that Christ with His body ascended to the heavens with the result that He there is limited to a certain place in heaven in such a way that before the day of judgment He neither wills nor is able to be present on earth, not even in His Supper, even though the words of institution sound that way. But Paul distinctly says: "Christ has ascended above all heavens so that He might fill all things" (Eph. 4:10), and according to Heb. 7:26 "He has been made higher than the heavens."

I am aware of a gloss the adversaries have added to the expression "above all heavens," namely, that He has ascended above the heavens which are visible, airy and starry, to the highest, fiery heaven, and there He is contained and kept. But according to this line of thought, we could say the same things of the assumption of Elijah that can be said of the ascension of Christ—Elijah ascended above all heavens, penetrated the heavens, was made higher than the heavens. But Paul speaks of Christ's ascension in a unique way (κατ᾽ ἐξοχήν): "He has ascended above all heavens," and with the express purpose "that He might fill all things" [Eph. 4:10]. Likewise: He has penetrated the heavens and "has been made higher than the heavens" [Heb. 7:26]. And Scripture does not use this common expression with reference to some localized enclosure in heaven, but with reference to the highest exaltation, the highest glory, majesty, and power, as in Ps. 57:5: "Be Thou exalted above the heavens, O God"; or Ps. 8:1: "Thou hast set Thy glory above the heavens"; Ps. 108:4: "Thy mercy is great above the heavens." And when Job wants to describe the highest divine majesty and power, he speaks this way in 11:8 and 22:12: "higher than the heavens." Chrysostom, *Sermo 11 ad Ephesios:* "He ascended above all heavens, beyond which there is nothing else, that is, except His power and dominion."[16] Primasius on Heb. 7:26: "He was made higher than the heavens when He was elevated above all heavens and above all orders of heavenly spirits to the throne of the Father's majesty, where He now sits in the fulness of honor and glory."[17]

Therefore it is not true that these statements: "He ascended above all heavens" or "He was made higher than the heavens," signify the local inclusion of the body of Christ in one place in heaven. And even more illustrative is the statement which Scripture teaches, that Christ ascended into heaven so that He might be glorified, not only with the glory which is bestowed on all the elect, but that He might be placed and seated at the right hand of the majesty and power of God and that He might be exalted above every name (Mark 16:19; 1 Peter 3:22; Eph. 1:20; Heb. 1:3-4; Matt. 16:27, etc.). Therefore, just as in the Creed, these two articles: "He ascended into heaven" and "He sits at the right hand of God the Father almighty," are joined together.

To be sure, some of our adversaries, though not the most recent ones, have tried to interpret "the right hand of God" in such a way as to prove from it that Christ with His body can be in only one place even in heaven, if the integrity of His body is to be maintained. But Calvin in discussing Eph. 1 clearly says that those are incorrect who try to prove from the session at the right hand of God that Christ is nowhere except in heaven, because, he says, the right hand of God does not refer to a place, nor does the session at the right hand refer to the localization of the body; but the right hand of God signifies the power which the Father has bestowed upon Christ, in order that Christ might administer the Father's rule over heaven and earth in His name. The session at the right hand expresses the highest authority for ruling, with which Christ is adorned. And since the right hand of God fills heaven and earth, it follows that the reign of Christ is diffused everywhere, and also His power. This is what Calvin says.

The opposition [to the position of our adversaries] is manifest. Basil, *De Spiritu Sancto;*[18] Ambrose, *De fide* [e.g., Bk. 5, ch. 15];[19] Jerome on Eph. 1;[20] Augustine, *De symbolo;*[21] and Cyril, *Thesaurus* [Bk. 8, ch. 2],[22] all dispute at great length and prove from Scripture that the session of Christ at the right hand does not refer to some physical localization or to a position and circumscription in a certain place. For God is not a corporeal substance who has a right or a left side. Thus how we are to understand the term "the right hand" is learned from Scripture.

In general the term indicates the greatest and highest degree of glory, dignity, authority, power, blessedness, and happiness. In keeping with human custom we usually find such excellent things located there: 1 Kings 2:19; Matt. 20:21; Ps. 45:9, "The queen stood at your right"; Matt. 25:33, "The sheep will stand at the right"; Sirach 12:12, "Do not place your enemy at your right, lest he seek your throne." When the right hand of God is mentioned, Scripture simply understands the power and omnipotence of God and His glorious manifestation (Ex. 15:6; Ps. 118:16, etc.). For because most outward works are performed by the arms or the hands, particularly the right, the term "right hand" is used in a general way to describe courage, vigor, strength, and power (Job 40:14; Ps. 89:13). Therefore when Christ is said to be seated at the right hand of God we understand "right hand" as the glory or majesty of God (Phil. 2:9-11; Heb. 1:3), divine strength or power (Luke 22:69), the highest excellence, the most glorious and powerful authority and administration of Christ's kingdom. (Eph. 1:20-22; 1 Cor. 15:24 ff.)

This is the way the ancients explained this article of the faith. For all the explanations of the ancients, if they were combined into one and summarized, would be found to describe the session of Christ at the right hand of God in a threefold sense.

First, with reference to the equality of the Son and the Father, that is, the divine nature in Christ, as when Basil, *De Spiritu Sancto,* on the basis of[23] Heb. 1 proves the deity of the Son of God by the session at the right hand.[24] And in this sense the person of the Logos is the right hand of God itself, or at least from eternity He has been at the right hand. But Scripture teaches that Christ in time was seated at the right hand of God, and the statements of Scripture are plainly speaking of the humanity of Christ, as Theodoret proves at length, *Dialogus 2;* and he cites the dictum of Athanasius: "It is the body of Christ to which it was said, 'Sit at My right hand.'"[25]

Therefore the ancients, second, interpreted the session of Christ at the right hand of God with reference to the highest dignity, glory, majesty, happiness, and blessedness. Thus Heb. 1:3 and 8:1 speak of the right hand of the Majesty. Ambrose, tom. 2, fol. 99;[26] Jerome, on Eph. 1;[27] and Augustine, *Epistola 222, De fide et symbolo,* ch. 7,[28] *De symbolo ad catechumenos,* Bk. 1,[29] *Contra sermonem Arrianorum,* ch. 12,[30] interpret it of "ineffable blessedness and happiness."

Third, they interpreted the session at the right hand of God with reference to the highest excellence, dominion, strength, and power over all created things, to which Christ according to His human nature has been exalted. Therefore it is called "the right hand of the power of God" (Luke 22:69); 2 Cor. 13:4, "Because He who was crucified in weakness now lives by the power of God"; Acts 2:33, "Exalted by the right hand of God"; likewise Acts 2:36, "He has made Him to be both Lord and Christ"; Acts 5:31, "God has exalted Him with His right hand to be Prince and Savior"; 1 Peter 3:22, "Who is gone into heaven and is on the right hand of God, angels and authorities and powers being made subject to Him"; Eph. 1:20-22, "God has set Him at His own right hand in the heavenly places, far above all principality and power and every name which is named not only in this world but also in that which is to come, and has put all things under His feet"; Heb. 2:7-8, "Thou didst set Him over all the works of Thy hands. . . . And in that He put all things in subjection under Him, He left nothing that is not put under Him"; Phil. 2:9, "God has highly exalted Him, and given Him a name which is above every name"; John 13:3, "Jesus, knowing that the Father had given all things into His hands"; Matt. 28:18, "All power is given unto Me in heaven and on earth."

These testimonies show most clearly what the session at the right hand of God is. Peter shows in Acts 2:33-34 that the correct explanation of the article of the ascension, what is included in it and to what purpose Christ ascended, must be derived from the article of the session at the right hand: "David did not ascend into heaven, but he says: 'The Lord said unto my Lord, "Sit at My right hand."'" [Ps. 110:1]

I want to repeat that I do not understand this highest exaltation of the human nature in Christ through the session at the right hand of God to be either a change of the humanity into the deity or an equation of the human with the divine nature. For the humanity is not the right hand of God, but it has been placed at the right hand, that is, it has been exalted to the highest majesty and power, after God and below God, as Cyril[31] and Luther say.

Now we must get back to the *status controversiae,* and this will serve to establish the argument: The words of the last will and testament of the Son of God in their proper and natural sense affirm the substantial presence of His body and blood in the Supper.

Because it is an article of faith that Christ ascended into heaven according to His human nature, therefore in order that He might exalt it to the right hand of God, having borne the state of humiliation and laid aside the infirmities, He bestowed upon it the highest majesty and power, above every name and with all things in subjection to it. Therefore [they say] because of the article of the ascension He could not, with the reality of His humanity intact, be present with His body and blood in the Supper which is celebrated here on earth, even though the words of institution so state.

Surely no one with a sound mind will say that there is any good reason for this conclusion to follow. This argument simply does not present sufficiently serious, certain, firm, or necessary reasons so that with an untroubled conscience we can depart from the proper and natural meaning of the testament of Christ. Indeed, this meaning is most strongly reinforced and confirmed on the basis of this article. He who according to His human nature through the ascension has been exalted to the highest majesty and power, all things having been subjected to Him, has said in His last will and testament: "This is My body; this is My blood." Therefore without doubt He can accomplish, while still preserving intact the integrity of His humanity, what the words declare, even though we do not comprehend how this takes place or can take place. For the exaltation, majesty, and power of His human nature are above every name.

These points are so self-evident and convincing that I do not see how they can be truly contradicted. Moreover, let it be considered how serious it is on the strength of such arguments to repudiate and condemn the natural meaning of the testament of the Son, when the guilt of divine judgment is declared to those who do not rightly discern the body of the Lord in the Supper. And certainly discernment cannot properly take place unless it is correctly understood in accord with the Word. In the same way this natural meaning is not overturned by the article of faith: "From thence He shall come . . ." [Apostles' Creed], or "You show forth the Lord's death till He comes" [1 Cor. 11:26]. For the angel in Acts 1:11 expressly adds the declaration: "He shall so come in the same way that you have seen Him going into heaven." He is, therefore, speaking of the visible and circumscribed form of the body of Christ with which He shall descend from heaven to judgment on the clouds of heaven with great power and glory, in such a way that the eyes of all will see Him (Matt. 24:30; Rev. 1:7). These things are evidently said regarding Christ's second advent for judgment, which is later called an epiphany (ἐπιφάνεια) and a revelation (ἀποκάλυψις). (2 Thess. 1:7; 2:8; 1 Tim. 6:14; 2 Tim. 4:1, 8; Titus 2:13; 1 Cor. 1:7)

But it does not follow that Christ meanwhile, until He descends from heaven for judgment in that visible and glorious advent, cannot be present in His Supper in any other way, since in regard to what is present, distributed, and received on earth in the Lord's Supper the Son of God Himself, who has already been received into heaven, pronounces: "This is My body; this is My blood." Therefore there is no conflict between these two concepts: He shall come from heaven on the last day for judgment with a visible and glorious descent and advent; and what is distributed in the Lord's Supper which is celebrated here on earth is the body of Christ, in another mode of presence, to be sure, which is past our comprehension and known to God alone; but both concepts are the Word of God.

And it is common in Scripture that according to the one or the other mode of presence God is said to be at the same time present and still to be coming. Nor does it follow with any validity that since He shall come, therefore He is not present; or since He is coming, He could not have been here prior to that time. But we must by no means rely on this kind of argumentation from the deity to the humanity without an express word; but because we do have an express word in the testament of Christ concerning the substantial presence of His body in the Supper, therefore we are right in saying that this meaning is not overturned by the article of His visible and glorious return to judgment.

C. The arguments from passages dealing with the departure of Christ from this world.

It is beyond controversy that the Lord's Supper is celebrated in this world, and Paul testifies to this fact in 1 Cor. 11. But Christ, after instituting the Supper, says that He is leaving the world (John 16:16 ff.) and that He will no longer be in the world (John 17:11 ff.). These statements must not be understood of His divine nature, which fills all things, but of His assumed human nature. Therefore [they argue that] Christ Himself after instituting the Supper gave us the declaration that the words of the Supper must not be undertood as they sound with regard to the substantial presence of His body and blood in the Supper.

Likewise in Matt. 26:11: "The poor you have always with you, but Me you do not always have." But if we do not have Christ with us after His ascension according to His human nature, then the words of the Supper must be interpreted and understood differently than they sound.

Reply

These arguments also have a great appearance of force. For Scripture is not of private interpretation, but it is the surest and safest analogy and rule for interpretation that the dubious and more obscure passages are to be explained and interpreted by means of the surer and clearer ones. But we must always keep in mind and repeat the Pauline statement in 1 Tim. 6:20, which we have already mentioned several times, so that when some seeming opposition (ἀντινομία) is raised as an objection from other passages of Scripture we do not immediately permit ouselves to be won over to another viewpoint than that which is taught and revealed by the proper and natural meaning of the words in those passages where the dogmas have their proper setting. But in this controversy the discussion deals with the words of the last will and testament of the Son of God, from which we surely must not rashly and lightly depart without some very weighty, certain, firm, and extremely necessary reason.

Therefore we must consider whether the statements of Scripture about the departure of Christ from this world are entirely unable to bear or admit the proper and natural meaning of the testament of Christ; likewise, whether those statements testify more clearly, certainly, and firmly in favor of the absolute absence of Christ than the words of His testament do in behalf of the true presence of His body and blood in the most holy Supper. For this absolutely must be demonstrated, if because of these passages we are to depart from the proper and natural meaning of the testament of Christ. So we shall take up these points in order, points that are simple, correct, and clear.

In the first place, it is certain that when Christ at the first Supper said to His disciples: "Take, eat, drink; this is My body, this is My blood," He then had not yet left the world. For in John 13:33, after the institution of the Lord's Supper, He says: "Little children, I am still with you for a little while." And it is certain that they had Christ with them at the time of the first Lord's Supper. Therefore that statement had not yet been fulfilled: "You will not always have Me with you" [Matt. 26:11]. So it is manifest that this argument cannot be applied to that first Lord's Supper.

Now I ask of our adversaries whether they concede that the words of institution in that first Supper had and retained their proper and natural meaning. I know they will answer no. For it would be absolutely absurd to imagine that there now is a different meaning and interpretation for the words of Christ's last will and testament, as far as its substance is concerned, than there was for the first observance of it. For there is nothing different which is offered and received in the Lord's Supper now than the apostles received at that first celebration. But if the adversaries want to apply this argument even to that first Supper, that the words of institution could not even then have retained the proper and natural meaning because Christ had already left the world, this is obviously false, as we have shown. Therefore if this argument does not conflict with, does not accomplish anything against the proper and natural meaning of Christ's testament in that first Supper, as is abundantly clear, let the reader now consider whether there is any serious, sure, convincing, or compelling reason, on account of these passages, now to interpret or understand the words of Christ's testament differently from the way they read. For it is absolutely certain that the meaning of Christ's testament is the same now as it was at that first Supper and must continue to be so until the end of time.

In the second place, what it means to "leave the world" [John 13:1] must not be learned from Aristotle but from those Scripture passages which speak of Christ's departure from this world and His going to the Father. For John does not use the word "world" in only one sense. Sometimes he understands it in the popular sense of the system of celestial and terrestrial bodies, as in John 1:10: "The world was made through Him," or John 17:24: "Before the foundation of the world." Sometimes he uses the word to designate the people who are in the world, as in 3:16: "God so loved the world," or 3:17: "That the world might be saved through Him," or 1 John 2:2: "For the sins of the whole world." Sometimes the term "world" involves the depravity of human nature which through Adam's sin has entered the world, and it is understood with reference to unbelievers, the reprobate, and the people who love the corrupted world, as in John 15:19: "The world hates you," or 1 John 5:19: "The whole world lies in wickedness," John 14:30: "The prince of this world," 1 John 2:15: "Do not love the world," 1 John 2:16: "Whatever is in the world is not of the Father." Sometimes the word is used to refer to the state and common condition of this world; or to the infirmities, miseries, adversities, persecutions, and all the troubles of every kind which customarily befall us in this life. Paul speaks of the "fashion" (σχῆμα) of this world (1 Cor. 7:31). Christ in John 12:25 puts eternal life and the world in opposition to one another, that is, the fleeting and miserable life of this present age; John 17:15: "I do not ask that You take them from the world, but that You keep them from evil"; John 18:36: "My kingdom is not of this world." Therefore when we read that Christ has left the world, we must not immediately run to the definition of "world" offered by the philosophers. But the antithesis and the position of the parts of the sentence in John 16:28 show what it means when Christ says that He is leaving the world.

The words: "I have gone out from the Father and have come into the world, and again I am leaving the world and going to the Father" are integrally related to one another and belong together. The statement: "I have gone out from the Father and have come into this world" is not made only with reference to the human nature in Christ. But it is made in such a way that we learn to recognize divine power and strength in Christ, that He is not only a man but also true God. He went out from the Father and, having assumed a human nature, He came into this world, not in the sense of having left the Father (John 8:14 ff.) or as though the Father who fills heaven and earth were not in this world. But He humbled Himself and did not exercise His divine majesty and power but was made in the likeness of men and found in the state or condition of man, burdened with human weaknesses, except for sin, subject to all human miseries and adversities, also exposed to the hatred and persecutions of the devil and the world. Finally He was put under the Law and pressed down by the wrath and curse of God, so that by His obedience and suffering He might be made a sacrifice for the sins of the whole world. All these things Christ included in the statement: "I have gone out from the Father and have come into the world." [John 16:28a]

On the basis of the antithetical aspect of this statement we can rightly and correctly gather what He wishes to say when He says: "Again I am leaving the world and going to the Father" [John 16:28b]—that the departure of Christ from this world is our righteousness. Therefore it is too trivial and inadequate to interpret these great passages as referring only to a change of location, for they actually teach that Christ by His completely perfect obedience and His most bitter suffering has opened the way of life to the Father. Thus after His work had been completed He Himself no longer remained in a state of perpetual humiliation, burdened down with weaknesses, subject to miseries, exposed to persecutions and injuries, but with the removal of the humiliation and the laying aside of the weaknesses He is exalted above all miseries and injuries to the highest degree of excellence, enters that glory which He had with the Father before the world began, and receives that power of which it is written in Dan. 7:13-14 and Matt. 28:18: "All power is given unto Me in heaven and on earth," in order that He might forever be our King and Priest, High Priest, Mediator, and Savior. Christ includes all these great concepts when He says: "Again I am leaving the world and going to the Father" [John 16:28b]. And John 13:3 gives us a succinct explanation of this when it says: "Jesus, knowing that the Father had given all things into His hands, because He had gone out from God and was going to God . . ." Even Calvin himself cannot deny that these points are included under this verse.

And thus if you wish to know whether this argument which we have now been discussing is so urgent and burning that it presents to our consciences a sufficiently weighty, certain, firm, and thus compelling reason on account of which we can and ought rightly, safely, and thus necessarily depart from the proper and natural meaning of the last will and testament of Christ, then take a look at the statement in John 16 in this way, that Christ has left the world and has returned to the Father; that is, with His humiliation laid aside and His infirmities cast off He is exalted to the highest excellence, so that He now reigns by the power of God in keeping with His statement: "All power is given to Me in heaven and on earth" [Matt. 28:18]. And now consider also whether and how this follows: Even though the words of Christ's testament in their proper and natural meaning affirm the presence of His body and blood in the Supper, yet because of this statement in John 16 we are to believe that this could not take place, and therefore we should give up the literal meaning of the words of Christ's testament. Indeed, the contrary most excellent conclusion follows: Because the Son of God in His testament has said: "This is My body; this is My blood," therefore He is able to perform this just as the words declare—for the very reason that He has left the world and gone to His Father in such a way that, with the humiliation laid aside and the weaknesses overcome, even according to His human nature He has received all power in heaven and on earth.

Finally, in addition to the things which have been said, a denial of the presence of Christ still seems to be implied in such statements as: "I am leaving the world" [John 16:28]; "Now I am no longer in the world" [John 17:11]; "You will not always have Me with you" [Matt. 26:11]; "For a little while I am still with you" [John 7:33]. "When I was with them in the world, I kept them" [John 17:12]. And the adversaries contend, to be sure, that these statements of Christ must be understood according to the human nature, since according to the divine nature He fills heaven and earth, and that therefore we must attribute to the words of Christ's testament some other meaning than the literal.

But our people say that just as God is without contradiction said to be absent in one way and present in another way at the same time, likewise at the same time to be present and to be going away, to be coming and to be present, so it can also rightly be said of Christ according to His human nature that He no longer sojourns among us as before His ascension He moved among His disciples in the familiar manner and as in glory He will come to judgment. This is the intent of these Scripture passages. But this in no way hinders Him from being present with us in the Supper also according to the human nature, in keeping with His own words, but in a different, supernatural, and heavenly manner, known to Him and incomprehensible to us. Thus in these passages it is not the denial of His presence but of a certain mode of His presence which is referred to. And therefore it does not follow that because according to His human nature Christ is not with us in His visible presence He therefore is absolutely not present, not even in His Supper, although it has His word regarding the presence of His body and blood. But because Scripture is not "of private interpretation" [2 Peter 2:20], there ought to be no authentic interpretations of it, regardless of who the authors or supporters of it are, unless such an interpretation can be proved by sure testimonies of Scripture.

Therefore if we could reproduce the actual words of Christ Himself as to the manner in which He would no longer be with us, would not this entire dispute be absolutely correctly decided and determined, so that rightly no more questions ought to be allowed? Surely Christ at the time when He said: "You will not always have Me with you" [Matt. 26:11]; "Now I am no longer in the world" [John 17:11]; "For a little while I am still with you" [John 7:33], etc., also asserted, indeed with the words of His last will and testament, that His body and blood would be present in the Supper. And indeed, even after these expressions ("I am leaving the world"; "You will not always have Me with you") had been fulfilled, He repeated the same assertion to Paul after His ascension. Therefore the interpretation does not rest on any sure or certain foundation that these statements must be understood as referring to the absence of the substance of Christ's humanity in the Lord's Supper. To this comes the very strong argument that Christ Himself clearly does not interpret these statements with reference to the complete absence of His humanity but rather with reference to the various other modes of His presence. He is expressly referring to these statements: "For a little while I am still with you," and "You will not always have Me with you," when after His resurrection, as He stands in the midst of the disciples, He says in Luke 24:44: "These are the words which I spoke to you while I was still with you."

You clearly hear that these statements were fulfilled at that time. But does this mean that the substance of Christ's humanity was then simply absent in every way? It is certain that at that time He was showing and demonstrating to the apostles that He was present with His body, so that He said: "Touch Me and see" [Luke 24:39]; again: "He showed them His side and His hands" and His feet [John 20:20]. And yet at the same time He affirmed that He now was not with them, that is, with the same mode of presence and familiar movement He had had with them before His resurrection. Thus Christ Himself interprets these passages of Scripture, concerning which we are dealing in this discussion, not in a simple way with reference to a total absence of His human nature, but with reference to one mode of presence and absence out of many. And therefore Christ from time to time adds a kind of appendix to these words which refers to His visible presence, e.g., John 14:19: "Yet a little while and the world will not see Me"; or John 16:17: "I go to the Father and you shall see Me no more"; or Mark 14:7, where these words are added: "For the poor you have always with you, and whenever you wish you can do good to them; but Me you do not always have," namely so that you can show My body the external benefits of the kind of loving care which is offered to the poor and which Mary has now performed in her anointing.

Thus we have the declaration by Christ Himself that these statements of Scripture must not be understood in a simple way of the total absence of the substance of Christ's humanity, but only of one mode of presence or absence out of many. For Calvin himself in interpreting the statement of Christ in John 17:12: "When I was with them, I protected them," says that this must not be understood in an oversimplified way of His care for them, as if Christ were now entirely divorcing Himself from this work, but it must be understood of the mode of His visible care. And Augustine in a similar way says the same thing about the statement in John 14:19: "Yet a little while I am with you," namely, it must be interpreted within the context of other related passages, for example, Luke 24:39-44:[32] "These things I have said to you while I was still with you." And Jerome in discussing Matt. 26 writes thus: "The question has arisen as to why the Lord after the resurrection said to the disciples, 'I am with you even unto the end of the world' [Matt. 28:20], and at this point is saying, 'You will not always have Me with you' [Matt. 26:11]. But to me He seems in this passage to be talking about His corporeal presence, which was not going to be with them after the resurrection in the way He was with them at that time in all interchange and familiarity."[33] But we shall speak shortly regarding the statements of the ancients, in a special section.

But now let us examine what the consequence would be if we put this in logical form: Christ no longer wills to move among us in a familiar way with the visible presence of His body, as before the resurrection He moved about here on earth and as He will return to judgment in glory; therefore He is simply and absolutely not present with His body in the Supper, even though He Himself in His last will and testament taught and after His ascension repeated the dogma of the presence of His body and blood in the Supper.

Whoever therefore because of these words disapproves and rejects the proper and natural meaning of Christ's testament will see and recognize from these explanations what weak, uncertain, unconvincing foundations he has for his opinion. And let him consider how he can keep his conscience in harmony with the testament of the Son of God as he stands before His tribunal. The proper and natural meaning of Christ's testament is therefore not shaken or overturned by these passages of Scripture; rather it is reinforced and confirmed. Because Christ has left the world, He is therefore not present in the Supper with His body in accord with the properties and conditions of this world, nor in accord with the concept of presence understood by this world. This we freely grant. But He has said: "This is My body; this is My blood." Therefore

He is not subject to the properties and conditions or the modes or presence of this world or age (for He has left the world) in such a way that He cannot in another, supernatural, heavenly manner, incomprehensible to us, accomplish those things which the words of His testament state, namely, that He be present with His body and blood in the Supper, as Bucer himself has so learnedly argued in his retractions.

D. The arguments from the doctrine of the spiritual eating, John 6.

These arguments are set forth in various ways. The explanations therefore must be accommodated to the chief reasons which the adversaries are accustomed to adduce in support of their position. Sometimes they formulate it thus: It is certain that the end and purpose of the communication of the body and blood of the Lord in the Supper is that His body, in as far as it is given for us, must become our possession and that His blood which was shed for the remission of sins be applied to us, along with all those things which He acquired by the giving of His body and the shedding of His blood. But we can obtain all of this by the spiritual eating of the absent and far distant body and blood of Christ no less truly and efficaciously than if it were substantially present in the Supper and received in our mouth. Therefore [they say] we can have the Lord's Supper no less truly and gloriously even if we should say the substance of the Lord's body and blood are farther away than heaven is from earth and imagine that we receive orally only the elements of the bread and the wine. Indeed, they say that we have a truer and more wonderful Supper in this way, because it is received through better instruments and more outstanding means, namely, not with the external mouth and body but with the mind, the intelligence, the spirit, and faith.

But when the argument goes in this direction, the answer is easy and clear. Christ has not set forth for us the aim and purpose of His Supper in such a way as to permit us the liberty of figuring out for ourselves how and through what means and instrumentalities we think He can approach us, or to argue among ourselves as to which method seems better, more feasible, or more efficacious. But in the very institution of the Supper Christ has prescribed and defined the mode and rationale. For when we take these words of institution in their proper and natural meaning: "Take, eat, drink; this is My body, this is My blood," then there is no doubt that they are speaking of the external reception which takes place by oral eating and drinking. Taken thus, this proper and natural meaning of the words confirms that the body and blood of Christ Himself are not far away and removed from us but are present in the very celebration of the Supper.

Moreover, in order that this reception may be salutary Christ commands that it be done in memory of His body which has been given for us and His blood which has been shed for the remission of sins. That is, He wills that the spiritual eating, by faith, be added, as we have clearly pointed out in preceding chapters, namely, that the words of institution, if they are taken in their proper and natural sense, teach that there is a double eating of the body of Christ in the Supper.

Now our adversaries contend that there is no need for this twofold eating of Christ's body and argue, therefore, that we must depart from the proper and natural meaning of the words of institution on the basis of this line of thinking, that it is sufficient that there be only one kind of eating of Christ's body in the Supper, that is, the spiritual.

But let us give ear and consider how surely and firmly this argument is set forth. We concur in the concept of spiritual eating, whereby the body of Christ together with all His merits and benefits becomes ours, and that therefore there is no need for that second kind of eating of Christ's body which flows out of the proper and natural meaning of Christ's last will and testament. The reason for this line of thinking has to be that whatever we can acquire as a result of the spiritual eating does not require any other means. And there is an axiom of the scholastics that it is a sin to do with many means what can be accomplished by few. But by the same kind of reasoning it would follow that there is no need for the distribution of the elements of bread and wine in the Lord's Supper at all or for receiving them by eating and drinking with the mouth, for we could achieve the purpose of the Lord's Supper by the spiritual eating alone.

But if they say that this argument has no force against the distribution and reception of the elements of bread and wine in the Supper because there is an express command in the words of Christ regarding them, then I say, for exactly the same reason, that this argument is absolutely inconclusive in proving anything against the proper and natural meaning of these words: "Take, eat; this is My body. . . ." For the same Christ in the same institution not only spoke regarding the bread and the wine, but at the same time He also affirmed what it is we receive in this Supper by eating and drinking: "This is My body, this is My blood. . . ." And certainly the presence of the body and blood of Christ in the Supper is of more importance than the presence of the bread and wine. Surely it is an incomparably greater thing if in the

Supper our mouth receives the body and blood of Christ than if it receives only the bread and wine. Therefore if because of the spiritual eating we are unwilling to remove what is less important in the Supper, namely, the elements of the bread and the wine, because we have a word regarding them, how can we then condemn and reject, because of this very spiritual eating, the natural meaning of Christ's testament regarding the substantial presence and reception of His body and blood in the Supper?

Further, let us give some thought to the point at issue in this controversy. It is an argument over these words of Christ: "Take, eat, drink; this is My body, this is My blood." And although it is perfectly clear what the proper and natural meaning of these words is, the adversaries contend that this natural meaning must be set aside, indeed repudiated, for this reason: because it would seem that there is no need for such eating of the body of Christ as the words call for, since the spiritual eating alone is sufficient. Likewise, they argue that there is no use for this eating, which the words of institution describe according to their natural meaning, that we cannot obtain equally, surely, and efficaciously by spiritual eating alone.

But Christ, who is the eternal Wisdom of God, has been made Wisdom for us by God. To Him faith certainly ought to attribute enough wisdom so that from Him we may learn what is useful and necessary for our salvation, in the midst of our infirmities. But in addition to the spiritual eating He has also instituted the following, indeed in His very will and testament: "Take, eat; this is My body." And the proper meaning of these words is that this reception ought to take place orally.

Now think what it means when the Son of God speaks to you, a poor and unworthy person, and says to you at His most holy table, where He Himself is both the Host and the Meal: "Take, eat; this is My body, this is My blood"—but you answer: "I indeed see and cannot deny the proper and natural meaning of Your words, but I want to denounce, repudiate, and reject it. For what useful and necessary purpose will such a presence and eating of Your body have for me, in keeping with the literal meaning of the words, since only the spiritual eating is sufficient and even better? Actually, I believe that this Supper of Yours will be more glorious for me if I can get away from the natural meaning of the words of Your last will and testament and if I can remove Your body and blood farther away from Your Supper than heaven is from earth." Think, I beg you, what kind of grace such a response would evoke at such a meal and before such a host! But it is altogether necessary that this be the thrust of the argument if we adopt a position contrary to the proper and natural meaning of Christ's last will and testament.

But by some of the adversaries this argument is set forth thus: The promise of the Gospel is not received with our hands or our body but only by faith. Likewise: As God offers Christ and His benefits in the Word and sacraments, so there is only one means or instrument by which we lay hold on Christ and His benefits in the Word and sacraments, that is, by faith. Therefore [they say] the body and blood of Christ are not received with the mouth as the words of institution declare, but only by faith, spiritually. The heart of this argument, if we conclude something against the words of institution, must be: Although the words of Christ's testament in their proper and natural sense do say that, when eating the bread and drinking the wine in the Lord's Supper we at the same time receive orally the body and blood of Christ, yet this cannot be correct. And their reason is that the Son of God neither can nor ought to institute another mode for the reception of His body and blood than the spiritual mode, which takes place by faith alone. But how is such a notion concerning the Son of God (that He neither can nor ought) to be proved? And unless this is proved, this argument is inconclusive in establishing anything against the natural meaning of the testament of Christ.

But if they say that it is not a question of power but of the will and that the will of Christ concerning the spiritual eating has been revealed with a sure and manifest word, again I say that this argument cannot prove the conclusion which the adversaries are trying to reach, unless it can be demonstrated that the Son of God by a sure and clear word has revealed that He absolutely does not will that His body and blood be received in any other way than only spiritually, by faith alone. But how can this be proved when the words of the last will and testament of Christ in their proper and natural meaning say and affirm that in the Lord's Supper the body and blood are received by oral eating and drinking: "This is My body; this is My blood"?

Therefore, because we have the word concerning the twofold eating of the body of Christ, both the spiritual and the sacramental, as we have demonstrated previously, it surely does not follow that the one kind of eating rules out and nullifies the other, in such a way that for this reason we have to give up the natural meaning of the testament of Christ; but rather both can stand, and indeed in such a way that the one supports the other. For in order that the sacramental eating of the body of Christ may be salutary we must add the spiritual. And the spiritual eating is sealed and confirmed through the sacramental eating.

Also, we must always keep in mind the point at issue in the controversy. We have the word concerning the spiritual eating of the body of Christ, and the words of the testament of Christ in their proper and natural meaning affirm the sacramental eating of the body of Christ which takes place orally. Now the question is: Can both forms of eating be maintained as the words declare, or does the one rule out and annul the other in such a way that it therefore becomes necessary to repudiate and reject the proper and natural meaning of the testament of Christ? This is the real issue, regardless of the colors or the pretexts under which this argument is made. And if the issue is described in these terms, a decision is easy and plain. It is true that the promise is received, and Christ is received in that promise, only by faith. And indeed our senses do not understand or comprehend that our mouth in the Lord's Supper along with the bread and wine receives the body and blood of the Lord, but faith on the basis of the words of Christ does recognize this and believe it. But I ask whether it follows: The promise is received by faith; therefore the substance of the promise must be a great distance away from us. For this distance ought to be as great as possible (to speak in the common manner) if it is to follow: The promise is received by faith; therefore the body of Christ is not substantially present in the Supper, even though the words of institution say so in their natural meaning. I ask again whether it is true: Because the promise is received by faith, therefore it is impossible that the content of the promise can be received by the body. Faith surely also lays hold on the promise of daily bread. And in the Gospel history the sick clung by faith to the promise of healing. But does it follow from this that therefore the content of the promise, namely, bread and healing, is not received by the body? Surely the promise of the Spirit is received by faith (Gal. 3:2). But does this make it false that the Holy Spirit was present under visible signs and that He sat upon the heads of the apostles and entered the mouths of the apostles (Acts 2:3)? Scripture certainly affirms both that the promise of the Spirit is received by faith and that the Holy Spirit does not dwell only in the souls but also in the bodies of the faithful (1 Cor. 6:19). Christ is received in the Word by faith, but He also says: "I will come and make My abode with him" [John 14:23], and again: "I will be and dwell among them." [1 Cor. 6:16]

Thus the explanations of these arguments, if they are correctly and clearly referred to the true issue of this controversy, are easy and plain, and the result is manifest, namely, that there are no sufficiently serious, sure, firm, and necessary reasons why, because of these arguments, we should repudiate and reject the proper and natural meaning of the last will and testament of the Son of God Himself.

But they propose this argument, the most specious of all the arguments they construct, on the basis of John 6. For it is certain that the truest analogy of the interpretation of Scripture is when one passage is illuminated and explained by another Scripture passage where the same concept or the same dogma is treated and explained. But now it is manifest that Christ is speaking of the same body and blood both in John 6 and in the words of the Supper. Likewise, He is speaking of an eating of His flesh and a drinking of His blood in John 6; and in the words of the Supper He is also speaking of an eating of His body and a drinking of His blood. Therefore [they say], because there now is a controversy concerning the mode of this eating and drinking in the Supper, or how we are to understand the words "eat and drink" in the Supper, from where can a better, more correct, and safer understanding be taken than from John 6, where the eating of the flesh of Christ is described both affirmatively and negatively? They also add that Christ in the words of the Supper spoke only of the eating of His body and the drinking of His blood; but how He willed that His body be eaten in the Supper and His blood drunk, this He did not explain in the words of the Supper, because He had dealt with that doctrine earlier, in John 6. This is a summary of their argument.

Later on we shall explain how and to what extent John 6 may correctly be referred and applied to the doctrine of the Lord's Supper. For the moment and for the sake of order we shall speak first concerning the chief points of this argument, and lay down this rule, that in such comparisons of Scripture passages it is necessary that the same dogma be dealt with by both. Moreover, I am aware that some of our adversaries contend that John 6 does treat the institution of the Lord's Supper, so that they may gain a more plausible appearance for saying that the words of institution of the Supper are not to be understood as they sound but rather must be interpreted from John 6.

But the basic point of this argument is manifestly false. For the Lord's Supper was instituted on that night in which Christ was betrayed. And although there had always been spiritual eating in the church, yet the dogma of the Lord's Supper surely was not in the church prior to that institution. But the sermon in John 6 preceded by more than a year that night in which Christ was betrayed, as the numbering and annotation of the festivals of the Passover in John very clearly demonstrates. Therefore their foundation falls apart, as though the same dogma, namely, that of the Lord's Supper, were treated both in John 6 and in the words of institution, so that we therefore could and should depart from the proper and natural meaning of the words of institution and seek an interpretation on the basis of John 6.

But they reply that whatever may have been the time of the delivery of the sermon in John 6, yet it manifestly is evident that Christ in both places treats of the eating of His flesh and the drinking of His blood, both in John 6 and in the words of institution. Therefore [they say], because the question concerns the mode of the eating in the Supper, the explanation is rightly sought in John 6.

There is no doubt that there is some relationship and connection between the words of institution and John 6. We shall shortly speak as to how and to what extent the eating in John 6 pertains to the Lord's Supper. At this point, however, we shall consider only whether such a parallelism and relationship between John 6 and the words of institution of the Supper should be set forth and admitted that those things which the words of institution in their proper, natural, and manifest sense teach and command are immediately to be rejected if they are not in all points in complete agreement with the sermon of John 6. Thus the things taught in the words of institution would be entirely the same as those taught in John 6, and the words of institution would simply be explained on the basis of the words of John 6. This is absolutely necessary if the argument is to come certainly, firmly, and necessarily to the conclusion the adversaries want.

Now there is mention of the bread and mention of the drinking both in the words of the Supper and in John 6. But if the words of the Supper concerning the bread and the drinking must be interpreted and understood in the same way as they are used in John 6, then there will be no need for the external or material elements of the bread and wine in the celebration of the Lord's Supper; and it will follow that Christ in the first Supper did not take material bread or physical wine. For it is beyond controversy that these words of John 6 are used in a figurative sense. Also the words "to eat" and "to drink" are simply metaphorical. Now the people of Capernaum were seeking an external eating. But Christ simply interpreted the eating as faith. But then a person could come to the absolutely false conclusion that the Lord's Supper could be celebrated without the external elements of bread and wine, and thus the physical mouth would receive absolutely nothing in the Supper. But this is beyond controversy false. And from this it becomes absolutely clear that we must not take the words of institution away from their proper and natural meaning, because of the words of John 6, in order either to remove or to change those things which the natural meaning of the words of institution prescribes and commands, because John 6 either does not deal with these matters or does not do so in the way they are handled in the words of institution.

But they say they concede this concerning the external elements of bread and wine, but concerning the eating of the flesh of Christ they contend that this is exactly the same in the words of the Supper as in John 6, so that the eating in the Supper must not be understood as the words sound but must be interpreted according to John 6. I hear them and I know that they argue this way, but it is one thing to assert and another thing to prove. Furthermore, let them show, if they can, on the basis of sure and certain principles, why the remaining words of the institution must be understood in a literal sense and not taken in accordance with John 6, but the eating of Christ's body must not be understood as having happened in the way described in the words of institution but must be taken in the sense of John 6. For my part, I can clearly demonstrate that when Christ speaks these words in the Supper: "Take, eat, drink," they cannot be interpreted simply as they are understood in John 6. For there they are simply metaphorical and do not signify taking something with the physical mouth, but only embracing it by faith. But it is false that the mandate of Christ in the Supper, when He says: "Eat," is satisfied if nothing is received with the physical mouth. And yet without any proof it is asserted with such strong statements that the eating in the Lord's Supper is precisely the same as that in John 6.

Let us consider what takes place because of this kind of axiomatic statement: The words of the last will and testament of the Son of God are twisted and perverted, since a comparison of the passages clearly demonstrates that there is one kind of eating in John 6 and another in the Lord's Supper, which was then first instituted. For the eating of John 6 is always and by all people done unto salvation. But in the Supper many people eat judgment to themselves and in the eating become guilty of the body of Christ. Likewise, the eating in John 6 is and ought to be an eating by all people in all places and at all times. But in regard to the eating in the Lord's Supper it is written: "As often as you eat it . . ." [1 Cor. 11:26]. Again: "When you gather together . . ." [1 Cor. 11:20]. For the eating of John 6 there is no need to show the elements of bread and wine, no need for those words: "The bread is My body; the wine is My blood." But these things are necessary requirements for the Lord's Supper.

Nor is it true that in instituting the Supper Christ spoke only in an indefinite way regarding the eating of His body and the drinking of His blood, that He did not show at all how He willed that His body be eaten in the Supper or His blood drunk, and that therefore this must be learned from John 6. For when He says: "Take, eat, drink," He wills and commands that we receive orally that which is offered. And when Mark says: "And they all drank from the cup," he understands that they drank from the cup orally. But in regard to that which is received orally in this way Christ pronounces: "This is My body; this is My blood." That this is the proper and natural meaning of the words is certain. Therefore Christ in the Supper has instituted a new and peculiar eating of His body, which we have fully described above in many places.

Nor does any necessity compel us for a sufficiently serious, certain, and firm reason because of the eating described in John 6 to repudiate, discard, and reject this eating which the proper and natural meaning of Christ's testament teaches and prescribes, since both accounts are found in the Word of God. There is no contradiction or incompatibility (so to speak) between them, whereby the one excludes or removes the other, but they have complementary functions toward each other. Thus in order that the eating which was instituted in the Lord's Supper might not take place unto judgment but rather unto salvation, it is necessary to add the spiritual eating which is described in John 6. So we receive and embrace the body of Christ, which we receive orally in the Lord's Supper, with the same faith with which, outside the use of the Supper, Christ wills that His flesh be eaten (John 6). Thus we may be certain that we are participants in all the benefits which He Himself offers us in the Supper by the giving of His body and the shedding of His blood, namely, His body to be eaten and His blood to be drunk. That is, the spiritual eating of John 6 is confirmed and sealed by this eating which was instituted in the Supper.

Cyril, *In Johannem,* Bk. 4, ch. 14, indeed deals with the doctrine of the Lord's Supper in his interpretation of John 6. But he does not do so in such a way that he condemns or rejects the natural meaning of the institution or interprets the mode of eating in the Supper on the basis of John. Rather he says that when the people of Capernaum without faith sought the manner of the mystery as to how Christ would give His flesh to be eaten, He did not in any way explain John 6. But He explained it for His believing disciples, even when they did not seek an answer, while He was giving them the pieces of bread in the Supper, by saying: "Take and eat; this is My body." But in John 6 He is teaching what great benefits they would lose if they did not eat with faith, and on the other hand what they would receive if they did eat with faith. Thus far

Cyril.[34] Thus the ancients did not interpret John 6 the way our adversaries do, but compared it in a far different way with the words of institution of the Supper.

But these things are clear and manifest. And the point at issue in the controversy must always be recalled to mind, as to what kind of eating of the body of Christ in the Supper the proper and natural meaning of the institution teaches—which is so manifest that not even the adversaries can deny it. Now the question is whether the discourse in John 6 absolutely cannot tolerate this kind of eating; or in other words, whether the discourse of John 6 causes and compels us absolutely to repudiate and reject the kind of eating which the natural meaning of Christ's testament teaches.

Here some cite the words of John 6:63: "The flesh profits nothing; it is the spirit that gives life," etc. And to these words they attach a meaning as if Christ by these words was trying to disapprove of and condemn the proper and natural meaning of His testament which He was going to establish a year later. But it is certain that the meaning of John 6 stands in opposition to the objections and imaginings of the people of Capernaum, and what He was trying to say can be correctly understood on the basis of that antithesis. Therefore the ancients, when the antithesis was considered, explained this statement in three ways.

1. The Capernaites, looking at the humility of Christ's flesh, opposed as most absurd what He taught, that the life of the world lay in the giving of His flesh and that eternal life could not be obtained unless it were derived from His flesh. Augustine, therefore, and Cyril [In Johannem, Bk. 4, ch. 14][35] interpreted this statement in this way: If the flesh of Christ were alone, or if it were only common flesh, then it could not give life, but because it has been hypostatically united with the Spirit, that is, with the Deity, it gains the whole power of giving life. It is the same thing that Christ Himself says: "I am the bread of life, because I am the bread which comes down from heaven" [John 6:48-51] This interpretation surely does not militate in any way against the proper and natural meaning of the words of the Supper.

2. The people of Capernaum departed from Christ because they could not understand with their reason or comprehend how a fountain of life, from which faith must drink, could be deposited in the flesh of Christ. Chrysostom therefore interprets the words: "The flesh profits nothing," in this way: Whatever powers reside in carnal man are of no help that the things which belong to the Spirit may be received (1 Cor. 2:12-14).[36] But it is necessary that the Spirit give man life and enlighten his mind. For in this way, and in no other, is faith conceived from the

Word, so that it can apprehend Christ. Christ Himself from time to time in the discourse of John 6 repeats this thought: "No one can come to Me unless the Father draw him. For it is written, 'They will all be taught by God.' Everyone who has heard and learned from the Father comes also to Me. There are some among you who do not believe. No one can come to Me unless it be given him by My Father," etc. [John 6:44 ff.]. Therefore Chrysostom's interpretation, which Luther also followed, renders and expresses the exact meaning of Christ's sermon. Moreover, it is manifest that by this statement we are strengthened in our retention of the proper and natural meaning of Christ's testament, even if our flesh cannot comprehend it.

3. Augustine [In Evangelium Johannis tractatus 27] explains this statement thus: "'The flesh profits nothing.' But how did they understand it? To be sure, they thought in terms of flesh being torn to pieces in a carcass or sold in a butcher shop, not as it is nourished by the Spirit, but as if He were going to cut off pieces of it from His body."[37] Therefore He realized that by this statement He was rejecting the notions of the Capernaites which without an express word, indeed contrary to His express declaration made in this discourse, on the basis of their own carnal notions thought of a Scythian butchering of the body and a Cyclopean guzzling of the blood of Christ, notions which horrify us and which we detest. But in no way does it follow that, if the notions of the Capernaites are condemned, we must at the same time by the same words condemn the proper and natural meaning of Christ's testament, that is, the substantial presence and the eating of Christ's body, which in plain and express words has been instituted in the Lord's Supper in a mysterious and heavenly manner.

Therefore the discourse of John 6 in no way removes or overturns the proper and natural meaning of Christ's testament. For in John 6 we take the word "to eat" in a metaphorical way, because in this very discourse it is manifest that a figure of speech is being used and explained. But in the words of the Supper this is not the case. In all those passages of Scripture in which the dogma of the Lord's Supper is repeated the proper and natural meaning is retained and established.

E. The arguments of the adversaries from certain statements of the ancients.

We have shown above what the thinking and confession of the ancient church was in regard to the Lord's Supper, on the basis of the clearest testimonies of that era. But our adversaries keep piling up various and different and often even obscure and ambiguous statements from the ancients in order that they may appear to have the consensus and favor of all antiquity for their opinion. But we shall not speak one by one of individual statements of the ancients, but rather we shall gather under general headings or arguments those things which they customarily set up in opposition from the writings of the ancients; and regarding those matters which are of prime importance and seem to have some appearance of validity we shall speak in proper order.

[1. In what way the bread is called a sign of the body of Christ.]

In the first place, therefore, they raise in opposition those statements in which the ancients called the bread and wine of the Lord's Supper signs, symbols, figures, and antitypes of the body and blood of the Lord. Likewise, statements which speak of the body and blood of the Lord as signified, shown, and represented by the bread and wine. And because such statements are not rare among the ancients, they try on this basis to prove that the ancient church did not believe in the presence of the body and blood of the Lord in the Supper but only in the bare signs of the absent and far distant body of Christ.

We will not hunt for the minute syllables in the statements of the ancients, but rather from the context and the actual statements of the ancients we shall gather the explanations as to what understanding they had in calling the elements of the Supper signs, figures, symbols, antitypes, etc. For the ancients recognized two things in the Eucharist, as was demonstrated above with their own words, namely, the external elements of bread and wine and also the very body and blood of Christ. And sometimes they speak of these two things together, as Scripture also does, but other times they speak of them separately, of only one part at a time. They discourse so clearly, so magnificently, and so often concerning the presence, distribution, and reception of the body and blood of the Lord in the Supper that they almost seem to forget the elements and scarcely seem to be aware of the bread and wine, with the result that from this the papalists seized the opportunity for their invention of a transubstantiation of the elements. But sometimes they do discuss the actual elements of the bread and wine. And because these are subject to our sense perception, and are not that principal good on account of which the Lord's Supper was instituted, the ancients show what their use is in the Supper and for what reason and to what end Christ willed to have them used in the Supper—that they are to be external, visible signs that bear witness to the invisible presence, distribution, and reception of the body and blood of the Lord in the Supper. For they call the elements signs of the body and blood of the

Lord in such a way that at the same time they affirm that the body and blood of the Lord are present there, as we have clearly shown above in ch. X on the basis of their own testimonies. Even Peter Martyr himself noted that the fathers say both that the body and blood of the Lord are signified in these mysteries and that they also are contained and possessed in these same mysteries.

They themselves explain the reason for the use of the term "signs," as for example Augustine, *De catechizandis rudibus:* "The signs of divine things are visible, but invisible things are honored in them."[38] In *Contra Adimantum,* ch. 12, he argues that the bread is a sign of the body of Christ just as blood is a sign of the soul (Deut. 12:23), namely, because the soul of the flesh is in the blood (Lev. 17:11). For it is false that the blood be only then called the soul when the soul or the life is separated from it.[39] Likewise, in the statements of Prosper he says: "The Eucharist consists of two parts and is made up of two things—the visible appearance of the elements and the invisible body and blood of our Lord Jesus Christ. Likewise in the outward appearance of the bread and wine, which we can see, we are actually honoring invisible things, that is, the flesh and blood of Christ."

Bessarion in his monograph on the Eucharist cites the statement from Augustine that the body of Christ is both a reality and a figure. It is a reality, to be sure, insofar as by the power of the Holy Spirit out of the substance of bread and wine the body is brought into being. But it is a figure in that it is subject to the external senses.[40] He also cites the statement of Hilary of Rome that the body of Christ in which we participate at the altar is a figure to the degree that the bread and wine are apparent to the external senses. But it is a reality to the degree that the body and blood are believed in truth of heart.[41] In the same vein Augustine says of the cloud and the flame that the Lord and the Holy Spirit, who are by nature invisible, were made manifest in those physical forms.

It is therefore a genuine distinction that certain signs only signify a thing, either future or past or absent, but certain signs are demonstrative, as when the dove is called a sign or a symbol because it is a sure guarantee of the invisible presence of the Holy Spirit. For when God willed that His Spirit appear at the baptism of Christ, He caused Him to be represented under the appearance of a dove. The ark is the symbol of the Lord of Hosts. The flames are signs of the Holy Spirit, not by reason of His absence but because there is a true connection between the symbol and the true reality of the thing it symbolizes.

The fathers in many places clearly distinguish between the things which in the Old Testament were figures of the future and absent body of Christ and the Eucharist itself. Origen, *Homilia 7 in Numeros,* says: "At that time the manna was the bread in a hidden way, but now the flesh of God is the true bread in public view."[42] Cyprian, *De coena Domini,* says: "In the sacramental meals the old and the new meet; the lamb having been consumed, in keeping with the ancient tradition, the Master distributes to the disciples the unconsumed bread. The food of immortality is then distributed, differing from common bread while at the same time retaining the appearance of the physical substance, but proving that the presence of divine power is there with its invisible efficacy. As far back as the time of Melchizedek the sacraments had been foretold: They ate of the same bread according to the visible form. But before the time of these words this common bread was useful only for the physical nourishment of the body. But after the Lord said: 'This is My body; this do in remembrance of Me'—as often as it is done with these words and with this faith, He offers this supersubstantial bread for the life and salvation of the whole man, a medicine and a sacrifice that exists for the curing of our infirmities and the purging of our iniquities."[43]

Ambrose, *De his qui initiantur mysteriis,* ch. 8, speaking of the Eucharist, undertakes a comparison between it and the manna. "Consider," he says, "whether the bread of angels is more glorious than the flesh of Christ, which surely is the body of life." And finally he concludes: "And thus light is more powerful than darkness, true reality more powerful than a sign, the body of its Creator more powerful than the manna from heaven."[44] Jerome, on Titus 1, in speaking of the Eucharist says: "There is as great a difference between the showbread and the body of Christ as between a shadow and the body, as between an image and reality, as between prophecies of the future and what the prophecies prefigured."[45] Cyril, *In Johannem,* Bk. 4, ch. 28, says: "The showbread particularly signified the most holy body of Christ, by which all are nourished unto life."[46] Augustine, *Liber quaestionum Veteris et Novi Testamenti,* quest. 95: "The manna is a symbol of the spiritual food which the reality of the Lord's resurrection made into the mystery of the Eucharist."[47] Ambrose, on 1 Cor. 10, says that the manna and the water from the rock are called spiritual things because they contain within themselves "a figure of a future mystery" which we now receive in memory of our Lord Christ.[48] Theodoret, *Dialog. 1* and *2,* calls the bread a symbol and a sign, but in such a way that "just as the person of Christ consists of a divine and a human nature, so the Eucharist consists of the bread and the body of Christ." Thus he in no way understands it as a symbol of an absent body. And in regard to 1 Cor. 11 he compares the paschal lamb and the Eucharist and says that the one is the type of the other.

Chrysostom, on John 6, comparing the blood of the lamb and the blood in the Eucharist, says: "If its figure had so much power in Egypt, how much more the reality! This blood in the figure cleansed sins and purified the holy of holies. If it had such power in the figure, if death was so afraid of the shadow, how much more, I ask, would it have shrunk from the actual reality?"[49]

From another standpoint and in another respect, it was not on account of the absence of the body and blood of Christ that the ancients called the bread and wine signs or symbols. For sometimes they used this simile: As bread nourishes, sustains, preserves, and strengthens the body to natural life, so the body of Christ distributed and received in the Supper nourishes, sustains, and strengthens the soul and the body to eternal life. Sometimes they argue that the external reception of the body of Christ is a figure or likeness of the spiritual ingrafting into the body of Christ, as Augustine, *Contra adversarium legis et prophetarum,* Bk. 2, ch. 9.[50] Sometimes they say that the entire action of the Supper is a sign of commemoration or memorializing of the death or sacrifice of Christ on the cross, as Chrysostom, *Homilia 82 in Matthaeum*[51] and *Homilia 17 ad Hebraeos.*[52] Often they argue that the body of Christ signifies the mystical body, that is, the church, as Chrysostom, *Homilia [24] in 1 ad Corinthios,* on 1 Cor. 10,[53] and Augustine, *Ad infantes*[54] and *De consecratione,* dist. 2, ch. 2, *Quia passus.* Since these things are so, let the reader note what sort of a line of thought it is that the presence of the body of Christ should therefore be excluded from the Supper because the ancients called the bread a sign of the body of Christ.

We have shown, therefore, in what sense the ancients spoke of the bread and wine in the Supper as signs of the body and blood of the Lord, and that never did they understand them as bare signs of the absent body and blood of the Lord. And it is worthy of note that in later times, when certain individuals tried to develop arguments on the basis of these statements of the ancients regarding signs, figures, or symbols in opposition to the presence of the body of Christ, Euthymius, John of Damascus, and Theophylact[55] were unwilling to concede that the bread is only a figure of the body of Christ which is actually absent; and for this reason they rejected such forms of speaking.

[*2. In what way the Lord's Supper is a sacrament or a mystery.*]

In the second place, they raise in opposition also those statements

of the ancients in which they call the Lord's Supper a mystery or
sacrament, a mystic benediction, and mystical food. Likewise, that the
body of Christ is present or received in or under a mystery or
sacrament. They [the adversaries] understand a "mystery" as a figure or
a sign of an absent reality. But the ancients called both Baptism and the
Lord's Supper mysteries, not with regard to the absence of anything but
because they could not understand them with their minds or grasp them
with their senses; rather, these sacraments occupied a position far above
and beyond the range of the senses and the mind and had to be
understood and judged by faith on the basis of the Word of God alone.
Thus Paul says: "We speak the wisdom of God in a mystery" [1 Cor.
2:7], and again he speaks of dispensers of "the mysteries of God" [1 Cor.
4:1; Col. 1:25-27]. Chrysostom, *Homilia 82 in Matthaeum,* says: "In the
mysteries of Baptism and the Lord's Supper we must not only look at
those things which are subject to the senses but we must particularly
believe that those things which are taught us by the Word are present
and bestowed upon us, even though to the senses and to reason they
seem absurd, for they are above our senses and our reason." [56]

Augustine, *Ad neophytos:* "That which you see on the altar of God
you also saw last night. But what it was, what He willed, what a great
thing the sacrament contained, you have not yet heard. Therefore what
you see is bread and a cup which your eyes bring to your notice, but
your faith demands that you be instructed: 'The bread is the body of
Christ and the wine is His blood.'" Again, in giving the reason why he
appeals to the sacrament of Baptism, he says that water is observed, but
He who is not seen is the Spirit at work. Chrysostom, discussing 1 Cor.
10:16, calls it a fearful mystery, not because it signifies the absent body
and blood but because the Word tells us, and faith believes, that what is
present in the cup of the Lord is the same as that which flowed from the
Lord's side. [57] And Cyril, *In Johannem,* Bk. 4, ch. 13, says: "In the
mysteries we must not inquire how this takes place or how it can take
place but simply and firmly believe what the words of Christ tell us
takes place and is and what they affirm the mysteries are." [58] Thus the
words "mystery" and "sacrament" in no way suggest the absence of
something.

[3. The confusion of spiritual and sacramental eating.]

In the third place, they say that the thinking of learned antiquity is
that the words of the Supper are not to be understood in the literal
sense, as they read, but must be interpreted figuratively. But they are
misleading the reader. For in regard to John 6 and concerning the eating

which is described in John 6, that beyond controversy it is metaphorical, the fathers were arguing against the Capernaites but not against the words of the Supper. Augustine, *De doctrina Christiana*, Bk. 3, ch. 16: "'Unless you eat the flesh of the Son of Man and drink His blood . . .' [John 6:53] seems to command an outrageous and disgraceful act. It is therefore a figure, commanding us to participate in the suffering of the Lord and to hold in sweet and beneficial memory the fact that His flesh was crucified and wounded for us."[59] Origen, *Homilia 7 in Leviticum*, in dealing with the words of John 6: "'Unless you eat My flesh . . . ' [John 6:53-54]. You must recognize," he says, "that these are figurative expressions which are written in the divine book. For even in the New Testament there is the letter which kills him who does not listen spiritually to the things that are spoken. For if you follow what is said here according to the letter: 'Unless you eat My flesh . . .' this letter will kill."[60] In the same way Chrysostom, *Homilia 47 in Johannem*, says that the people of Capernaum erred in that they understood the eating in John 6 in a simple way, in keeping with the literal meaning and without any figure of speech.[61]

These things are rightly stated in regard to the eating in John 6, but our adversaries cite them as though they had been spoken about the words of the Lord's Supper; but this they cannot establish on the basis of the ancients. The reader should carefully beware of this trick.

[*4. What Augustine calls the essence* (res) *of the Sacrament.*]

In the fourth place, Augustine from time to time calls the substance of the Sacrament *(res sacramenti)* the very body and blood of Christ, as in the Sentences of Prosper. But more commonly in speaking of the substance of the Sacrament he understands the power, efficacy, benefit, and usefulness of the Sacrament. And in this sense he says that the unworthy receive the Sacrament but not the substance of the Sacrament.[62] But the Sacramentarians interpret this statement against the intention of the author as referring to the very body and blood of Christ, although the statements of Augustine and the rest of the ancients most clearly teach that the unworthy receive in the Supper the very body of Christ, even though not to their salvation but to their judgment, as we have noted in several statements in ch. X. Thus they twist the thinking of the ancients regarding the spiritual eating of the body of Christ against the sacramental eating of His body and do so in such a way that by this confusion they thereby destroy and remove it. For example, Augustine says, *In Evangelium Johannis tractatus 26:* "To believe in Him is to eat living bread." Again: "This is to eat that food and to drink that drink, to remain in Christ and have Him remaining in you. And thus he who does not remain in Christ obviously does not eat His body spiritually."[63] You hear that Augustine clearly explains that he is thinking of spiritual eating. But it does not follow that because the unworthy do not eat the body of Christ spiritually they therefore do not eat it in any way at all.

[5. *How the ancients spoke in regard to the bodily and local absence of Christ.*]

In the fifth place, the fathers, when they speak of the eating in John 6 or when they are disputing against the imaginings of the people of Capernaum, are accustomed to speak in the following way. Augustine, *In Evangelium Johannis tractatus 25:* "Why do you prepare your teeth and your stomach? Believe, and you have eaten."[64] Or, *De verbis Domini in Lucam tractatus 33:* "Do not prepare your throat but your heart." Cyprian, *De coena Domini:* "We do this often; we do not sharpen our teeth for eating, but with sincere faith we break the holy bread and divide it among us."[65] These and similar statements of the ancients, namely, that the flesh of Christ is not chewed up or digested in the natural way, as food is in the stomach, so that it becomes nourishment for the body, the Sacramentarians twist to make it appear that the ancient church held that in the Lord's Supper the mouth and the body do not receive the body of the Lord but only bread and that the body of the Lord is received in the Supper only by the spirit and by faith alone. They do this even though the ancients, as we have demonstrated above, affirmed with many very clear statements that the body of the Lord is received in the Supper not only with the heart, the soul, and the spirit but also with the physical mouth and that in the Lord's Supper our bodies receive not only the bread and wine but at the same time the body and blood of the Lord, but not in a Capernaitic way.

[6. *Negatively, the absence of Christ's body in the Supper cannot be demonstrated clearly in the writings of the ancients.*]

In the sixth place, statements of Augustine, Cyril, Fulgentius, and Vigilius are brought forward to argue that according to His human nature Christ with His body, according to the flesh, locally and with bodily absence has departed from the world and is not here. And it is true that among all the arguments they produce from the writings of the ancients there is none that influences our minds with an attractive outward appearance as much as this one. But we must watch that this appearance of plausibility, which at first glance this argument seems to possess, does not force itself upon us with insufficient consideration of the real facts. Thus also in the case of this argument we must go back to the point of the controversy. It is a question of the words of the last will and testament of the Son of God. And it is a serious matter to tamper with anything in this testament and change it to something different from what its proper and natural meaning states. I therefore ask whether the ancients understood those statements of theirs concerning the bodily, local, and physical absence of Christ, and wanted them understood, to mean that therefore they did not retain and did not think we could or ought to retain the proper and natural meaning of Christ's testament in regard to the substantial presence, distribution, and reception of the body and blood of the Lord in the Supper. For this must be clearly, surely, and firmly established from the ancients if the argument is to be settled as the adversaries contend.

However, I have not discovered among the ancients that this kind of argumentation is expressly or clearly used or established, namely, that Christ with His flesh or His bodily presence has locally left us and is absent, and that therefore the proper and natural meaning of the words of the Supper in regard to the substantial presence, distribution, and reception of the body and blood of the Lord in the Supper can in no way be sustained, but that what is present on earth in the Lord's Supper and what is given us in the external distribution and received orally is only the bread and wine, and this in such a way that the body and blood of the Lord are not present nor offered nor received orally for us to eat in the Supper which is celebrated among us here on earth. I do not find in the ancients that they drew the consequence that Christ has left the earth with His flesh and that therefore now in His Supper He is present with us and joined to us only according to His other nature, namely, only according to His divinity, but in no way with His body and blood.

I have investigated with considerable diligence, but I have not been able to find such lines of argumentation and consequences among the ancients where they dealt with the Lord's Supper. And thus it is still my duty, in the absence of any definite and firm reasoning, to hold to the words of the last will and testament of the Son of God without any deviation from their literal sense. Indeed, I see and find that the ancients who do speak of the bodily departure and absence of Christ in keeping with what has been said nevertheless contend with serious assertions that we must hold with firm faith to those words: "Take, eat, drink; this is My body, this is My blood," even though they may seem absurd and above our senses and reason. Nor must we in the Jewish manner seek how this can take place and how this can be, but rather grant to Christ alone the way and the understanding of His own work; cf. Cyril, *In Johannem*, Bk. 4, chs. 13—14;[66] Chrysostom, *Homilia 85 in Matthaeum.*[67] Likewise, the ancients assert that not only the bread and wine but also the very body and blood of Christ are present on that sacred table and are received orally by those who partake. They also exclaim that it is a great miracle for Christ to be present with His flesh at the same time both in heaven and in His Supper which is celebrated among us here on earth. We have noted these statements in ch. X.

Augustine, *Confess.*, Bk. 9, ch. 13, says: "From the altar is given that second victim by which the handwriting against us has been destroyed and by which He has triumphed over His enemies."[68] *In Evangelium Johannis tractatus 28:* "From the table is taken the body of the Lord."[69] And he says that the reception takes place orally, *Epist. 118, Sermo 215.*[70] The Nicene Canon says that on the altar the lamb of God is present. Chrysostom, *Homilia 24 in 1 ad Corinthios*, says: "On the altar that body is present which the Wise Men worshiped in the manger."[71]

Likewise, the ancients with long discussions asserted and confirmed the fact that Christ is joined or united to us not only in the Spirit or only with His deity by faith, but that in the Lord's Supper He offers His very body and blood to us in such a way that bodily, by nature, and by natural participation, that is, with the very nature or substance of His body, He is joined and united to us. In ch. 10, above, we noted those statements from Hilary, Chrysostom, and Cyril, and we warned against all corruptions. Cyril says: "It was surely necessary that not only the soul through the Holy Spirit ascend into a blissful life but even that this rude and earthly body, related to Him by taste and touch and food, be returned to immortality. The life-giving nature of the Word, joined to the flesh in that ineffable manner of union, makes the flesh life-giving, and thus the flesh gives life to those who participate in it. When we eat it, then we have life in us, when we are joined to Him who has created life. But if by a mere touch of the flesh of Christ those who were sick were restored, how can it be that we will not live who both taste and eat that flesh?"[72] And we have noted, above, several other passages from Cyril which illustrate these points.

Therefore I recognize the statements of the ancients concerning the bodily, fleshly, and local absence of Christ, but I neither recognize nor accept the conclusions which are fabricated from these statements in opposition to the natural meaning of Christ's testament concerning the substantial presence, distribution, and reception of His body and blood in the Supper. There are two reasons, perfectly clear, sure, and firm: 1. because when the ancients speak about the Lord's Supper they never at any time draw these conclusions; 2. because the ancients themselves distinctly, clearly, and evidently in their most weighty discussions affirm that Christ is in the Supper not only with His deity but also with the substance of His body, that it is received in the mouth of those who eat, and that it is united and joined to us, just as when a person pours new wax into wax which has already been melted. Moreover, they seriously reprove and refute those who believe that Christ dwells in us only spiritually or with His deity. These things have been clearly demonstrated above.

When I discovered these things in the writings of the ancients, I surely did not dare to fabricate under the title and name of antiquity, nor could I accept, those conclusions of the Sacramentarians whereby they proscribed the body and blood of Christ from the Lord's Supper which is celebrated on earth and removed it very far away from us. For I see that the ancients, when they speak about the Lord's Supper, do not draw conclusions of this kind but rather on the contrary assert and confirm these very things with strong convictions.

This is a simple, clear, correct, sure, firm, and solid reply to those statements of the ancients, nor do I see with what kind of conscience, under the pretext of the authority of the ancients, we can on the basis of these citations disprove and reject the natural meaning of the last will and testament of Christ, which is surely a most serious and awesome responsibility.

In the writings of Cyril there are statements which occur very frequently concerning the bodily, fleshly, and local separation and absence of Christ. But the same Cyril argues with great force in regard to the bodily union of Christ with our bodies in the Supper. And in an epistle to Calosyrius he writes thus: "Therefore it was fitting that Christ be united with our bodies in a certain way, through His sacred flesh and His precious blood which we receive in the life-giving blessing in the bread and wine." In the same letter: "We should not tremble at the flesh and blood which have been placed on the holy altar, where God condescends to our weaknesses and fills us with the power which is given unto life, converting it into the true nature of His own flesh, so that it is found to be the body of life, a kind of life-giving seed, in us. And do not doubt that this is true, when He clearly says: 'This is My body,' but rather receive the words of the Savior in faith."

But you say: How can these statements of the ancients concerning the bodily, fleshly, and local departure and absence be reconciled with those that deal with the Lord's Supper so that there is no implication of contradiction? For my part, even if I could not demonstrate this, yet I judge that those statements which I have cited from the ancients are sufficient for me so that in the last will and testament of the Son of God I am not compelled to try something different from what the words say. However, I have noticed that the ancients themselves have demonstrated how they want these sayings to be understood, so that they are not in conflict with the natural meaning of Christ's testament and do not overturn it.

First, Augustine says to Dardanus: "Of course the body of Christ is in a certain place in heaven,"[73] but he adds that this takes place in keeping with the mode of a true body, that is, according to the physical properties of a human body. But because Christ according to His humanity is sitting at the right hand of the majesty of God, has entered into His glory, and has been glorified with that glory which He possessed with the Father before the world began, therefore Augustine does not deny that Christ according to that majesty of His can be present in the Supper with His body in another way than according to the physical properties of a body, even though it is not omnipresent like His deity. For it has been falsely attributed to Augustine that he thought and said that the body of the Lord in which He rose from the dead had to be in only one place. For in *In Evangelium Johannis tractatus 30,* where such a statement occurs, he is only saying that the body of the Lord in which He rose from the dead can be in one place.[74]

Second, in *In Evangelium Johannis tractatus 50,* explaining the statement of Christ: "You will not have Me with you always," even though he says that according to the presence of His majesty we always do have Christ but that this statement: "You will not have Me with you always" is spoken with reference to the presence of His flesh,[75] yet he does not dare to say this in opposition to the words of Christ's testament. For in the same place he says: "The church holds to Christ only by faith, not by sight. You have Christ in your presence by faith, through the sacrament of Baptism, through the food and the drink of the altar, but you will not always have Him if you live an evil life."[76] Likewise Chrysostom, *Homilia 60 ad populum Antiochenum,* when he has discoursed in many ways concerning the substantial presence, distribution, and reception of the body of Christ in the Supper, brings up that statement of Christ: "You will not have Me with you always," but he does not conclude from it that the body of Christ is absent from the Supper, but he raises another statement of Christ: "Lo, I am with you always, even to the end of the age." This we must carefully note.

Third, the ancients interpreted their statements regarding the bodily and local departure and absence of Christ as referring to the visible, bodily, and fleshly fellowship, presence, and conversation of Christ, as when He showed the apostles that He was present. Augustine, *In Evangelium Johannis tractatus 50:* "For a few days He walked among the apostles according to the presence of His body."[77] *In Evangelium Johannis tractatus 102:* "He came into the world, for He showed the world His body."[78] Cyril, *In Johannem,* Bk. 11, ch. 19: "Present and living in His flesh among the apostles, He was a manifest consolation to them when they beheld Him with their eyes. For the human soul is accustomed to trust not in hidden things but in what can be seen with the eyes."[79] And it is such a bodily presence of Christ which he says the apostles desired, ch. 22. [80] And this is what he says in ch. 3: "He could not live among the apostles in the flesh when He ascended to the Father."[81]

Augustine from time to time explains such statements as referring to the mode of presence and absence, as for example *In Evangelium Johannis tractatus 64,* dealing with the words of Christ: "For a little while I am still with you" [John 13:33]. He says: "Christ is not here speaking of that kind of presence with His disciples by which He is with them to the end of the world, but either of His mortal weakness by which He was with them up to the time of His passion, or of the bodily presence by which He was going to be with them up to the time of His ascension; whichever of these options one chooses is not in conflict with the faith. But if this interpretation seems to someone to depart from the truth, let him note Christ's words also in another gospel, where He says: 'I said these things to you while I was still with you' [Luke 24:44], as if He then were not with them although they were standing, seeing, touching, and talking with Him. Therefore, what does it mean when He says: 'while I was still with you' except: 'while I was still in the mortal flesh'?" Thus Augustine.[82] And in *Tractatus 95 de Justitia* [John 16:8] he says: "'Because I go to the Father and you will not see Me' [John 14:28]. But surely we will not say that Paul was wrong when he confessed that he saw Christ after the ascension [1 Cor. 15:8]. Surely Stephen was not wrong when he said: 'I see the Son of Man standing at the right hand of God' [Acts 7:56]. What then does it mean: 'I go to the Father and you will not see Me,' except: 'You will not see Me as I am now when I am with you'? Therefore they were not going to see this Christ, that is, this form of Christ, when He departed from this world and went to the Father. 'When you see Me as I will be, you will not see Me as I am now with you, for you will not see Me in My humility but in My exalted state.'"[83]

Augustine says the same thing when speaking of the Lord's Supper, in that He distinguishes the mode of presence but does not remove the presence itself, as in *In Evangelium Johannis tractatus 50,* where he says: "At the present time we possess Christ through the food and drink of the altar," and he prefaces this with the words: "The church possesses Christ only by faith; it does not see Him with the eye."[84] Likewise in *Sermo III,* 140, in speaking of the breaking of the bread in the Supper, he says: "The absence of the Lord does not mean He is absent. Have faith, and He whom you do not see will be with you." And in the *Sententiae* of Prosper, *De consecratione,* dist. 2, the statement is repeated from time to time: "The Eucharist consists of the invisible body and blood of Christ." Likewise Chrysostom in regard to those things which they perform in the church says: "On that table Christ is present invisibly."

Cyril, *In Johannem,* Bk. 11, chs. 21—22, in explaining the words of Christ: "When I was with them, I kept them in Your name" [John 17:12] indeed says: "We can be preserved by reason of the deity, not by the presence of the flesh." Likewise: "Because the preserving is attributed to the deity, you ought not desire the presence of the flesh for this reason."[85] But I ask, does Cyril simply and totally omit the flesh of Christ and exclude it from the work of preservation? This he denies by many very clear statements which we have noted in ch. X and in our monograph on the hypostatic union,[86] namely, that the Word ($\lambda \acute{o} \gamma o \varsigma$) has joined His life to ours but has done this through His flesh, which has been made life-giving. And he explains this sufficiently in the very same passage: "For the apostles had regard to the flesh of Christ and their daily relationship with Him on a man-to-man basis, not with special regard to His deity, and they thought that being deprived of His bodily, familiar, and visible presence would be the cause of many troubles for them in the future." Thus Cyril says that the role of preserver is attributed to Christ not in as far as He is a man, nor is it attributed to the flesh as flesh. But does he thereby take away from the Supper the presence of the flesh of Christ and its benefits, so that we are entirely dependent on His deity? Not at all. But he says: "The flesh of Christ was not holy of itself, but having been, in a sense, conformed to the virtue of the Word by union with the Word, it is the cause of salvation and sanctification for those who participate in it." Again: "We do not say these things because we do not highly regard the body of the Lord, but because we believe these marvelous actions should be attributed to the glory of the deity. For the body of Christ itself is sanctified by its union with the virtue of the Word and thus is made an active agent in the mystical blessing so that it can bestow its sanctification upon us in the Supper." And in another place: "As we have shown, Christ is joined bodily with our bodies by His flesh in the Supper."[87]

So also Theodoret, *Contra Eutychianos,* argues that the body of Christ has dimensions as well as the other natural properties of a true body. And yet at the same time he demonstrates by many very clear statements from the ancients that this body in addition to these natural properties has received infinite and supernatural prerogatives.[88] And in explaining the doctrine of the Lord's Supper in 1 Cor. 11 he clearly teaches that the most holy body of Christ is taken up in the hands and received into the mouth of those who eat.

Fulgentius also says that Christ according to His flesh has locally departed from the earth, just as by reason of the humanity it was local when He visibly walked among us here on earth. But it does not follow that because Christ with His body is not locally present on earth, that therefore His body is in no way present in the Supper. For Fulgentius when he is talking to Monimus says that the coming of the Holy Spirit must not be thought of as something local, and yet he is not thereby simply denying the true presence of the Spirit. Indeed in the same passage he says: "God is nowhere locally, and yet He truly is everywhere."[89] And in Bk. 2, *Ad Monimum,* he says in regard to the presence of the body of Christ in the Supper: "By the very body of Christ, which is the church, the very body and blood of Christ are offered in the sacrament of the bread and the cup." And Fulgentius adds his rationale: "For the cup which we drink is the communion of the blood of Christ, and the bread which we break is a participation in the body of the Lord."[90]

Therefore I have cited these declarations of the ancients which expressly show that they did not mean their own remarks about the bodily, fleshly, and local departure and absence of Christ to oppose the substantial presence, distribution, and reception of the body and blood of the Lord in the Supper, nor did they want others to understand them in such a way. I concur in these declarations, and with a little explanation of those statements which are gathered from their own words I rest my case. For articles of faith must not be established on the basis of individual jots and tittles in the ancients. Bucer plainly follows the same line of reasoning, for he says: "Because the fathers state that we have Christ present through the food and drink of the altar; therefore when they elsewhere deny the presence of His flesh, they understand that which is perceived by the senses." And he very properly adds: "[This is true] even if the holy fathers are found to have written something regarding a definite place where Christ dwells in heaven." As for what goes beyond what Scripture clearly teaches—I do not wish to reject it in an irreverent way, and yet I pray that no dogma may ever be established from it and that I may be allowed to remain in the simple teaching of the written Word of God.

These are the chief arguments which are raised from the statements of the ancients. And it is evident that if these arguments are examined with even a meager amount of care it can in no way be demonstrated from them with certainty and finality that the ancient church disapproved of, rejected, or condemned the natural meaning of the testament of Christ and the substantial presence, distribution, and reception of the body and blood of the Lord in the Supper, as our adversaries are doing. For it is certain that the adversaries in all the literature of antiquity cannot certainly, clearly, and explicitly show that denial of theirs, that the true body of Christ is not present in the Supper and that, while preserving the integrity of His body, it cannot be present both in heaven and on earth at the same time.

Peter Martyr is in the habit of bringing in a statement of Chrysostom, *In Sanct. Matthaeum,* in an incomplete work: "In the holy vessels the true body of Christ is not present, but only His mystery is contained there." But this work is not by Chrysostom, and Erasmus has noted many spurious statements in it. Furthermore, this statement does not speak of the Lord's Supper but of the consecrated vessels of the Old Testament which Balthasar in Dan. 5 had profaned. Thus we should carefully note that when he cannot prove his denial from the fathers, he does not hesitate to use fraudulent and false testimonies to delude his reader. Moreover, he cites Augustine on Ps. 89: "You will not eat this body which you see," etc. But in this very passage Augustine says: "Christ received His flesh from Mary's flesh, and this same flesh He has given to us to be eaten for our salvation." And why he says: "Not this body which you see," etc., he soon explains by the use of the adverbs "visibly" and "invisibly." It is the same thing with the statement, *In Evangelium Johannis tractatus 50:* "They were not going to see this Christ, that is, such a Christ, namely, in His humiliation."[91] We have cited those words previously.

F. The arguments from the analogy and the similarity to the other sacraments.

With much colorful rhetoric the adversaries declaim that, because there is a certain similarity among the sacraments, therefore the words of the Supper must be explained and understood not in their proper and natural way but in such a manner that an analogy with the other sacraments is preserved. And they add that Scripture in every instance where it deals with the sacraments possesses a definite and particular way of speaking, that is, the words are not to be understood according to their literal meaning. They affirm these points with ill-defined and sweeping assertions, but when it comes to the proof, they adduce only individual and particular examples from which no universal and rational conclusion can be drawn. For example, there is the lamb of the Passover and similar things. But against this notion I assert a true, sure, and firm rule which cannot be denied: There most certainly is some similarity or relationship between the sacraments. Therefore, as a result of this, they share a common appellation, that they are called sacraments. But it does not follow from this that there is no difference at all between them, for otherwise they would not be similar but the same. But what the similarity is and what the difference is between the individual sacraments has to be considered and determined not on the basis of passages which indicate similarities or relationships but on the basis of the clear Word of God and the institution of the individual sacraments. And the similarity or relationship consists in this, that the sacraments are made up of the Word and the external elements, in which one thing is perceived by the senses and another thing is understood from the Word and according to the Word. Likewise, they are seals (σφραγίδες) of the promise of grace, an exercise and confirmation of faith, and notes of external profession in the church. But this similarity or relationship does not constitute an obstacle which prevents each sacrament from possessing its own proper and peculiar material and form.

But what are those things which we must learn and establish as being peculiar and proper to each sacrament on the basis of its institution? There is this correct, sure, and firm rule: In no way does it follow from the similarity or relationship of the sacraments that we can make a statement in regard to the material and form of any sacrament while disregarding its institution, purely on the basis of a similarity. Much less is such a similarity or relationship to be extended to the point that because of it the words of institution of each sacrament are deserted and repudiated.

But if they say that it is an analogy which applies for all times to all sacraments that those words of Scripture in which the sacrament is dealt with must be taken in a different sense than their literal meaning, my reply is that this is not always true. The words of institution of Baptism retain their proper and natural meaning. For where is the figure of speech, or in which words does the figure occur, when Christ says: "Baptize them in the name of the Father and of the Son and of the Holy Spirit [Matt. 28:19], or: "He that believes and is baptized shall be saved" [Mark 16:16]? Nor is it true that it is a perpetual and universal analogy which applies to all sacraments and signs that they speak of and deal with things that are absent. For Baptism is the washing of regeneration by the Holy Spirit. But not because the Holy Spirit is far distant or because, in His absence, regeneration is only signified; but as Christ Himself explains: "We are born again of water and the Spirit" (John 3:5). For through this means the Spirit is poured out, so that He confers, applies, and seals regeneration (Titus 3:5). Hence Chrysostom, *Homilia 1 in Acta,* calls the Holy Spirit the chief part of Baptism, because through Him the water is also made efficacious.[92] Thus the dove is a symbol, the flame of fire is a symbol, but the analogy between the sign and the thing signified is not that the substance of the Holy Spirit is far removed and separated from these symbols. The relationship and analogy of the sacraments therefore in no way effects or compels us to conclude that the substantial presence of the body and blood of Christ in the Supper, which the proper and natural meaning of the words of institution affirms, must be denied and repudiated. For here is the point of the dispute: Is such an analogy of the sacraments so sure, perpetual, and universal that it cannot bear the proper and natural meaning of the words of the last will and testament of Christ concerning the substantial presence of His body and blood in the Supper?

They also make much use of the argument that the sacraments of the Old Testament were different from those of our era as to their signs but were the same as ours in respect to the substance of a sacrament. Augustine also speaks this way extensively in many places. But in the Old Testament sacraments the body of Christ was not substantially present because at that time Christ had not yet become incarnate. Therefore [they say] the body and blood of Christ are not present in the Lord's Supper.

I am always stressing that the point at issue in the arguments against our adversaries is this: Are we to desert and repudiate the proper and natural meaning of the last will and testament of Christ? Therefore let us see if that is surely and firmly accomplished by this argument. This would have to be the train of thought: Because the sacraments of the New Testament otherwise would have some kind of superiority and prerogative over the sacraments of the Old Testament, or because it is not said of the manna: "This is My body," therefore we must not believe this regarding the bread of the Lord's Supper. But because Christ did say of the bread of the Lord's Supper: "This is My body," the adversaries contend that we must therefore depart from His words lest there be a total difference between the manna and the bread of the

Supper in respect to the substance of the sacrament.

However, the reader should consider what kind of reasoning this is and on what foundations it rests. They cite the passage in 1 Cor. 10:3: "They all ate the same food and drank the same drink." But does Paul actually say what the adversaries are trying to prove? Surely the text expressly and clearly deals with the point that the ancients among themselves had the same sacraments. For he says: "Our fathers all ate the same food." And the ancient church fathers, except for Augustine, interpreted this passage this way. Even Oecolampadius says with regard to this statement of Paul: "We must not make a comparison with ourselves, as certain commentators do, that the Old Testament people ate the same thing we eat. But the comparison must be made among them, that the food which Moses ate was not denied to Korah or Abiram or the women." Thus Oecolampadius. But Paul applies this statement to his own situation in this way: Just as the same sacraments were held in common by all in the Old Testament, so also we in the New Testament all have the same sacraments, namely, Baptism and the Lord's Supper. But just as then in the Old Testament God was not pleased with all who used these sacraments (for many of them were struck down in the desert, when they gave themselves over to murmuring, debauchery, fornication, and idolatry), so also in the New Testament debaucherers, fornicators, idolators, etc., should not delude themselves because they have the same Baptism and the same Supper as the pious use. It is perfectly clear that Paul instituted and proposed this in order that he might take away from the Corinthians that false delusion that debauchery, whoring, communion with idols, etc., could not hurt them since they had been baptized and used the same Lord's Supper as did the truly pious. But in no way does what the adversaries attach to it follow from this.

And I must warn concerning the meaning of the passage in 1 Cor. 10, that the reader may consider the nature of the foundations of the opinion of our adversaries. There is attributed to Paul in 1 Cor. 10 a meaning which he does not have in this passage, as we have demonstrated, and because of that meaning we imagine that we are compelled to give up and reject the proper and natural meaning of the last will and testament of Christ and that the bread symbolizes the body of Christ in the same way as the rock in the desert was a figure of Christ.

But, someone says, Augustine's meaning, which is the true meaning of Scripture itself, is that the real object of faith in the Word and the sacraments, both in the Old as well as in the New Testament, is

Christ Himself. My reply is that without Christ there would not have been any promise of grace at all in the Old Testament nor in the sacraments attached to it, nor did the people of the Old Testament have a different Christ than we have in the New Testament. For Christ is yesterday, today, and forever (Heb. 13:8). "Abraham saw My day and was glad" (John 8:56). There is no doubt, of course, that the ancients also had the spiritual eating. (Is. 55:1 ff.)

These points are true, and there is no controversy about them. But the point is that it is necessary that there be a connecting chain in the argument of the adversaries if we are to conclude anything contrary to the proper meaning of Christ's testament, namely, whether for us in the New Testament era Christ is offered and distributed in the sacraments in exactly the same way and in no other way than in the Old Testament. They [in the Old Testament] believed in the Christ who was to come; we in the Christ who is shown to us. At that time He was not yet incarnate; but now the Word has been made flesh. They believed that Christ would be killed (Dan. 9:26); we believe in the Christ who has died and risen again. Therefore, even though the same Christ is in the sacraments of the Old and the New Testament, yet no one can deny that there is some difference in the mode. But is it permissible to circumscribe this difference with certain limits and boundaries in accord with our own opinions? Many are trying to do this entirely on their own authority and in an exceedingly audacious manner. But the surest, firmest, and safest rule is that in regard to the mode and the difference in the distribution and reception of Christ in the sacraments either of the Old or the New Testament we make our decision on the basis of the clear word by which each of the sacraments is instituted. And who can deny this rule, as if Christ were not permitted in the sacraments of the Old and the New Testament to institute and ordain His own distribution and reception with whatever differences He wills? Surely in the institution of the Supper the Son of God speaks in the form of a command in regard to the oral reception: "Take, eat, drink; this is My body, this is My blood." And it is clear what the proper and natural meaning of these words is.

But our adversaries reject that meaning in this argument which now concerns us, on the ground that this mode of distribution and reception did not occur in the sacraments of the Old Testament. But concerning the bread and wine of the Lord's Supper we have the word: "This is My body; this is My blood," an expression which does not occur in regard to the manna. But they say that even though there is this word concerning the bread of the Supper, yet it must not be understood according to its literal meaning, because such a mode of distribution and reception did not exist in the Old Testament. This line of reasoning will be necessary, if it is to prevail against the words of institution, that to the Son of God there has been permitted absolutely no difference, in the manner of distributing and receiving Him, between the sacraments of the Old Testament and those of the New; but no one will dare to say this. Or it follows that there is absolutely no difference between the sacraments of the Old and the New Testament, so that as a result we should depart from the words of institution of the sacraments rather than admit the slightest difference. For unless this is put in the strongest terms (so to say), the argument has no force against the natural meaning of the words of institution of the Supper. But both of the following points are true: 1. As Augustine says, the sacraments of the Old and the New Testament are different in their outward symbols, but equal in the thing which they signify. For the same faith, the same Christ, and the same salvation which exists in the New Testament was also in the time of the Old Testament. 2. This is also true, which several of the fathers taught, that there is some difference between the sacraments of the Old Testament and those of the New and that the sacraments of the New Testament have a certain preeminence. But from where can this difference and preeminence be more correctly and rightly established than on the basis of the words of institution?

Origen, *Homilia 7 in Numeros,* says: "Then, in a glass darkly, the manna was food; but now, in the full brilliance, the flesh of the Word of God is the true food."[93] Ambrose, *De his qui initiantur mysteriis,* ch. 8: "Consider which is the more outstanding, the bread of angels or indeed the flesh of Christ, which is most certainly the body of life. . . . To the people of that time the water flowed from the rock, to you the blood from Christ."[94] Jerome, on Titus 1, in speaking of the Eucharist, says: "There is as great a difference between the showbread and the body of Christ as between a shadow and the body, as between an image and reality, as between prophecies of the future and what the prophecies prefigured."[95] Chrysostom, on 2 Cor. 5: "For the manna we have the body of the Lord; for the water of the rock, the blood from His side."[96] Theodoret, on 2 Cor. 11, compares the Supper of the Passover, which was a type, and the Lord's Supper and says that the latter is the true archetype of the type. But this is not our line of argumentation: There is some kind of difference between the sacraments of the Old and the New Testament; therefore in the Lord's Supper the body and blood of the Lord are substantially present. But because the words of the institution of the Supper in their proper and natural meaning speak of such a presence, we say that we cannot depart from this meaning because such a presence, distribution, and reception did not take place in the sacraments of the Old Testament. For it is certain that there is some difference between the sacraments of the Old Testament and those of the New. But this cannot be determined more correctly or more certainly than from the words of institution. Therefore the manna and the water from the rock do not displace or overturn the proper and natural meaning of what Christ said concerning the bread and the wine of the Lord's Supper: "This is My body; this is My blood."

G. Various arguments which are gathered by the adversaries from various places and in various ways.

The arguments of the adversaries which we have evaluated up to now are the principal ones, those that have a good outward appearance; therefore the sources of the explanations had to be shown more diligently and at some length. But the adversaries are accustomed to scrape together many other additional arguments, in some way twisted to their cause, as though they want to have it evaluated not so much by the weight as by the number of the arguments. We could certainly have ignored arguments of this kind, for they are not of sufficient value to make it necessary to describe and refute each of them. But I wanted to gather them together in this one section and to make brief comments about them individually. For thus we can get some idea of the kind of thinking which can build on such arguments as on a foundation, and can present a clear judgment as to the kind of support which the human mind seeks and constructs for itself when once it has determined to depart from the Word of God.

Always keep in mind what the point of controversy is in the explanation of these arguments, namely, do these arguments offer sufficiently serious, certain, firm, and compelling causes and reasons to make us depart from, disapprove, and repudiate the natural meaning of Christ's last will and testament? We shall therefore consider the various arguments of our adversaries in order.

1. Christ says in regard to His Supper: "This do in remembrance of Me." But memory deals with things which are not present, which are past or absent. Therefore we must not believe in the presence of the body and blood of Christ in the Supper, even though the words of institution say so.

My answer is: It is not universally true that memory or a record of things simply and necessarily includes a denial of the presence of the thing which is to be remembered. Surely the people of God are commanded constantly to remember the Lord their God. Pious believers often pray, "Lord God, remember me." But are we then going to say that God is not present with His people? God instituted the festivals of the Old Testament for a remembrance, a memorial, and a record of Himself. But does this mean that He is far away? Surely in the first Lord's Supper Christ was visibly present, and yet He said: "This do in remembrance of Me." Paul in 2 Tim. 1:6 uses this very word (ἀναμιμνῄσκω): "I put you in remembrance of that gift which is in you." Certainly in that passage the word ἀναμιμνῄσκω does not include a denial of the presence. Oecolampadius himself admits the imbecility of this argument. He says: "Memory is often of things which are present, as also the poet says: 'Ithacus was forgetful of himself by so great a difference.'" Furthermore, Paul interprets this remembrance thus in 1 Cor. 11:26: "You will proclaim the Lord's death until He comes." Thus there can certainly be a remembrance of a past action which yet does not overturn the natural meaning of these words: "This is My body; this is My blood."

2. They use this argument on the basis of 2 Cor. 5:16: "We no longer know Christ according to the flesh," or John 3:6: "That which is born of the flesh is flesh." Therefore, after the work of redemption has been completed in the flesh of Christ, there is no efficacy or usefulness in the flesh of Christ for vivification. For "that which is born of the flesh is flesh." And thus as a consequence there is no need for the presence of the body and blood of Christ in the Supper, but His deity alone suffices.

Calvin himself acknowledges that this argument is false, as we shall show more fully in another book, on the hypostatic union.[97] But it is blasphemy to twist things around so that what is said of the corruption of our flesh: "That which is born of the flesh is flesh," is applied to Christ's flesh. And yet they at one time brought these arguments forward in their first line of battle. But Paul in 2 Cor. 5 is either speaking of the carnal imagination concerning the reign of Christ or is saying that many thought that there is nothing more excellent about Christ than they could imagine on the basis of the weakness of Christ's flesh during the time of His humiliation. And yet because of this statement some have departed from the words of Christ's last will and testament.

3. Gal. 4:9: "How is it that you have been turned again to the weak and beggerly elements?" Col. 2:4, 8, 18, 20: "Let no one deceive you according to the elements of the world." In the Lord's Supper there

are the elements of bread and wine. Therefore [they say] in the Lord's Supper we must not seek Christ and His efficacy.

It is certain that Paul is speaking about Mosaic ceremonies, whose observance, even after the coming of Christ, some imagined was necessary for salvation. Even *ex opere operato* they attributed much to them. But with what kind of conscience will we twist such statements to apply them to the Lord's Supper, which consists not only of the elements of bread and wine but also of the very body and blood of Christ, as the ancients said? But how is the absence of Christ's body in the Supper proved from these passages?

4. Christ has promised that He would send the Holy Spirit as His representative (*vicarius*). Therefore [they say] He Himself is not present with His body and blood in the Supper, but only with His deity.

But Christ is not speaking there of His deity, but of the person of the Holy Spirit. For He says: "I will send you another comforter" [John 14:16]. Therefore the same thing will follow concerning the whole person of Christ and also concerning His deity, namely, that it would not be present—and this is certainly false. Christ does not send His representative in order that He Himself may be entirely absent. For just as the passage in John 14:23 still stands: "I and My Father will come and make our dwelling with him," so the Holy Spirit as the representative will not overturn what Christ has said: "This is My body."

5. "God does not dwell in temples made with hands" [Acts 7:48]. Therefore [they say] the body of Christ is not present in the Lord's Supper along with the bread and wine.

But one should consider how diverse the goals of this argument are. The deity is not fenced in or contained locally in temples made with hands. And yet He is present everywhere, and He dwells in the humble. But how will it follow from this that therefore the body of Christ absolutely is not present in the Lord's Supper although the words of His last will and testament expressly so state?

6. "If someone says to you: 'Lo, here is Christ!' or 'Lo, there!' do not believe him. For false prophets shall arise . . ." [Luke 17:23; Mark 13:21-22]. Therefore [they argue] that they are false prophets, to whom no credibility must be given, who retain the natural meaning of the words of institution and teach that Christ is present in the Supper.

But by the same reasoning it follows that we must not teach that Christ is in heaven either. For Mark and Luke have: "Lo, here!" and "Lo, there!" Nor could it be said that Christ dwells in the hearts of believers. But Christ's meaning is crystal clear; for He is predicting to

His followers that before the devastation of Jerusalem many would arise who would take unto themselves the title of Messiah and would promise to the people an external deliverance from the oppression of the Romans. And from this it would follow that they would gather many followers, some in the deserts and some secretly in the corners of their homes. And many would join themselves to these false prophets because of their imaginings regarding an external physical reign of the Messiah in the land of Judah. Christ therefore forewarns His own that they should embrace no Messiah other than Himself, lest they join themselves to another, whoever has followers and success. And to their notions concerning a physical liberation and a certain place for the Messianic kingdom in Judaea He opposes His own kingdom (Luke 17:20-21), which He does not want judged by an observing of its external and visible majesty and happiness nor circumscribed by a defined location in the land of Judah. For He says that His kingdom is spiritual and that it is in us, and He predicts that this kingdom shall be spread throughout the whole world, from the east to the west, that it shall come with sudden power, as the lightning shining from the east immediately fills also the west [Luke 17:24]. But the visible majesty of His kingdom, He says, is to be revealed only on the last day, when He Himself shall come to judgment. This is the meaning of Christ's sermon, as the circumstances of the text show and as a comparison with the description in Luke 17 points out.

But how can we on the basis of this prediction regarding false Christs conclude that therefore the body of the true Christ is not present in the Supper, although the very words of His last will and testament in their proper and natural sense affirm this? Nor does such a denial follow from the passage: "Do not believe it if someone says to you: 'Lo, here is Christ!' or 'Lo, there He is!'" [Matt. 24:23; cf. Luke 17:23]. For Christ in Luke 17:20-21, where He is speaking of His kingdom as being bound to no definite place and as not being recognized by an external and visible majesty, indeed says that people will not say: "Lo, here!" or "Lo, there!" But He does not conclude from this that His kingdom is far removed from us, for He immediately adds: "The kingdom of God is in the midst of you." Therefore this expression in no way nullifies the natural meaning of Christ's testament concerning the presence of His body and blood in the Supper. For otherwise it would also nullify the statement in Eph. 3:17: "Christ dwells in your hearts through faith," and also: "We shall come and make our abode with him." [John 14:23]

7. Col. 3:1-2: "Seek the things which are above, where Christ is, sitting at the right hand of God. Set your minds on things that are above,

not on things that are on earth." Thus [they say] Christ must be sought not in the holy Supper but above the heaven of heavens.

But what Paul understands by "the things which are above" must not be sought on the basis of philosophy. For he himself clearly shows it by his antithesis, so that there is no need for guesswork on our part. He is dealing with salvation and life; he is contending against philosophy, against human traditions and Levitical ceremonies, now abrogated by the death of Christ. He calls these things "the elements of the world" [Col. 2:20] and "the things that are on earth." He adds that he has in mind the old man with his concupiscence and actions when he refers to "the things that are on earth." And to these he opposes "the things which are above." These points are certain and manifest.

But now do we include under the Pauline phrase "the things that are on earth" such things as the Word, Baptism, and the Lord's Supper? Besides, by "the things which are above" Paul there does not have in mind an interval of space, that is, those things which while we still live in this world are far removed and distant from us. For among them he mentions the new man, the knowledge of God, love, the peace of God in our hearts, the Word of God, the words and deeds of believers which are done in the name of the Lord, etc. These things are certainly among us and in us while we live on earth. Therefore it is absolutely clear from Paul's own explanation that this statement of Paul in no way nullifies the presence of the body and blood of Christ in the Supper as it is taught and affirmed by the proper and natural meaning of the words of institution. For according to this expression of Paul the Lord's Supper is not something of the earth but something above, even though it is celebrated on earth; that is, it is not something earthly but a heavenly action, just as the Word of God, the peace of God, the knowledge of God, the new man, etc., are things above and not things of the earth. Therefore nothing concerning the Word and the sacraments should be judged according to philosophy, for philosophy is not a thing above but an earthly thing, as Paul puts it.

8. Matt. 15:11, 17: "Whatever enters into the mouth of a man cannot defile him because it does not enter into his heart but goes into the stomach and out through the digestive process." This statement, which Christ pronounces about external, physical, and natural food on the basis of the common order of nature, some people impiously twist and apply to the reception of Christ's body in the Lord's Supper—as though the wisdom of the Son of God did not know and His power were not able to bring it about that His very body is received in the Lord's Supper for eating with the mouth, as the words say, in another manner

(supernatural and heavenly) than the natural way common physical foods are received. For this must be proved if on account of this statement we ought to repudiate the proper and natural meaning of Christ's last will and testament.

Surely the ancients, who affirm that the body of Christ is received orally in the Supper, do not play games with the testament of the Son of God with such profane language. No one from the ancient church ever reasons from this statement of Christ that the body of Christ is not received orally in the Supper; indeed, they reverently distinguish between the body of Christ and the elements of bread and wine. Origen confesses that the latter in the normal way go into the stomach and are ejected in the digestive process. But concerning the true body of Christ, which our mouth receives at the same time along with the bread in the Supper, Chrysostom, *De encoeniis,* asks: "Does also that, like other food, go out through the digestive process?" He answers: "God forbid!"[98]

9. Only they eat the body of Christ for whom He was crucified. But [they say] He was not crucified for the ungodly. Therefore those who eat unworthily do not receive the body of Christ but only the bread in the Lord's Supper.

But it simply is false to say that Christ was crucified only for the elect. For He is "the Lamb of God who takes away the sin of the world" (John 1:29). "Christ is the propitiation not only for our sins but for the sins of the whole world" (1 John 2:2). "He gave Himself as the ransom for all people" (1 Tim. 2:6). "One died for all" (2 Cor. 5:14). "I will give My flesh for the life of the world" (John 6:51). And the ungodly shall be damned, not because Christ was not crucified and put to death for them, but because: "They loved the darkness more than the light" (John 3:19); "He who does not believe will be condemned" (Mark 16:16). For the merit of Christ is one thing and the application of that merit is something else. The unbelievers are going to undergo greater judgment because they spurned this propitiation which was accomplished for the sins of the whole world. Paul surely says expressly that Christ died even for those who perish: "Lest for the sake of food you destroy him for whom Christ died" (Rom. 14:15); "And thus the weak brother for whom Christ died will perish because of your knowledge" (1 Cor. 8:11). As for what Christ says in John 17:9, that He is not praying for the world—He means that those will not have life who do not believe the Gospel. The very context of that passage shows this is the meaning.

These are just about all the Scripture passages which are twisted by our adversaries against the proper and natural meaning of Christ's testament. Whatever arguments they bring in besides these, based on the judgment of reason and on absurdity, are not worthy of refutation. For the question is not how it appears to our reason, either in agreement with it or absurd, but the question concerns the meaning of the words of Christ's last will and testament, which has to be taken from Scripture and from no other source. This is beyond controversy among the pious.

10. Therefore we are in no way impressed when the argument is made that it is unworthy of the glory of Christ's body if it is received in our physical mouth as the words of institution declare. For also the Holy Spirit does not disdain to dwell in our physical bodies as in His temple. (1 Cor. 6:19)

11. We are correct in refusing to admit the following argument against the words of institution, taken from the popish doctrine of concomitance: It is impossible to understand how the body of Christ in the bread and the blood in the wine can be substantially present, distributed, and received without any physical pulling asunder or tearing apart of the body and blood of Christ. Therefore [they say] the proper and natural meaning of Christ's last will and testament must rather be repudiated.

But if, because of unexplainable absurdities, we are forced to depart from the clear word of God, nothing will remain safe among the chief articles of our faith.

12. It is ridiculous that some people in publicly printed documents have gloried in the fact that the opinion of Zwingli concerning the Lord's Supper has been confirmed by the judgment and approval of the emperor of Turkey, as if he stood in the position of one who could make pronouncements on such a matter. For they tell the story that when the Turkish emperor had carefully listened to a certain merchant explaining both our position and that of Zwingli on the Lord's Supper, he at last pronounced that the position of Zwingli was the more convincing to him. Nor is this something to be wondered at, for the Arab Averroes has also pronounced that no race is more degenerate than the Christians, for they devour the God they worship. And some of our adversaries have declared that they are marvelously pleased with this statement of Averroes. Therefore, if it pleases them, let them have the approval of all philosophy and even of the emperor of Turkey himself; for us the words of the last will and testament of the Son of God are sufficient. For when His mouth speaks, heaven and earth ought to rejoice; yea, before His face all flesh should be silent.

And although it is not only a serious but also a very dangerous matter to attempt to read into the last will and testament of the Son of

God something other than the words actually say, I have up to this point calmly and without bitterness shown that there are no sufficiently weighty, sure, firm, and compelling causes and reasons on account of which we can with a quiet conscience desert, condemn, and repudiate the proper and natural meaning of Christ's last will and testament. And since many other true, clear, serious, and strong reasons demonstrate that the natural meaning can, indeed must, be retained, I rest my case in that natural meaning in the simple obedience of faith. And when my mind is disturbed by arguments to the contrary, I repeat what has been truly and seriously said regarding secular wills: "In times of doubt it is safer not to depart from the words." And I pray the reader seriously and attentively to consider these things, "without favor and partiality" (1 Tim. 5:21), in the fear of the Lord. Then judgment will be right and equitable.

To God the glory!

Notes

Dedicatory Epistle

1. 1561.
2. *Repetitio sanae doctrinae de vera praesentia corporis et sangvinis Domini in Coena.*

Chapter II

1. MPL 34, 70.
2. Ibid., 219—221.

Chapter IV

1. Chemnitz has "Exod. 17."
2. *Luther's Works,* American Edition, 37, 151—372. The page numbers given in the text are by Chemnitz and are, of course, not applicable to modern editions of Luther's works.
3. In *De Trinitate,* Bk. 8, ch. 14; MPL 10, 247.

Chapter V

1. MPL 42, 918, but we were unable to find this quotation there.
2. Cf. *Contra adversarium legis et prophetarum;* MPL 42, 658.
3. There are several references to Chrysostom's *De encoeniis.* I was unable to locate a work by this title. However, according to Miss Margaret Schatkin, who graciously did extensive research on this question at my request, this work of Chrysostom "is no longer extant but in some form equals Homily 9, *De poenitentia;* MPG 49, 343—50." She adds, "The quotation which Chemnitz gives in Latin may therefore be found in Greek in *De poenitentia;* MPG 49, 345."
4. *De corpore et sanguine Domini;* MPL 120, 1267—1350.

Chapter VII

1. MPL 34, 71.
2. Ibid., 74.
3. MPL 24, 250.
4. Chemnitz has "Luke 10" instead of the Luke 12 reference.
5. MPL 34, 71.
6. Ibid., 39.
7. I was unable to find this statement in *Contra epistolam Petiliani;* MPL 43.
8. Ibid.
9. Instead of *non incepte* we are reading *non inepte,* as later editions do.
10. Cf. *Luther's Works,* American Edition, 37, 305 f.
11. MPG 7, 802.

Chapter VIII

1. *Ennaratio in Evangelium Johannis,* Bk. 13, ch. 23; MPG 124, 160. Probably a reference to Ex. 12:11, which speaks of eating the passover in a position of preparation to move at once.
2. MPL 40, 555.

Chapter IX

1. *Homilia 24 in 1 ad Corinthios;* MPG 61, 199.
2. Ibid., 202.
3. Ibid., 200.

Chapter X

1. MPL 43, 489—90.
2. Otto, 1, 178, ch. 65.
3. MPG 7, 1029.
4. Ibid.
5. MPG 7, 1027.
6. Ibid., 1124.
7. MPG 93, 886.
8. MPG 83, 284.

9. MPL 183, 682—83.
10. Otto 1, 228, ch. 10.
11. There are five references in this work to a *De coena Domini* attributed to Cyprian. Cyprian wrote no work with such a title, and no modern edition even mentions such a work as spurious. Cyprian has one treatise on the Eucharist, namely, *Epistola 63* (MPL 4, 383 ff.), but no citation quoted by Chemnitz is found in this epistle. Nor has the translator been able to find the work from which Chemnitz quotes.
12. MPG 52, 757 ff.
13. MPG 85, 1186 ff.
14. MPG 83, 105 ff.
15. There are four *Sermones ad neophytos* by Augustine in MPL 40, 1203—14. Some words similar to those quoted are found in Augustine's *Sermo 227, Ad infantes de sacramento;* MPL 38, 1099—1101.
16. *Homilia 24 in 1 ad Corinthios;* MPG 61, 200.
17. Ibid.
18. Cf. ch. V, note 3.
19. MPG 61, 203.
20. MPG 48, 754.
21. MPL 16, 458.
22. Ibid., 463.
23. MPG 48, 642.
24. MPG 61, 204.
25. Ibid., 205.
26. MPG 49, 46.
27. MPG 63, 131.
28. MPL 187, 1756.
29. Basel Ed., p. 355.
30. Ibid., p. 597.
31. MPL 189, 1766.
32. MPG 49, 380.
33. Cf. ch. V, note 3.
34. MPG 58, 557—66, but I was unable to locate this quotation there.
35. This may be a wrong reference. I was unable to locate it.
36. MPL 4, 963—66.
37. This is a wrong reference. Cf. *De sacramentis,* Bk. 5, ch. 12; MPL 16, 468.
38. MPL 37, 1265.
39. MPG 61, 200.
40. Cf. ch. V, note 3.

41. MPG 61, 205.
42. Ibid., 206.
43. Ibid.
44. MPL 77, 428.
45. *Adversus haereses,* Bk. 4, ch. 18; MPG 7, 1029.
46. MPL 2, 806.
47. MPL 42, 658.
48. MPL 54, 452.
49. I was unable to locate this sentence.
50. MPL 4, 479.
51. Cf. note 11.
52. MPG 61, 231.
53. Ibid., 607.
54. Basel Ed., p. 551.
55. MPL 10, 246 ff.
56. Ibid.
57. Basel Ed., p. 498.
58. Ibid., p. 500.
59. Ibid.
60. Ibid., p. 566.
61. Ibid., p. 565.
62. MPG 58, 743.
63. MPG 59, 254.
64. MPG 49, 15 ff., but we were unable to find these thoughts there.
65. MPG 58, 516.
66. Ibid., 743.
67. Basel Ed., p. 566.
68. MPG 61, 201.
69. In *Adversus haereses,* Bk. 5, ch. 2; MPG 7, 1124—25.
70. Ibid., Bk. 4, ch. 18; MPG 7, 1028—29.
71. Ibid., 1125—26.
72. Ibid., 1028—29.
73. Ibid., 1125—26.
74. Basel Ed., p. 181.
75. Ibid., p. 201.
76. Ibid., p. 203.
77. MPL 32, 742.
78. MPL 54, 357.
79. Cyril, *In Johannem,* Bk. 3, ch. 36; Basel Ed., p. 180.
80. Ibid., p. 203.
81. Ibid., p. 180.
82. Ibid., p. 201.
83. In *De resurrectione carnis;* MPL 2, 795 ff.
84. MPL 2, 806.
85. MPL 43, 146.
86. Ibid., 255.
87. MPL 41, 741.

88. MPL 35, 1614.
89. MPL 38, 453.
90. MPL 35, 1611.
91. MPL 38, 453.
92. MPL 43, 181.
93. MPL 38, 453.
94. MPL 43, 766.
95. MPL 36, 135.
96. MPL 33, 329.
97. MPL 43, 298.
98. Ibid., 657.
99. MPG 83, 271.
100. MPG 58, 741.
101. MPG 61, 231.
102. MPG 118, 808.
103. MPG 12, 1386.
104. Ibid.
105. MPL 4, 498.
106. Ibid., 493.
107. Ibid.
108. MPG 31, 1577.
109. Ibid., 1196.
110. MPG 62, 28—29.
111. MPL 28, 1134.
112. MPL 35, 1802.
113. MPG 118, 808.
114. MPL 54, 279—80.
115. MPG 125, 336.
116. MPG 93, 1139.
117. MPG 59, 262.
118. MPG 61, 203.
119. MPL 33, 171.
120. MPL 43, 462.
121. MPL 54, 279—80.
122. MPG 118, 808.
123. MPG 31, 1584.
124. MPL 43, 181.
125. Ibid., 766.
126. Ibid., 462.
127. MPL 35, 1432.
128. MPL 43, 146.
129. MPG 12, 1386—87.
130. MPG 49, 390.
131. MPL 28, 1134.
132. Cf. note 11.
133. MPG 43, 117.
134. MPG 58, 743.
135. Basel Ed., p. 199.
136. In *Liber de mysteriis;* MPL 16, 424.

Chapter XI

1. *In Johannem,* Bk. 10, ch. 13; Basel Ed., p. 500.

2. See *The Two Natures in Christ,* trans. J. A. O. Preus (St. Louis: Concordia Publishing House, 1971), pp. 11, 20.
3. Basel Ed., p. 203.
4. MPL 35, 1614.

Chapter XII

1. In *Epistola VIII;* MPL 65, 361.
2. Otto 4, 62.
3. *Quaest. et regs. ad orth.;* Otto 3, 2, 190.
4. Ibid. 192.
5. Cf. ch. XI, note 2.
6. Ibid.
7. MPL 41, 784.
8. Ibid., 801.
9. Following MPL we are reading "volet" instead of "valet."
10. Following MPL we are reading "decere" instead of "dicere."
11. Ibid.
12. MPL 41, 151.
13. MPL 40, 1029—30.
14. MPL 36, 252.
15. MPG 61, 204—05.
16. MPG 62, 82.
17. MPL 68, 732.
18. MPG 32, 89—90.
19. MPL 16, 714.
20. MPL 26, 491 ff.
21. MPL 40, 646.
22. Basel Ed., p. 103.
23. We are reading "ex" instead of "et."
24. MPG 32, 89.
25. MPG 83, 179.
26. Cf. *De fide,* Bk. 5, ch. 15; MPL 16, 714.
27. MPL 26, 491.
28. MPL 40, 188.
29. Ibid., 634.
30. MPL 42, 692.
31. E.g., *Thesaurus,* Bk. 8, ch. 2; Basel Ed., p. 103.
32. In *Evangelium Johannis tractatus 75;* MPL 35, 1829.
33. MPL 26, 199.
34. Basel Ed., p. 201.
35. Ibid.
36. *Homilia 7 in 1 ad Corinthios;* MPG 61, 59.
37. MPL 35, 1617.
38. MPL 40, 336.

39. MPL 42, 144.
40. MPG 161, 499.
41. Ibid., 494—95.
42. MPG 12, 613.
43. Cf. ch. X, note 11.
44. MPL 16, 422.
45. MPL 26, 603.
46. Basel Ed., p. 215.
47. MPL 35, 2289.
48. MPL 16, 1274. Not exact quote.
49. *Homilia 46 in Johannem;* MPG 59, 261.
50. MPL 42, 658.
51. MPG 58, 739.
52. MPG 63, 131.
53. MPG 61, 200.
54. MPL 38, 1099—1101.
55. MPG 123, 444.
56. MPG 58, 742—43.
57. *Homilia 24 in 1 ad Corinthios;* MPG 61, 199.
58. Basel Ed., p. 199.
59. MPL 34, 74—75.
60. MPG 12, 487.
61. MPG 59, 262 ff.
62. MPL 51, 481.
63. MPL 35, 1614.
64. Ibid., 1602.
65. Cf. ch. X, note 11.
66. Basel Ed., p. 199 ff.
67. MPG 58, 753.
68. MPL 32, 778.

69. MPL 35, 1614.
70. MPL 33, 203.
71. MPG 61, 204.
72. *In Johannem,* Bk. 4, ch. 14; Basel Ed., p. 201.
73. MPL 33, 833—34.
74. MPL 35, 1632.
75. Ibid., 1763.
76. Ibid.
77. MPL 35, 1763.
78. Ibid., 1899.
79. Basel Ed., p. 537.
80. On John 11:22; ibid., p. 554.
81. On John 11:3; ibid., p. 531.
82. MPL 35, 1807.
83. Ibid., 1872.
84. Ibid., 1763.
85. Basel Ed., p. 552.
86. Cf. ch. XI, note 2.
87. Basel Ed., p. 552.
88. MPG 83, 438.
89. MPL 65, 186.
90. Ibid., 190.
91. MPL 35, 1763.
92. MPG 60, 21.
93. MPG 12, 613.
94. MPL 16, 422.
95. MPL 26, 603.
96. MPG 61, 476.
97. Cf. ch. XI, note 2.
98. Cf. ch. V, note 3.

Indexes

By Delpha Holleque Preus

SUBJECT AND NAME INDEX

received prerogatives from hypostatic union
with divine nature 202, 203
Scripture asserted what we must believe
concerning 204
true integrity of, retained as Christ wills 201
we must believe whatever Scripture asserts
regarding 204
Human reason
cannot comprehend divine omnipotence 199
devises absurd interpretation of dogmas 71
must not force way into dogmas 72
understands only physical eating 57
Hypostatic union
See also Union; Union, bodily; Union,
heavenly
of God and man 46
of two natures of Christ has power of giving
life 240
on personal union in Christ 53
opinions on 40, 41
Hypostatic union of Christ, on prerogatives
added because of 202-206

Ignatius described heretics 152
Interpretation, analogy of
given in Scripture 89
in first line of battle 66
preserved by Holy Spirit 88
preserve with same rationale as Holy Spirit
92
specific method where dogmas have particular location 77
Invisible entity, predicate 51
Irenaeus 65
called wrong who deny salvation of the
flesh 168
calls bread also body of Christ 152
explains "body and blood" 152
entire apostolic Scripture foundation of our
faith 94
Eucharist consists of earthly and heavenly
things 151, 152, 161
not speaking of nourishment for this life 169
safe principle that Scripture has clear
language 87
says Christ now designates fruit of the vine
as His blood 98
when bread receives call of God it is
Eucharist 169
Is *(est),* explains what is distributed and
received 95

Jerome 220
charged with sacrilege by envious 26
dogmas not established purely on figures of
speech 79
on Scripture explaining itself 69
on showbread and body of Christ 244, 261
speaks of Christ's corporeal presence 230

those who pollute Lord's body despise
Lord's Table 181
unworthy pollute body and blood of Christ
178
John of Damascus, bread in Supper not figure
of absent body of Christ 245
John 6
compared with Lord's Supper 238
effect on natural meaning of Christ's
testament 240
metaphorical eating 238
sermon preceded night Christ was betrayed
236
"to eat" and "to drink" metaphorical 237
Judas received good body of Christ 180
Judgment
See also Guilt; Guilt of judgment
brought by sacrifice to idols 142
for not discerning body of Christ in Supper
81, 126, 133, 148
for not eating spiritually through faith 171
for unworthy eating in Supper 129, 171-183,
247
from eating only sacramentally 37
incurred by eating, not rejecting in Supper
130
on violations of will and testament of Christ
20, 28
Paul relates to words of institution 132, 133
threatened those who handle mysteries
wrongly 27, 28
Judgment, day of
Christ comes in visible, circumscribed body
223
no conflict with presence of Christ in
Supper 223
Justification
humanity of Christ pertains to work of 204
understood from its proper setting in
Scripture 33
Justin 153
bread and drink called Eucharist 151
faith leans on clear divine voice 195, 196
our blood and flesh are nourished by
Eucharist 170

Lamb of God
placed on sacred table 155, 156
present on altar 250
Last Supper, order described 109
Last will and testament
See also Law; Law, doctors of; Law, Greek;
Law, imperial
adversaries oppose impudence regarding
civil wills 29
force of can be drawn from words 83
is no testament if uncertain 86
men often err trying to read mind of testator
19, 84